D1294015

Executive Power

*How Executives Influence
People and Organizations*

Suresh Srivastva
and Associates

169595

Executive
Power

658.4
5774

Jossey-Bass Publishers
San Francisco • London • 1986

Alverno College
Library Media Center
Milwaukee, Wisconsin

EXECUTIVE POWER
How Executives Influence People and Organizations
by Suresh Srivastva and Associates

Copyright © 1986 by: Jossey-Bass Inc., Publishers
433 California Street
San Francisco, California 94104

&

Jossey-Bass Limited
28 Banner Street
London EC1Y 8QE

Copyright under International, Pan American, and
Universal Copyright Conventions. All rights
reserved. No part of this book may be reproduced
in any form—except for brief quotation (not to
exceed 1,000 words) in a review or professional
work—without permission in writing from the publishers.

Library of Congress Cataloging-in-Publication Data

Srivastva, Suresh (date)
   Executive power.

   Bibliography: p. 331
   Includes index.
   1. Executives—Addresses, essays, lectures.
2. Power (Social sciences)—Addresses, essays, lectures.
I. Title.
HD38.2.S75   1986   658.4'092   85-45914
ISBN 0-87589-691-X (alk. paper)

Manufactured in the United States of America

The paper in this book meets the guidelines for
permanence and durability of the Committee on
Production Guidelines for Book Longevity of the
Council on Library Resources.

JACKET DESIGN BY WILLI BAUM

FIRST EDITION

Code 8620

A joint publication in
The Jossey-Bass Management Series
and
The Jossey-Bass
Social and Behavioral Science Series

Consulting Editors
Organizations and Management

Warren Bennis
University of Southern California

Richard O. Mason
Southern Methodist University

Ian I. Mitroff
University of Southern California

Preface

The organizational life of an executive is full of seemingly simple questions and answers. Almost every day, in business meetings where decisions are said to have been made, one can randomly observe exchanges such as these:

Q. Who is making the decision around here?
A. It looks like we all are.

Q. Who's really in charge of this project?
A. It all depends.

Q. Where did you get that information?
A. From many sources.

Q. Why don't you just do what I have asked?
A. Because I can't.

Q. How do we get people to agree to this strategy?
A. Maybe we need to change our ways of working together.

Q. Why don't you get people involved?
A. I've tried, but people aren't participating.

Q. Who should be invited to this meeting?
A. Everyone who reports to you.

Q. Where does his power come from anyway?
A. He has the ears of the chief and direct access to decision makers. Moreover, he is just a nice person.

Such typical answers and questions are deceptively simple. This book is an attempt to unravel the mysteries that give rise to such conversations and to show how the very nature of these conversations transforms the quality of interaction among people working with each other.

Executive power is not obtained, bestowed, or wielded. It is certainly not found in job titles or positions. Executive power is a form of enactment of social and human relationships at the workplace. When executive power is thriving, these enactments are nurtured by an ongoing organizational culture that supports the transforming and evolutionary nature of human relationships. While organizations attempt to define relationships in terms of roles and assignments, the actual behavioral expression of relationships is driven by cultural and interpersonal learning experiences between members. This book attempts to focus on just this: executive power as it exists in the ongoing, developing relationships among people.

The book is presented in three sections, each focusing on a major function of the executive: sources of executive power (Part One), the maintenance of executive power in use (Part Two), and the transformation of executive power (Part Three). In the concluding chapter, where executive power is defined as a functioning part of organizational life, the executive is seen as a consensus seeker, a commander of cooperation, and a transmitter of a visionary culture. The themes implicit in the book's main sections correspond to a number of fundamental questions: What are the sources of executive power, and how is it initiated and used to *empower* others? Second, once initiated, how is power maintained, strengthened, or preserved over time? Also, how is power used *unobtrusively,* in order to prevent the escalation of open conflicts, which then might require more overt expressions of executive intervention? Finally, how have executives reacted when past paradigms of power have become outmoded or tarnished? Why does power not function in the ways it once did? What are the alternatives?

The chapters do not provide executives with simple lists for gaining influence or winning long-term success; rather, they encourage executives to be open to these larger questions and, in the process, to rethink some of their most basic assumptions about power. For those who accept the challenge offered here, newer, richer possibilities for organizing will become imaginable. This book will encourage executives to consider new modes of organizing, for it calls their attention to consequences of human interaction that have too long remained unnoticed.

The book is also important, we believe, for the field of organizational behavior. Originally, the choice of executive power as a theme for this work was guided by an effort to distinguish the field of organizational behavior from contributions to organizational theory by psychologists, sociologists, and others. It was against this background that in 1984 some of the leading thinkers in the field assembled at Case Western Reserve University for an international symposium on executive power. The chapters in this volume—which provide an integrated view of the omnipresent concept of power—are a culmination of the ideas developed and shaped at this important conference.

As the chapters will make clear, organizational behavior is a field that strives to appreciate both ideas and the living processes of organizing, building theories that emerge from action, and engaging in actions that feed into the formulation of new theories. Further, the field of organizational behavior has become distinctive both through theory-building processes and through its commitment to innovative processes of inquiry. Most of the work in our field has been characterized by an activist approach to organizational change and by the implicit, normative assumptions about human behavior in our methods of inquiry. The major efforts in understanding organizations have been process oriented, problem centered, and developmental in nature. We have not taken a hands-off attitude toward our subjects of inquiry but, rather, have taken advocacy positions for organizational change. In a sense, we have assumed that research itself is an intervention for the better within an organization. These assumptions have served to support our research action and our action research strategies. This book is true to the same tradition. It offers insightful theories that enlighten complex human behavior; at the same time, for the reader, this volume itself is an important intervention into the active processes of organizing.

The theme of executive power seems especially pertinent because much of the knowledge and research in our field have emphasized active and normative involvement. Such basic terms as "action research," "organization development," and "planned change" communicate many ideas telegraphically, although the underlying processes involved in managing influence and working with human beings who exercise power in organizational life are fundamental to strategies for organizational change. These underlying processes receive refreshing intellectual revisits in this book.

Although all of us—as individuals, as practitioners, and as theoreticians—have a basic grasp of the nature of power as it exists in organizations, organizational behaviorists have as a group been somewhat tentative in grappling with this elusive concept and considering its relationship to such humanistic values as openness and trust, participation and involvement, and social action and change. As our field has grown and matured, we no longer need to banish power to a murky underworld or to unresearchable arenas. This volume provides an opportunity to develop new hypotheses and theoretical frameworks in the exploration and proactive creation of the field of organizational behavior, particularly in the area of functioning aspects of executive power.

Hence, the book should appeal to both the academic and the executive worlds. For the academic world, it provides suitable material for advanced graduate courses but more likely a standard reference that will help to formulate research and action ideas. For the executive world, it is a call to revisit some of the premises of authority, influence, and power and provides ideas for experimenting with new ways of organizing relationships toward the furtherance of organizational life. It gives hints to executives, pleads with them, cajoles them, and simply presents an appreciation of their efforts in managing complex issues of importance to the society of men. This is a book that is timely, given the current level of interest in discovering more effective means of managing organizations, but also timeless in that the basic issues and dilemmas described will always have relevance to those in executive positions and to those who study them.

Pursuing the provocative questions raised in this volume implies not just rethinking old theories but changing the very way we live together, the way we proceed to organize ourselves. For this reason, understanding this topic of executive power is a *social responsibility*. It entails paying attention to the developmental potential inherent wherever there are human relationships. We often think that philanthropic contributions to society are reserved for special moments outside the workplace. However, a true understanding of executive power in the workplace is itself an important humanitarian contribution to the larger social world. Once we become aware of the processes underlying human interaction, an important corollary is not far behind: we increase our potential for creating richer, more nurturing worlds for ourselves.

The spirit behind the preparation of this volume needs special notice. In addition to maintaining exacting standards of excellence in writing individual chapters, the participants exhibited many resourceful characteristics that made the book a gathering of ideas from colleagues who are inclined to celebrate knowledge and learning. The authors have used appreciative modes of inquiry and interaction; and their ability to learn from the ideas of others and their commitment to shared meanings are very noticeable in this volume.

A volume of this nature depends largely on the good will and unreserved support of friends and colleagues and on a proper environment for inquiry. During the conception period, I was supported most ably by all my faculty colleagues in the Department of Organizational Behavior and in the Weatherhead School of Management at Case Western Reserve University. My faculty colleagues included Eric Neilsen, Barbara Bird, David Cooperrider, Michael Manning, David Kolb, Ronald Fry, Mitchell McCorcle, Michelle Spain, William Pasmore, and Donald Wolfe. Splendid support was provided by a group of students in my integrative seminar, which included Thomas Blue, Harry S. Jonas III, Christopher Barlow, Leo Duncan, Jared Florian, Shirley Graves, Lennox Joseph, Jacquie McLemore, Jeanne Neumann, Richard Rosen, and Dorothy Siminovitch. These students acted as shadow scholars to invited authors and created the community for exciting learning opportunities. Two of my graduate students, Harry S. Jonas III and Karen Locke, carried the major task of organizing and managing the conference; and their thoughtful diligence and personal commitment was at the core of our success. Mitchell McCorcle was a splendid colleague to me in administering the final write-up of chapters, and his personal support was very valuable. Dean Scott Cowen of the Weatherhead School of Management provided personal encouragement and part of the financial support. I am grateful to all and to many others who remain unmentioned.

Warren Bennis, Richard O. Mason, and Ian I. Mitroff, who are consulting editors for the Jossey-Bass Management Series, have been continuously supportive, thoughtful, and generous with their ideas and time. And, of course, our administrative staff—Amanda Brown Rowans, Debbie Ptak, Retta Holdorf, and Carol Shurmer— deserve all the cheers for their help in preparing this manuscript.

Cleveland, Ohio   SURESH SRIVASTVA
January 1986

Contents

Part Two: Executive Power in Use

Part Three: The Transformation of Executive Power

The Authors

Suresh Srivastva is professor of organizational behavior in the Department of Organizational Behavior of the Weatherhead School of Management, Case Western Reserve University, serving as chairman of the department from 1970 to 1984. He received his Ph.D. degree (1960) from the University of Michigan in social psychology. In addition to his work as a consultant for industrial enterprises and health care systems in the field of organization development, he is the author of numerous articles in the area of psychology and management problems. His major books include *Behavioral Sciences in Management* (1967), *Human Factors in Industry* (1970), *Anatomy of a Strike* (1972, with I. Dayal and T. Alfred), *Job Satisfaction and Productivity* (1975, with others), *Management of Work* (1981, with T. Cummings), and *The Executive Mind* (1983, with others).

Frank J. Barrett is a Ph.D. candidate in organizational behavior at the Weatherhead School of Management, Case Western Reserve University. He received his B.A. degree (1975) in government and international relations and his M.A. degree (1977) in English from the University of Notre Dame. He is also an active jazz pianist. He has worked with the Cleveland Clinic, university hospitals, General Electric, and municipal and county government agencies. His current research interests include the role of language, metaphor, and myth in group processes and the creative management of conflict.

David E. Berlew is a cofounder and president of Situation Management Systems, Inc. (SMS), a Plymouth, Massachusetts-based firm that develops, publishes, and distributes training and development programs for business and government organizations. He received his B.A. degree (1956) from Wesleyan University in psychology, his M.A. degree (1958) from Harvard University in clinical psychology, and his Ph.D. degree (1960) from Harvard University in social psychology. Berlew is the author or coauthor of numerous chapters in edited volumes, book reviews, and articles; codeveloper of the Positive Power and Influence Programs and the Positive Negotiation Program, distributed internationally by SMS; and coeditor of *Interpersonal Dynamics* (1964, 1968, 1973).

L. David Brown is professor and chairman of the Department of Organizational Behavior at Boston University. He is also president of the Institute for Development Research and of the Organization Development Division of the Academy of Management; a director of the NTL Institute for Applied Behavioral Science; and an associate editor of the *Journal of Applied Behavioral Science*. He received a B.A. degree (1963) from Harvard University in social relations and an LL.B. degree (1969) and a Ph.D. degree (1971) in organizational behavior from Yale University. In addition to numerous articles and chapters, he has authored or coauthored *Group Relations and Organizational Diagnosis* (forthcoming), *Managing Conflict at Organizational Interfaces* (1982), and *Learning from Changing* (1975).

W. Warner Burke is a member of the faculty at Teachers College, Columbia University. Prior to his appointment there, he was chairman of the Department of Management at Clark University in Worcester, Massachusetts. He received his B.A. degree (1957) from Furman University in psychology and his M.A. (1961) and Ph.D. (1963) degrees from the University of Texas in psychology and social psychology, respectively. He has been an organization and management development consultant to a variety of organizations; is editor of the journal *Organizational Dynamics*; and has published numerous articles, book chapters, and books. His latest book is *Organization Development: Principles and Practices* (1982).

He holds the Diplomate in Industrial/Organizational Psychology, American Board of Professional Psychology.

David L. Cooperrider is assistant professor of organizational behavior in the Weatherhead School of Management, Case Western Reserve University. He received his B.A. degree (1976) from Augustana College in psychology; his M.S. degree (1982) from George Williams College in organizational behavior; and his Ph.D. degree (1985) from Case Western Reserve University in organizational behavior. Recently he has been engaged in research on the relationship between organizational ideology, executive power, and the management of change. Cooperrider is the author of a number of articles on alienation and authenticity in organizations and is coauthor of an experiential book and training manual, *Developing Organizations for High Performance* (1985). He is also very active as a management educator and consultant.

Robert T. Golembiewski is research professor of management and professor of political science at the University of Georgia. He received an interdisciplinary B.A. degree in social sciences (1954) from Princeton University and his M.A. (1956) and Ph.D. (1958) degrees, both in political science, from Yale University. He serves on the editorial board of the *Academy of Management Journal* and several other journals; on the advisory board of the Institute of Organization Development; and in various regional and national roles with Certified Consultants International. Alone or with collaborators, he has authored or edited over forty books, including *Approaches to Planned Change* (2 vols., 1979) and *Humanizing Public Organizations* (1984). He has also published numerous scholarly articles, case studies, and research notes.

Larry E. Greiner is professor of management and organization in the School of Business Administration at the University of Southern California. He received a B.S. degree (1955) from the University of Kansas and M.B.A. (1960) and D.B.A. (1965) degrees from the Harvard Business School. He is the author of numerous publications on the subject of organization change and development, including the *Harvard Business Review* classics "Evolution and Revolution as Organizations Grow" and "Breakthrough in Organization Development." His most recent publication is *Consulting to Management* (1983, with Robert Metzger). Currently, he is on the board of directors of Management Analysis Center, an international management consulting firm, and on the editorial board of *Organization Dynamics*.

John P. Kotter has taught at the Harvard Business School since 1972. He received his B.S. degree (1968) from Massachusetts Institute of Technology in electrical engineering, his M.S. degree (1970) from MIT in organizational psychology, and his Ph.D. degree (1972) from Harvard University in organizational behavior. Since receiving his doctorate, Kotter has completed six books, written more than a dozen articles, and designed two new courses for the M.B.A. curriculum. His books include *The General Managers* (1982); *Power in Management* (1979); and *Organizational Dynamics: Diagnosis and Intervention* (1978). Two of his *Harvard Business Review* articles were selected for McKinsey awards for being among the best of the year: "Power, Dependence, and Effective Management" (1977) and "Managing Your Boss" (1980, with John Gararro).

Meryl Reis Louis serves at Boston University as an associate professor in the School of Management, a research assistant at the Center for Applied Social Science, and a fellow of the Human Resources Policy Institute. She has been a management consultant on the staff of Arthur Andersen and Company and a counselor in a community mental health center. She received her B.S. degree (1967) in business, her M.S. degree (1968) in management theory, and her Ph.D. degree (1978) in organizational sciences, all from the Graduate School of Management at the University of California at Los Angeles. She is a member of the board of directors of the Organizational Behavior Teaching Society and is on the editorial review boards of the *Academy of Management Review, Administrative Science Quarterly,* and *Exchange: The Organizational Behavior Teaching Journal.* Her work has been published in *Organizational Dynamics, Human Systems Management, Administrative Science*

Quarterly, Academy of Management Review, Wharton Magazine, and several edited volumes.

Eric J. Miller has been on the staff of the Tavistock Institute of Human Relations since 1958. He received his Ph.D. degree (1950) from Cambridge University. At the Tavistock Institute, his principal interests have been organizational change and development and the relatedness of the individual to the group and the organization. He is director of the Group Relations Training Program at the institute and is also policy adviser to the Organisation for Promoting Understanding in Society (OPUS). His books include *Systems of Organisation* (1967, with A. K. Rice), *A Life Apart* (1979, with G. V. Gwynne), *Task and Organisation* (1976), and *A Life Together* (1981, with T. Dartington and G. V. Gywnne).

Eric H. Neilsen has served on the faculties at Katholik University of Leuven, Belgium; Harvard Business School; and Case Western Reserve University, where he was director of the Master's Program in Organization Development and Analysis. He received his B.A. degree (1965) from Princeton University in sociology and his M.A. (1970) and Ph.D. (1970) degrees from Harvard University in sociology. He is the author of *Becoming an OD Practitioner* (1984) and has also published articles in numerous professional journals and in anthologies. He has served on the editorial board of *Exchange: The Organizational Behavior Teaching Journal* and in 1982 was the conference coordinator for the Ninth Annual Organizational Behavior Teaching Conference.

William A. Pasmore is associate professor of organizational behavior in the Department of Organizational Behavior of the Weatherhead School of Management, Case Western Reserve University. He received his B.A. degree (1973) in industrial management and his Ph.D. degree (1976) in administrative science, both from Purdue University. As a certified consultant, he has worked with many diverse organizations. In addition to numerous articles, he is coauthor of *Sociotechnical Systems: A Sourcebook* (1978, with Jack Sherwood) and is currently working on an additional volume, *Using Sociotechnical Systems to Design Effective Organizations* for the Wiley Series on Organizational Assessment and Change.

Andrew M. Pettigrew is professor of organizational behavior and head of the OB group at the School of Industrial and Business Studies, University of Warwick, Coventry, England. He was trained in sociology and industrial sociology at Liverpool University and received his Ph.D. degree (1970) from Manchester Business School. Pettigrew is on the editorial board of *Administrative Science Quarterly* and is a member of the Industry and Employment Committee of the British Social Science Research Council. He is the author of *The Politics of Organizational Decision Making* (1983), *Implementing Strategic Decisions* (1975, with Enid Mumford), and *Context and Politics in Organizational Change* (1984). He has also written numerous book reviews, articles, and chapters in edited volumes.

John Van Maanen is a professor of organizational studies in the Sloan School of Management at Massachusetts Institute of Technology and is currently a Fulbright scholar in the Department of Sociology at the University of Surrey, engaged in a study of the supervision of police work in England. He earned his B.A. degree (1965) from California State University at Long Beach and his M.S. (1968) and Ph.D. (1972) degrees from the University of California, Irvine, all in sociology. He serves on the editorial boards of various journals; is the coauthor of *Varieties of Quantitative Research* (1982) and *Essays in Interpersonal Relations* (1979); and has written numerous research articles, chapters in edited works, book reviews, and popular essays.

Executive Power

*How Executives Influence
People and Organizations*

INTRODUCTION

Ways of Understanding
Executive Power

Suresh Srivastva, David L. Cooperrider

Over the past quarter century, we have all witnessed the erosion of faith in traditional concepts of power associated with a bureaucratic system of hierarchical obedience and command, subordination and superordination. The erosion of faith is attributable to many factors: unprecedented rapid changes in technologies and communications; increasing diversity and specialization of people at work; a better-educated, professionalized work force; widespread concern for more democratic life-styles; the desire for truly meaningful work; irreversible global interdependence; and the recognition that executives are all too human—not the omniscient or perfect beings we often wish them to be. The list goes on. But perhaps most illuminating is the widespread disenchantment with past management practices *as voiced by executives themselves.* As indicated by a number of authors in this volume, the attack on traditional bureaucratic management practices is frequently being led by executives themselves, who are risking their own careers to experiment with new and more effective ways of organizing. Leaders at the very senior levels of management in all industries are being called on to act as "change masters," "pathfinders," "statesmen," and "innovators" of the boldest sort. They are being asked to envision alternatives that have never yet existed, to challenge current notions of what is possible, to ignite the spirit of collective renewal, and to harness turbulent environmental forces to help move their organizations to higher levels of development.

There is reason, then, for a fresh look at the concept of power; and so the authors of this book have not been content merely

1

to add repetitious rhetoric to the overstated theme that "autocratic management is now history" or to sound the trumpet that a crisis exists in the executive suite. In fact, each, in his or her own manner, has approached the issue in a twofold way. Like the Chinese, who have two separate characters for the word "crisis"—one indicating danger, the other symbolizing opportunity—the contributors take us beyond the current malaise that surrounds many discussions of leadership. The strength of the book, therefore, rests squarely with the authors' capacity to articulate innovations in the functioning of executive power and to recognize the opportunities inherent in our modern-day context of rapid change. Just as important, they do this without denying the complexities, the subtleties, or the problems of power. The message that unites the authors is clear: Since the world in which power operates has become increasingly complex, so must our conceptions of power.

Implicit in each chapter are a number of themes, which run *throughout* the book. These themes, while largely tacit, are important to highlight because, amidst the diversity inherent in the separate works, the commonalities shed light on an intriguing question, a question that is nowhere specifically addressed—namely, *why the conjunction of the word "executive" with the notion of power?* In other words, is there something that distinguishes *executive* power from power in general? If not, there may be little point in employing the term "executive" to recognize a distinct kind of power in use.

What emerges from the tacit dialogue is a conception of power that has normative significance for a theory of executive work. That is, executive power is distinguished from "raw" power by its unique *intentionality* or focus. To the extent that the primary task of the chief executive is the *perpetuation and development of the organization as an active social whole,* then the term "executive power" refers to that which is directed to creating an active organization, sustaining an active organization, and transforming an organization in the direction of its fullest potential. Normatively, executive power is therefore entirely bound up with the practice of helping the organization become what it can potentially become—in human, technological, economic, and moral terms. The functioning of executive power therefore consists of understanding what the organization is, envisioning or generating ideas about what it can or should become, and initiating processes that bridge ideals with actual practice. Executive power is therefore directional instead of chaotic, thoughtful instead of blind, holistic instead of egocentric, empowering instead of oppressive, and choiceful instead of random.

In conceptual terms, we find that the functioning of executive power is embedded in processes of communicative exchange among human beings and is tempered by a set of culturally learned responses for managing situations involving interdependent actions among individuals. What this means in practice, as a number of the authors have argued, is that executive power is embodied or carried forward in and through three fundamental elements of organizational life: consensus, cooperation, and culture.

Consensus potential refers to an organization's capacity to generate alignment between members and the organization on matters of general policy, direction, mission, and general task requirements. An organization is high in consensus potential when it has the capacity to synthesize the commitment of multiple constituencies and stakeholders in response to specific challenges and aspirations. In this realm executive power is embodied in the *management of ideas,* the *management of agreement,* and the *management of groups and participatory processes. Cooperative potential* refers to an organization's capacity to catalyze cooperative interaction among individuals and groups. In this realm executive power is embodied in the *management of social arrangements* (structures, task designs, resource allocation, and reward systems) that support and encourage cooperative action vertically, horizontally, and through voluntarily emergent networks. *Cultural/spiritual potential* refers to a sense of timeless *destiny* about the organization, its role in its own area of endeavor as well as its larger role in its service to society. Through the *management of meaning* (symbols, beliefs, myths, ideals, and values), the executive is powerful to the extent that he or she can create a passionate culture, whereby all those in the organization are convinced of the human significance of their existence as organizational participants.

Taken together, these three "embodiments" of executive power form an indispensable conceptual scheme for building an appreciation of the enormous complexity of the executive role. As an ideal image of executive power, this reinforcing system of elements gives the executive a focus for creating, maintaining, and developing an organization as a sociocultural reality. Far from complete, this broad framework represents perhaps a beginning in a line of inquiry that recognizes that in a postindustrial world the ultimate frontier for the functioning of power is not technological, geographical, or economic, but social.

As indicated, the picture presented above is broad and is primarily intended to add to a deeper reading of the issues presented among the various authors. The specific issues discussed and highlighted by the authors not only bring this background alive but provide a rich diversity of thinking that no single conception could ever hope to capture.

The chapters have been organized into three sections representing the most significant common elements uniting groupings of authors. These dimensions, related to the functioning of power, include: (1) the initiation of executive power, (2) the maintenance of executive power, and (3) the transformation of executive power. The themes respond to a number of fundamental questions, respectively: First, what are the sources of executive power and how is it initiated and used to empower others? Second, once initiated, how is power maintained, strengthened, or preserved over time? Also, how is power used *unobtrusively* in order to prevent the escalation of open conflicts which then might require more overt expressions of executive intervention? Finally, how have executives dealt with the situations where past paradigms of power are outmoded or tarnished? Why doesn't it function in the ways it used to? What are the alternatives?

As noted in the preface, each section of the book emphasizes a function of executive power within the context of organizational life. That is, each area describes processes that are basic to the perpetuation and development of the organization as a whole. From this perspective executive power is treated less as an individual property and more as an evolving social process initiated in order to bring something new into the world, maintained in order to ensure continuity and stability, and transformed through ongoing processes of cultural evolution.

Sources of Executive Power

A number of years ago, the celebrated French philosopher Gabriel Marcel suggested that social existence, that life itself, is not so much a problem to be solved as a mystery to be engaged in, a paradox to be experienced. Indeed, much about the delivery of executive power is at present enigmatic. And there is paradox.

One such paradox, touched on by every author in this section, is that research into executive power inevitably leads one to considerations of powerlessness—the powerlessness of executives and the powerlessness of followers. From the executive perspective, there is growing respect for and acknowledgment of the simple truth argued by Barnard (1938): that executives are essentially powerless until the time comes when followers grant their leaders the authority to lead. Organizations, as he brilliantly described them, are essentially cooperative systems designed to accomplish tasks that cannot be achieved through individual effort. Cooperation entails choice; it is a voluntary act. Thus, power in a cooperative system is exercised only when those who are the target of power give their consent to the use of that power.

But that is not the only paradox. The other is what has been called the "empowerment paradox." According to this view, the key executive task is not so much to acquire power as to deliver power to followers, who might otherwise experience a sense of powerlessness. As McClelland (1979, p. 81) notes, there exists "the ultimate paradox of social leadership and social power: to be an effective leader, one must turn all his so-called followers into leaders."

The polarities of the two paradoxes appear logically unresolvable, and perhaps they are. But their juxtaposition invites an intriguing set of questions: Can executives use their power in order to free and mobilize the voluntary development of others—to heighten others' sense of efficacy, esteem, capacity for self-management, and aspiration level? Can executives liberate personal and organizational energy without using tactics of control over resources or punishments? Can they employ power in the service of participation, for engendering in others a sense of active responsibility for the creation of more cooperative, collaborative organizational cultures? These are just a sampling of questions that come to mind as one reads the chapters by John Kotter, David Berlew, Warner Burke, Eric Neilsen, and Meryl Louis. What these chapters have in common is their concern for the *sources* of power— that is, how executive power is actually acquired and set in motion to enable, activate, and empower others and thereby bring something novel into the world of organizing.

John Kotter challenges us immediately with the following proposition: The responsible development and use of power is *the central* executive task. The core of executive work is to acquire and maintain the necessary power, so that inevitable conflicts among interdependent and diverse groups can be managed in ways leading to creative outcomes, serving as many legitimate stakeholders as possible. This, he writes, is what leadership in our society is all about.

People who have not experienced or directly studied executive work, Kotter argues, cannot readily appreciate the precarious position our society puts such individuals in. Social and organizational reality has become so complex that no longer does the "authority" vested in the job represent enough power to get things done. The difference between the power granted through position and that required to conduct business effectively—that is, "the power gap"—has widened in recent years, primarily through unprecedented increases in the interdependence among diverse sets of individuals and organizations throughout the world. The effective executive, as indicated by Kotter's research, is therefore one who is skillful in acquiring sources of power far beyond the formal power that comes with the job. The additional bases of power are never freely granted the executive but are continuously amassed and constructed through constant attention, experimentation, and observation. In a sense, the effective executive becomes a full-time student of power, seeking to develop it by (1) acquiring information and ideas, (2) creating good working relations, (3) envisioning intelligent agendas for action, (4) sharpening personal skills in diagnosis and interpersonal influence, (5) constructing networks of cooperation, and (6) maintaining a good image and track record.

Kotter discusses each of these in detail; however, the key insight he offers us is that the sheer volume of power-oriented activity associated with executive work will continue to increase dramatically in the coming years, so much so that the acquisition and maintenance of power may in fact be the definitive feature of executive life.

David Berlew, in Chapter Two, begins by asking a significant question—one that is raised by almost every organizational executive: "What can I do that will affect the way others, who may be several levels or thousands of miles away, conduct our business?" The answer to this question, suggests Berlew, is best formulated by defining executive work as the "management of energy." He distinguishes between two types of energy—PUSH energy and PULL energy—that executives exercise in the influence of others. At the organizational level, PUSH energy is a dynamic equated with structural management systems, such as job descriptions, policies, and formal reward structures. These systems are equated with PUSH energy in that they *prescribe* actions to be taken or procedures to be followed. On the other hand, PULL energy is an influence process expressed in the culture and spirit of an organization. It has to do with the shared values and visions that members aspire to attain. Both PUSH and PULL energy are essential to creating energy alignment among an organization's members; however, organizations frequently become encrusted in the repetitious use of structural management systems and hence are often dominated by the use of PUSH energy. What is needed, Berlew suggests, is the enactment of "common-vision leadership," especially when missions are mundane, tasks are dull, employees are cynical, or members are being asked to cut back on resources yet need to accomplish more. Under these conditions there is no management solution in the use of power, only a leadership solution.

Common-vision leadership begins with an inward examination, whereby executives ask themselves: "What do I want to create? What excites me to the point that it could become a personal cause or mission? Fairness? Quality? Excellence? Service to others?" Second, the executive must translate an emerging system of ideas into a *common* vision. The challenge is to discover the superordinate values of a group or collectivity—values that tap into the hopes and dreams of individual members and thus bind them together. Third, common-vision leadership is generated through participatory processes and through face-to-face communications, which lend integrity and excitement to the vision. Finally, the executive must "walk the talk." Common-vision leadership is an act of caring; "it depends on love." An executive without integrity will fail to ignite the imaginations and passions of his or her followers. Common-vision leadership, Berlew sums up, is a close relative of "spiritual leadership." People are empowered through the articulation of significant ideals.

Warner Burke, in Chapter Three, explores the process of empowerment within a larger context: the movement throughout the postindustrial world toward greater participation, delegation of authority, and democracy at the workplace. For Burke, to empower implies the granting of power; indeed, the sharing of power, perhaps by definition, means to *empower* others. Interestingly, Burke reverses Lord Acton's famous axiom that "power corrupts" to highlight that powerlessness corrupts as well. The solution to the problem of powerlessness is to create conditions where people can feel powerful. The antidote to powerlessness is obviously empowerment. But what exactly does this mean?

Burke grapples with this complex question by arguing that first we need to distinguish between management and leadership. After an extensive review of a number of classics, he offers a clear conceptual distinction between the empowerment dimensions of managing versus those of leading. The analysis has a number of direct parallels to Berlew's PUSH and PULL types of energy. For example, *leaders* provide direction for followers via ideals, vision, inspiration, and intense feelings involving passions of both love and hate. *Managers,* on the other hand, are noted for having less personal involvement with subordinates, greater detachment from the world of ideals and values, and a greater propensity to rely on formal reward structures as a means for directing others' activities. The difference between management and leadership is a simple one, but in practice it is a difference that can make *all* the difference, especially in the realm of innovation and change.

Above all, leaders are transformational. They are, according to Burke's review, "visionary, solitary, inspirational figures consumed with certain ideals and goals." By definition, they never leave the world as they entered it. Change is the order, Burke insists, not the exception.

The logic of empowerment is refined further in Chapter Four. Eric Neilsen provides a most articulate analysis of the "stages" of empowerment, including a sociological explanation of the special relevance of empowerment to our modern-day corporate world. Neilsen claims that executives today face an understandable crisis with respect to the initiation of power. The crisis is summed up in the concepts of authority and responsibility—and their dynamic interrelationship. In brief, executives today are being held responsible by more and more constituencies; at the same time, the authority that followers are willing to grant executives has considerably decreased. Multiple factors have contributed to making blind deference to any authority less viable, with the result that executives are caught in an almost untenable position.

Neilsen discusses two possible actions that executives can take in response to the crisis. First, the executive can accumulate sources of power *other than positional power* until enough power has been acquired to match his or her responsibilities. Second (the alternative that Neilsen clearly advocates), the executive can attempt to empower members of the organization, so that there is a sharing of responsibility as needed to ensure the system's long-term welfare. While the first strategy resonates with the Western ethic of rugged individualism, Neilsen believes that the second approach holds special promise because of the unique interdependencies defining our postindustrial future.

Neilsen bases his treatment of "empowerment strategies" on a theory of group development that highlights the need for executives to understand the dynamic stages of growth that social systems undergo. As a system grows from birth to maturity, there are differing approaches to empowerment that may be more or less relevant. That is, each successive stage of development requires a distinct type of leadership, which then *empowers* the group to move on to a more complex, mature level of development. Like Berlew and Burke, Neilsen sees the initiation of power as moving from prescription to inspiration, from PUSH to PULL, and from managing to leading. Neilsen, however, introduces more complexity into the analysis by taking into account an important life reality: groups and organizations develop at different rates and thereby have differing needs in relation to the exercise of executive power.

Ultimately, inquiry into the phenomenon of power must take a normative stance: What is the right use of power? What is the best kind of social order? As we engage in the delivery of power, we need continuously to concern ourselves with the value-laden issue: The initiation of power—for what? Toward what ends should executives be working?

Meryl Reis Louis, in Chapter Five, goes further than any of the other contributors in trying to make explicit what usually remains tacit. She does this by pursuing an "action-in-context" approach, which assumes that the phenomenon of power has little if any meaning apart from the purposeful and experiential context in which it operates. Too often, she argues, we discuss power in impersonal terms removed from real-life experience, in the sterile arena of Weberian bureaucracy, where human beings are related to each other like cogs in a machine. For Louis, research of this type (including traditional leadership frameworks in general) lacks a sense of some larger mission or mandate. More fruitful research, in her view, would attempt to discover the experiential continuities in organizational life; such research promises fruitful knowledge about the genuine human and social ends toward which executive action ought to be committed. Executive power, she suggests, must at once be humanized and humanizing; that is, it should function along with the informed consent of the governed and become an enlightened partner in the development of people and community. The action-in-context approach is therefore an appeal for the development of a truly significant—a humanly significant—applied science of administration. It is a daring appeal.

Accordingly, Louis takes a few tentative steps in outlining her viewpoint. Beginning with a "revised calculus of individual performance," she urges executives to use their power to help create person-job relationships characterized by notions of harmony and flow. Four features contribute to such experience: (1) job situations that afford people a sense of contribution, of making a real difference; (2) job situations that are marked by experiences of fun, play, and pleasure; (3) job situations that stretch the individual; (4) contexts that provide developmental support for the individual. Going further, Louis asks about the initiation of power at the *organizational* level: Toward what *organizational* aims should executives direct their actions and otherwise exercise power? Drawing on the work of Harrison (1983), she talks about the needs for "alignment" and "attunement." Alignment refers to the intimate connection between organizational members and mission, while attunement calls attention to the connection among members. Both of these highlight the need for worker input, initiative, and involvement in order to develop a climate of caring, ownership and cooperative work relations.

Executive Power in Use

Indeed, executives are powerful actors and shapers of the organizational society in which all of us live (Useem, 1984). Therefore, it behooves us—as social scientists, executives, and responsible citizens—to understand the phenomenon of power, including the sources of power and the ways in which power is maintained. For some of us, inquiry into the very topic of power is frightening; for others, it is a call to adventure. But for most, the lure of power has an almost primordial appeal. Indeed, the study of power is one of the oldest professions in the world. It was tales of power that Herodotus, the first historian, delighted to portray (Curtis, 1961). Yet, for all its attraction and significance, there remains a troublesome fact: We have relatively little firsthand, empirical knowledge concerning the maintenance of power at the very senior levels of management.

The theme of maintenance refers to processes through which executive power is strengthened, sustained, and preserved over time. What the chapters in this section show, however, is that the durability of executive power does not equal stability. The theme of maintenance does not refer to something static but is entirely bound up with such active processes as (1) continuously cultivating new sources of power, (2) managing through unobtrusive power relations, (3) maintaining and regenerating executive teamwork, and (4) supporting nonbureaucratic relationships in the form of "organizational time-outs."

The authors whose chapters are included in this section are Andrew Pettigrew, Larry Greiner, Robert Golembiewski, and John Van Maanen. Each chapter adds a unique dimension to our understanding of the sources, patterns, and ways in which executives maintain their power.

Andrew Pettigrew, in Chapter Six, treats us to a fascinating account of the acquisition and maintenance of business power in Great Britain. Specifically, he offers insight into the role of senior executives in generating strategic change in Imperial Chemical Industries (ICI), one of Europe's largest manufacturing firms. The research on which Pettigrew bases his chapter represents a landmark in the scientific study of executive power. He draws on longitudinal data from interviews, documents, and observations covering a period of twenty-four years, 1960–1984.

Pettigrew argues that it is the use of *unobtrusive power* by key executives which lays the groundwork for major, strategic organizational change. Unlike the overt use of power, which is used to produce preferred outcomes in the face of active conflict, unobtrusive power is used to *prevent* conflict from occurring. The use of power in this sense revolves around attempts to create agreement and legitimacy for certain arrangements, so that they are never questioned by others. Power is used to prevent conflicts by shaping the preferences, perceptions, and beliefs of potential opponents in such a way that alternatives do not even occur to them. The source of such power lies with the executive's capacity for managing ideas, myths, ideologies, and other systems of meaning. For example, the power of myths can be used to discredit opponents and also to prevent or defeat *potential* opposition.

After demonstrating that little is known empirically about the maintenance of power by very senior-level executives, Pettigrew offers data that destroy the mythical "commander" view of executive work. In managing strategic change, he shows, executives rarely operate as omnipotent commanders in charge of a linear problem-solving process; instead, they skillfully and incrementally operate at an ideological level *before* crisis sets in, attempting to create agreement and justification for a new order of things. Executives are consensus generators, not commanders, and their power in this realm rests on many sources: building awareness of need, legitimizing new viewpoints, building coalitions of support, capitalizing on environmental disturbances, creating educational opportunities, designing forums for dialogue, building climates of commitment, and so on. In short, the development of strategic change in the firm takes on the character of "a political-learning process."

The political process within the executive group is considered by Larry Greiner in Chapter Seven. In his view, executive power is essentially a *social* phenomenon, the product of a group context rather than purely individual attributes. Executive power is neither acquired nor maintained in a social vacuum. To understand executive power, we need to understand the executive group.

As an organization change theorist, Greiner maintains that many well-intended attempts to improve organizations are thwarted because of our lack of knowledge about patterns of power operating at the top level. Top-management politics, he contends, is a subject about which management scholars have been strangely silent. He argues the importance of astute political diagnosis during the start of any change project and calls for new directions in research and consultancy at the senior-management level. His chapter, containing "an in-depth case description of a consultant's intervention in a major corporation," is offered as an initial step in this direction.

In Chapter Eight Robert Golembiewski tells the story of his work with a fast-track public works project. As consultant to the Metropolitan Rapid Transit Authority (MARTA), Golembiewski argues that executive power needs to be constrained in order to gain focus and that it requires mutual trust in order to be maintained. His real concern lies with investigating the human and social costs to executives engaged in high-pressure, temporary project-type organizations. Golembiewski's treatment of the theme "mainte-nance" thereby differs from the others in this section. He looks not so much at sources or patterns of executive power as at ways to maintain the executive group as a healthy well-functioning social system. He points out the importance of team building, including the development of a set of values needed for sustaining "regenerative interaction systems at work."

The final chapter in this section (Chapter Nine) is a distinctive piece of work by John Van Maanen. In a fascinating account of power relations in a police department, Van Maanen addresses the issue of power in lucid detail by using ethnographic methods of social description. According to Van Maanen, it makes little sense to try to understand power through the abstract concepts often used by social scientists; instead, one must first enter the scene directly, open to learning about real-world complexities and ambiguities.

An intriguing finding of Van Maanen is that bureaucratic power relations are largely maintained through what he calls "organizational time-outs." By linking the observed social patterns of drinking among police officers to the negotiation and maintenance of power within the organization, Van Maanen shows, paradoxically, that bureaucratic power relations (at least in the organization studied) are maintained primarily through interactions that are themselves nonbureaucratic—that is, through interactions where people are able to cast aside their prescribed roles and meet each other outside of hierarchical constraints. In other words, the maintenance of bureaucracy might well depend on nonbureaucratic processes of interaction. The implication of this finding begins to stretch the imagination and certainly calls into question the very premises of bureaucratic organization at a deep and basic level.

Transformation of Executive Power

The topic of power has been studied from the earliest times of recorded history. Interestingly, questions about the phenomenon have consistently been raised during periods of crisis—economic, cultural, spiritual, or political. Sir Leslie Stephen's aphorism sums up the essence of this observation perfectly: thinking about power is the offspring of revolution—or the signal of an approaching one (Curtis, 1961). In this section William Pasmore, Eric Miller, and L. David Brown delve deeper into "the crisis of executive power" and raise issues about its future functioning. These authors have effectively combined their own grounded observations with speculative thought—a type of reasoning Whitehead ([1933] 1967, p. 82) recommends for converting the decay of one order into the birth of its successor: "It is the essence of such speculation that it transcends immediate fact. Its business is to make thought creative of the future. It effects this by its vision of systems of ideas, including observation, but generalized beyond it."

Specifically, the authors look at the many societal transformations that, taken together, are contributing to a dramatic reshaping of the paradigm of power. This inquiry, therefore, is of utmost and immediate importance, since executive power has direct relevance to a myriad of life-threatening global problems and to the illumination of human purposes in our technologically sophisticated nuclear age.

William Pasmore, in Chapter Ten, argues that the rafters supporting the power structures of traditional American organizations are shaking. But he also takes a realistic look at what we may be leaving behind. First he considers the forces that are both attacking and supporting traditional uses of executive power. He concludes that there are as many compelling reasons to believe that executives will continue along the traditional path as there are to believe that the functioning of executive power will undergo monumental transformation. This is especially true, he argues, in organizations with long-linked technologies in which simple tasks are performed repetitively and coordination is best achieved through standardization. Such standardization and bureaucratization leave little room for people to make changes in how things are done. However, peering in the other direction, Pasmore builds an equally convincing argument. Here he looks objectively at the forces supporting and hindering the movement toward democracy in the workplace and concludes that, after undergoing transformation, executive power and workplace democracy probably will turn out to be mutually supportive rather than mutually exclusive. The "tea leaves," he therefore suggests, indicate that there will be a blending of more traditional executive roles with more democratic ones. In essence, Pasmore argues that the future will demand a strong type of executive leadership based on vision and appeal to follower values. That leadership will invoke a type of power that resides in the collectivity, not in the individual; that is, it will be consensual, not autocratic, in nature.

In Chapter Eleven Eric Miller postulates that traumatic changes of the past five years have enabled individuals to take a more autonomous position in relation to organizations, reflecting a rather broad-based demolition of the myth of authority. In a masterful account of social trends occurring in Great Britain from the end of World War II to the present, Miller sees reason for hope in the new "self-authority" that individuals are exercising in organizations. The older system of power relations—based on passive compliance and blind conformity—is no longer seen as viable. For instance, given (1) the complexity of problems that organizations must now tackle and (2) the adaptive task orientation that is required to survive, a system of power relations based on the myth of omniscience at the top of the hierarchy is untenable. Hence, obedience, he writes, is the "kiss of organizational death."

Miller sweeps us along quickly into a substantial analysis of the British *dependency culture* emerging shortly after the war. Drawing on his experiences as director of the Tavistock Institute, where he has been engaged in research with a group called OPUS (Organisation for Promoting Understanding in Society), Miller documents both the rise and the failure of the culture of dependency. "Failed dependency" is the concept he develops to describe the transformation leading to the breakdown of certain beliefs about the dependability of organizations and the unlimited security offered by the "bountiful national breast." Miller shows that excessive unemployment rates, leading to business retrenchment and constrained career progression, have forced many workers to redefine their identity in the direction of greater autonomy and self-management. In this regard Miller envisages a possible "third role" for people in organizations: a role where people are seen not as employees or members of a work group or a union but as "citizens" of the organization as a community. However, with a sobering note of constraint, Miller reminds us that such changes will not happen automatically or inevitably because locked deep inside all of us are very primordial needs for security and dependency.

In Chapter Twelve L. David Brown offers us a rare glimpse into the dynamics of executive power functioning *outside* the boundaries of traditional organizational influence paradigms. While he does not go so far as to describe or suggest an ideal alternative to traditional practices, he does accomplish something that is probably even more of an achievement: he outlines, in detail, the unique skills that executives actually use in situations where *they* must help create new paradigms of power. That is, instead of prescribing what the future paradigm should look like, Brown superbly articulates the competencies needed to manage the process of transformation itself.

The chapter is based on Brown's research and consultation with executives in "community partnerships." These partnerships are best described as social inventions that bring together organizational representatives from different sectors—public, private, education, union, neighborhood—to solve broad problems that none could solve themselves. The use of community partnerships is on the rise throughout society (for example, a recent survey in Massachusetts showed more than a hundred public-private partnerships operating in that state alone). However, the truly significant aspect of these systems for purposes of our study is that they represent organizational forms where executives have virtually no position power or distinct control over resources. In fact, because such partnerships are relatively "unorganized," they fail to have a firmly entrenched "influence paradigm," which provides the blueprint that most corporations routinely use to determine who has organizational power and how such power should be exercised. Drawing on the theoretical work of Lukes (1974), Brown argues that, to understand executive power outside traditional organizational frameworks (which tend to emphasize power through *control over resources*), we need to understand two other dimensions of power: (1) control over *access and agendas* for decision making and (2) control over *awareness*. Thus, executive power in community partnerships may require skills for which organizational experience is poor preparation. Executive power in a partnership situation derives more from *personal credibility* than it does from position. To exercise power successfully, Brown demonstrates, executives must (1) use interpersonal skills to facilitate open discussion, (2) show genuine interest in others as people, and (3) display empathy in their efforts to understand the situation and others in it. Other critical skills carefully described by Brown include capacities for participation in building *inclusive visions,* organizing *shared decision* processes, and *balancing power* distributions in ways that promote task accomplishment. Creating partnerships that permit such participation and shared influence requires a complex set of human skills in managing the *access* and *awareness* dimensions of power, dimensions that many executives have yet to master. Brown concludes on a practical note, arguing that the competencies required to create successful partnerships are precisely the skills executives need in order to successfully transform the older paradigms of power in organizations where traditional practices have become illegitimate in the eyes of its members.

Toward a Normative Conception of Executive Power

Good social research, someone once said, has a dual task to accomplish: to lead us out of naiveté and into a more profound affirmation of life. It is in this spirit that the concluding chapter, by Suresh Srivastva and Frank Barrett, needs to be read. For, according to these authors, what we are dealing with in our study of power is something more than sterile abstraction. When we grapple with power, we are dealing with real and often dramatic interactions among human beings—interactions that give shape and direction to the course of human history. As an experience in living, issues of power are reported daily in the media and are contributing to an awareness of the intensive interdependence of all people in all parts of the world. Indeed, as a civilization, ours is the most interdependent *and* powerful the earth has ever known. Yet our power, it seems, is often contradicted by our experiences of powerlessness. As we are reminded so often today, we are the first civilization that has not only the capacity to contribute to history but also the power to end it. Because of this, propose Srivastva and Barrett, we need to bring to our study of power a keen affirmation of life: the aim of the student of power is and must be the constructive development of the human condition of the world.

Thus, Srivastva and Barrett take an integrative, pragmatic, and normative look at the functioning of executive power. For them, the key to executive effort is not to get people to do things they *would not* otherwise do; rather, the primary thrust of executive power is to enable organizations to do things they *could not* otherwise do. The challenge, they argue, is not one of domination but one of enablement.

The essential calling of the executive role—the element that distinguishes it from all others—is to act on the interests of an organization as a unified totality in order to help move our productive social systems to higher stages of development. The authors elaborate on this perspective by noting the incredible complexity, ambiguity, and contextual plurality of modern-day executive work and then go on to advance an applied focus intended to help executives make use of the learnings offered throughout the book. They present a series of principles that link the functioning of executive power to the management of ideas and organizational agreement (consensus); to the management of social arrangements for the maximization of interdependent action (cooperation); and to the management of meaning, which lends significance and definition to lives of organizational participants (culture/spirit). The functioning of executive power, in this sense, is one of the highest activities of human expression. It is also one of the least understood.

Like the other chapters, this concluding chapter is marked by a spirit of faith in human possibility. While scholars in the past have tended to debase the currency of power, this chapter affirms that there is an element of hope in the very articulation of the concept itself. For executive power—normatively conceived and dynamically understood—assumes an element of human choice in socio-cultural affairs; it assumes that situations are not totally determined by tragic forces beyond our conscious control; and it provides affirmation that people, together, can create social-organizational arrangements congenial to the human spirit.

The study of power, therefore, is a truly meaningful study precisely because it places us in a world that is dynamic and unfinished. It reminds us that the evolution of human culture is primarily and undeniably a human task. It reminds us that we live in a world where we can each assume some measure of joint authorship in the future, if we so choose.

ONE

Why Power
and Influence Issues
Are at the Very Core
of Executive Work

John P. Kotter

This chapter will argue four basic points. First, that the responsible development and use of power is *the* central executive function. Second, that this aspect of work is becoming a larger and larger part of almost all managerial, professional, and technical jobs today. Third, that because of the complex social milieu surrounding such jobs, developing and using power in a responsible way can be an enormously difficult task. Finally, that far too many people today are unaware of these realities—a condition that benefits very few of us.

The two main concepts employed in making the argument, other than the basic concept of power itself, are *diversity* and *interdependence*. The first refers to differences among people with respect to goals, values, stakes, assumptions, and perceptions. The latter is defined as a state in which two or more parties have power over each other because they are, to some degree, dependent on each other. Interdependence can be contrasted with a state of independence, where parties have no power over each other, and with a state of unilateral dependence, or some form of dominance, where one party has power over another, but not vice versa.

These two concepts are of central importance because it is the high degree of diversity and interdependence existing today that makes power issues so important and so difficult. The logic, which extends the original use of these concepts in an organizational setting (Lorsch and Allen, 1973), is as follows. The more interdependent relationships associated with a job, the more one cannot act unilaterally or simply demand that others cooperate. With a great many interdependencies, one is constantly forced to take into account the power of others and to look for ways to deal with that power. When those many interdependent relationships are in a highly diverse group of others, conflict (or at least potential conflict) becomes the norm, not the exception. With great diversity, finding ways to influence people and events so as to resolve all the conflicts in efficient and reasonable ways becomes enormously difficult. Diversity and conflict easily evolve into adversity, a we-them and win-lose mentality, power struggles, bureaucratic infighting, and parochial politics. And that is precisely what we find far too often in complex organizations today.

To some degree power struggles have been with us a long time. One can find instances of people or groups in primitive societies fighting for dominance. But the sheer volume of power-oriented activity associated with work, the number of people involved, and the complexity of it all, have increased dramatically in the very recent past—basically because work-related diversity and interdependence have grown enormously in the last century. The recentness of the change is one of the key reasons why many people are only partially aware of the realities described in this chapter.

The fundamental force behind these shifts is probably technological change. The technological revolutions of the eighteenth and nineteenth centuries helped undermine traditional concentrations of power (with kings and popes) and helped create the organizational society that is the hallmark of the twentieth century.

We often forget how much has changed in the past century and a half (see Robertson, 1955, and Chandler, 1980, for a more complete review of change during this period). The world of work for a typical person before 1840 was a struggle against nature. That person, and most of his forebears during the preceding 10,000 years, was a poor farmer. He spent most of his time working with things, not with people. There were some work-related interdependent relationships, but not many. And the people involved in those relationships tended not to be a very diverse lot; they often had similar educational, religious, ethnic, and national backgrounds. Conflicts among these parties certainly existed from time to time, but they were few in number and relatively straightforward in content. Work energy mainly went into plowing, seeding, mending, feeding, and the like.

Of course, "executives" in 1840 (and before) faced a considerably more complex milieu. But there were not that many executives back then; those helping to run organizations employing 500 or more people numbered in the hundreds (or a few thousand at most) in 1840, versus possibly over a million today. And for most of them, the number of important interdependent relationships, and the diversity of the people in those relationships, was very small compared to today.

An executive of 1840 would typically have to deal with a very limited geographical market. Transportation and communication difficulties made serving a larger market either impossible or uneconomical. He probably would have had to depend on a few local suppliers, but not many. Products and services were technologically simple and did not require a significant number of different inputs. Some form of government could not be ignored, but it was undoubtedly small and limited in its demands. Inside the organization the executive would have been somewhat dependent on key employees, but there would have been very few of them. Relatively uncomplicated technology, simple products, and small volumes required a small number of simple jobs, which could often be staffed by easily replaceable people. And the employee group would have been relatively homogeneous overall, drawn from a relatively homogeneous local labor pool.

A typical executive today works in a completely different world. A century and a half of technological evolution has produced communication and transportation technologies that make our entire planet a global marketplace. Medical, agricultural, and other industrial technological advances have increased the population in that market dramatically and have given most people a vastly increased purchasing power. Industrial technologies, beginning with the steam engine, have led to larger and larger factories to produce products for that marketplace. As industrial and retail organizations have grown in size and number, more and more organizations of a different sort have emerged, either to provide services for these firms (for example, accounting services) or for their increasingly urbanized factory-oriented labor force (services such as schools, hospitals, and local government) or to regulate their behavior (the function of organizations such as the Federal Trade Commission or the United Auto Workers).

As a result of this technologically driven set of changes, a typical executive today has to deal with thousands of interdependent relationships—linkages to people, groups, or organizations that have the power to affect his job performance. And the diversity of goals, opinions, and beliefs among these players is typically enormous (Kotter, 1982).

It is not unusual for an executive today, even in a relatively small company, to have to deal with hundreds of different markets in dozens of countries. He or she might serve these markets with 20, 200, or even 2,000 different technologically complex products or services, which demand a huge network of suppliers for parts, people, and money. In addition, there might be any number of unions, government units, even media organizations that are relevant and important and powerful. Inside the firm this person will be dependent on a highly specialized labor force organized into subunits that have different missions. The labor force will typically include both young and old, black and white, men and women, MBAs and high school dropouts, United States citizens and noncitizens. And many of these people will work in complex jobs where they cannot be quickly or easily replaced.

Although this social complexity peaks in executive jobs, it is found to some degree today in almost all managerial, professional, and technical work. Particularly since World War II, the growth of increasingly complex organizations has forced executives to "decentralize," which means asking more and more middle-level managers and professionals to help deal with some of the diversity and interdependence. And dozens of different trends have increased either diversity or interdependence at almost all levels during the past twenty-five years—trends such as corporate diversification, growth of government, increasing international competition, and more and more women and minorities entering the labor force at higher levels (see Kotter, 1985, especially chap. 2).

With this great increase in social complexity has come a corresponding (and predictable) increase in conflict among people at work and in the effort spent trying to deal with this conflict. Decreasing autonomy has forced people to allocate more and more time seeking to get others to help or to cooperate or to comply with their decisions. But diversity has made this a more and more difficult task. A new product specification decision that satisfies the engineers in a firm is often unacceptable to the marketing people. A delivery time decision that satisfies one customer often has unacceptable consequences for another customer or for certain manufacturing managers. A policy decision that satisfies one set of government regulators is often unacceptable to those managers who must carry out the policy and is sometimes unacceptable to yet another set of government regulators. Wage decisions that please a union upset stockholders. Resource allocation decisions that increase capital spending in one division of a firm upset managers in other divisions. Affirmative action policies that please minorities and women displease many white males. A new product design that pleases customers in Germany is unacceptable to customers in Brazil.

The sheer magnitude of all this conflict is staggering. Each and every day, millions of conflicts emerge, sometimes over the most trivial issues (where to put the water cooler) and sometimes over issues of monumental importance (nuclear arms). In complex organizations today, it is a rare decision issue or implementation issue that is devoid of at least the potential for conflict.

The burden for resolving all these conflicts in sensible and efficient ways falls broadly. All managerial, professional, and technical personnel in organizations are involved. But the burden falls most heavily on those in executive jobs—jobs that link their incumbents interdependently to the largest and most diverse groups of others. This burden is highly complex, especially if compared to the conflict resolution problem under conditions of little diversity and interdependence. When few people are involved (a very limited amount of interdependence), and when the differences among those people are small (very limited diversity), resolving conflicts in both efficient and effective ways is relatively easy today. The problem has been well researched, especially by specialists in organizational development (OD), and the solution now is reasonably clear. The parties should get together, confront the issues in a straightforward way, and search for a creative solution that satisfies the key needs of all the people involved. Or they can defer to the person who has the most relevant knowledge or expertise; that person will then search for the optimum solution and, once he or she has it, present it to the others.

When there are a lot of people involved (lots of interdependence), *and* when the differences among the people are great (a high level of diversity), resolving the conflicts in efficient and effective ways becomes much more difficult and complex. In such a case, the people involved will rarely agree on a single "expert" to whom they can defer. Different groups will propose different experts. Getting all the relevant parties together to discuss the issues usually becomes impractical, because of the number of people involved and because of time and geography constraints. If representatives of the key constituencies get together, great differences in outlook make discussion difficult, time consuming, and frustrating. Under those circumstances, people typically begin looking for other ways to resolve the conflict. Sometimes they will try to negotiate a nonoptimum compromise. Or they will try to force their opinions on others. Or they will allow the other parties to make the decision, with the implicit expectation that in the future those others will return the favor. Or they will try to manipulate the other parties into accepting their point of view. Or they will try to persuade others that some solution is really best for everyone. Any of those tactics can, under the right circumstances, resolve a conflict. But they often do so at a serious price. Forcing a solution on others invites retaliation in the future. A compromise is by definition not an optimum solution. Persuasion often takes a lot of time and effort. Manipulation can lead to a loss of trust among people, making conflict resolution more difficult in the future. And, when the level of diversity and interdependence is great enough, these tactics can simply fail, leading to a protracted power struggle characterized by bureaucratic infighting and parochial politics.

Coping with this difficult social reality is at the very heart of executive work today because it affects *everything*. Planning, organizing, staffing, directing, and evaluating are all subject to severe conflicts caused by diversity and interdependence, as are strategic decision making, resource allocation, and operational control. As such, *contrary to popular stereotypes*, the core of executive work is not narrow economic decision making, or bossing people around, or using technical tools learned in MBA programs, or overseeing highly formal and rational planning processes, or serving the interests of only one of the parties involved (for example, shareholders). *Executive work involves managing complex interdependencies among diverse groups of people so that destructive conflicts and power struggles are minimized, so that inevitable conflict leads to creative solutions that serve the interests of as many legitimate stakeholders as possible, and so that all conflicts are resolved with a minimum waste of scarce resources.* This is what leadership in our society is all about.

This concept of executive work is not widely recognized or accepted today. The most common beliefs about executive work are rooted in the past, in what used to be. Notions of the business executive as boss, as economic decision maker, and as a maximizer of shareholder wealth make sense in a world with limited interdependence and limited diversity. They make sense in the world of Adam Smith. But such a world is gone forever.

What little we know about people who handle today's challenge well suggests that the key to their success lies in their capacity to develop and use power responsibly (Kotter, 1979, 1982; Gabarro and Kotter, 1980; Kotter and Schlesinger, 1979). Effective executives develop and then use power bases (sources of potential influence) that far exceed the power that automatically comes with executive jobs. In this way they are able to manage in a milieu that is in many respects almost unmanageable. Because of this extra power, unlike their less effective colleagues, they do not operate from a position of weakness and they do not end up pawns in a set of power struggles they cannot control.

People who have not experienced or studied executive jobs often fail to appreciate the vulnerable position that such jobs put the executive in. I personally remember reading an article over ten years ago on the vulnerable position of executives (McMurray, 1973) and thinking to myself that the argument was rubbish. That was *before* I had spent hundreds and hundreds of hours in the field, observing and talking to executives. The naive simply do not realize that, despite the considerable power attached to such jobs (in rights to hire, fire, and reward; in budgets; in exposure to sensitive and important information), an executive today is surrounded by many powerful others who have conflicting priorities, beliefs, and interests. As such, the power that comes with the job is often considerably less than the power one needs to do the job well. In big and complex executive jobs, this built-in "power gap" is quite large. Just surviving under these circumstances requires some additional clout. Performing well requires more. Leading demands still more.

This power, of necessity, comes in many forms. It has multiple bases, including ones associated with information or knowledge, good working relationships, personal skills, intelligent agendas for action, resource networks, and good track records.

In terms of information, the truism "knowledge is power" certainly applies to executive jobs. But the knowledge that is particularly important is not just the kind one finds in books or in educational programs. It is detailed information about the social reality in which the job is imbedded. There is no way that one can perform well in an executive job today without a keen understanding of the diverse and interdependent milieu surrounding the job. This means knowing who *all* the relevant parties are, even though there may be thousands of them. It means understanding the different perspectives of all the relevant groups: what they want, how they look at the world, and what their real interests are. It means seeing where the various perspectives are in conflict—where important differences lie. It also means knowing what sources of power each group has to pursue its own interests and how prepared it is to use that power.

This information, along with a sensitivity to its importance, is a key to sensible decision making. It allows one realistically to answer such questions as "Whose cooperation will be needed to implement any idea under consideration? Whose compliance will be necessary? Will any of these people be inclined to resist cooperating or complying? If yes, why? How strongly are they likely to resist? Am I in a position to reduce or overcome this resistance? Which ideas, then, are feasible? Are any of those feasible ideas in everybody's best interests? If not, why not? Who has to pay what cost?" Without answers to these questions—answers that do not come automatically with the job—an executive takes himself and his people blindly through a mine field.

But information alone is not enough. One can know precisely what should be done and yet not be able to do it unless he or she has access to those whose cooperation and compliance are required, unless they are willing to listen to his or her point of view, and unless they are inclined to believe what he or she says. In other words, one also needs the power associated with credible relationships with most of the parties involved: bosses, subordinates, subordinates of subordinates, peers in other parts of the organization, outside suppliers or customers—indeed, anyone on whom the job makes one dependent. The greater the dependence, the more important the relationship.

Based on some combination of respect, admiration, perceived need, obligation, and friendship, good working relationships are a critical source of power in helping one get things done. Without these relationships, even the most optimum idea possible could be rejected or resisted in an environment where diversity breeds suspicion and in which interdependence precludes giving orders to most of the relevant players. And since these relationships serve as important information channels, without them one may never be able to establish the information base one needs to operate effectively.

Developing and then using these sources of power in turn require certain skills—skills that serve as still another important source of power. These skills include the ability to determine who really has power that is relevant to any particular issue, to assess differences among people and their roots, and to identify directions of mutual interest. They include the interpersonal skills associated with building good working relationships with many different kinds of people and then maintaining those relationships despite physical separation, limited face-to-face interaction, and the normal stresses and strains of modern life. They also include a wide variety of influence skills—skills associated with knowing precisely how to use information, relationships, formal authority, and other power sources in any specific situation.

These skills, the information base, and all the cooperative relationships supplement the power sources that automatically come with a job and allow an executive to do what he or she needs to do in order to lead in a highly complex social environment. These power sources allow one to create an agenda for action that minimizes destructive power struggles and resolves conflicts in creative ways, so that the interests of as many people as possible are served. They also allow one to create the resource network that is needed to implement such an agenda. They give one the ability to attract good people, needed financing, and new product ideas and to direct those resources toward a sensible agenda. In the final analysis, this resource network and this agenda are the ultimate power sources that allow an executive to perform well (Kotter, 1982).

Developing all the power sources needed to create strong agendas and networks is not easy. It takes time and effort and *constant* attention. With hundreds or thousands of people involved, and with a volume of relevant information that would fill a small library, developing information and relationship-based sources typically takes years of effort. The relevant skills involved are only to a limited degree learned early in life. They are largely refined and developed on the job, through lengthy trial and error and by watching capable role models.

From what little we know about effective executives, it appears that this development process typically takes the following form. First, people get into a context—an industry, a company, and a job—that fits their interests, values, and skills to some minimum degree. This "fit" makes it easier for them to begin building the information power base, because the information is perceived to be interesting. It helps them to develop good working relationships, because relating to the people is easy. It also helps them to perform well and therefore to attract the attention of potential mentors. The good initial performance, perhaps aided by a mentor-like figure, leads to a promotion or a larger assignment. The new assignment and the mentor stretch and develop new skills and provide access to new people and information. The expanding skill, information, and relationship base helps one perform well again. The good track record and expanding reputation make it easier to develop and maintain good working relationships—perhaps to even more mentor-like figures—relationships that in turn put one in contact with a larger information network and a larger group of role models. All this leads to a larger job and the greater power associated with it. And the process repeats itself again and again and again.

Maintaining the power sources developed early in one's career is also not easy. Attention is required constantly, day after day, hour after hour. One single bad decision in a stream of many decisions can hurt one's reputation, destroy dozens of good working relationships, and leave one without the power base needed to follow through on commitments already made. Effective executives seem to be very sensitive, if only intuitively, to these realities; their less effective counterparts often are not.

I would now like to address some of the more important implications of the previous discussion.

First of all, the increased attention that power issues have received in the literature on organizational behavior (OB) is very healthy (see, for instance, Mintzberg, 1983; Pfeffer, 1981b). This book, which focuses directly on power and executives, will surely be helpful too. But we must be careful. Just as many traditionalists in OB/OD made little progress for years on this most important topic because of their naive biases, many of the new generation of more "scientific" OB people may also be less effective than they should be because of their cynical inclinations. As we all know, people sometimes self-select into academic vocations, where they can operate with an unusual degree of independence, because of a deeply rooted temperamental distrust of authority figures. When these people study authority figures, such as executives, their feelings can easily overwhelm any data if they are not extremely careful. The outpouring of cynical pseudoscientific rhetoric on the functions of executive power would obviously be tragic.

In the past few years, mostly as a result of the increased attention paid to power in the OB literature, the amount of management training that has focused on power and the executive has increased greatly. Surely this is also a very good trend (as long as the training is not serving up cynical or naive distortions). But we still have a long way to go. The typical MBA program today admits basically naive people and then graduates basically naive people. In some ways it even strengthens their naiveté with technical courses that *implicitly* assume implementing decisions is easy, that differences among people are small, and that managers operate with considerable independence.

The situation is different but not better in executive education. The argument presented here suggests that discussions of power and influence, of coping with diversity and interdependence, of developing power bases, and of using power responsibly should be *the central* part of all general executive education. They are not today. Possibly it is not even possible to make these topics central given our current state of knowledge. But that should be our ultimate objective.

This line of thinking also has important implications regarding the ways in which aspiring executives should manage their own careers. The central issue for them during the early career stage is developing a good power base and learning how to use power effectively and responsibly. I fear that all too often young executives-in-the-making focus much too much on money and promotions during their early career years and not enough on other key indices of power—such as relationships, relevant information, track record, and skills. They also seem to spend precious little time thinking about what the responsible use of power means in an executive setting.

And that brings me to my last point. It seems obvious to me that organizations have both a responsibility and a very practical need to do a better job developing people for executive positions. There is absolutely no reason to assume that, if one simply hires "well-educated" people and then promotes "the best," one will end up with a sufficient number of executives who can provide the kind of leadership that organizations need today. More likely, one will end up with a few excellent executives, along with many who have not developed a strong enough power base to provide strong leadership in their jobs, and still others who have never learned how to use their power either effectively or responsibly. In a world with strong international competition, such an executive force is clearly inadequate.

A *major* challenge for organizations in the immediate future is to figure out how they can systematically develop more high-quality leadership for their executive ranks. This means leadership that brings with it to executive jobs enough power to make up for the power gap inherent in those jobs; leadership that knows how to use that power effectively and is dedicated to using it responsibly; leadership with a historical and contextual perspective, that recognizes why power issues are generally important and in what situations they might be more or less central. I am convinced that this kind of leadership could reduce bureaucratic infighting and make our corporations more competitive and our governments more responsive. I think it could make a real difference.

TWO

Managing Human Energy:
Pushing Versus Pulling
David E. Berlew

About twenty years ago, a senior Coca-Cola Company executive asked for my advice on how to "manage from the center." He told me that, in order to do his job well, he had to influence the behavior of thousands of people whom he could never hope to meet face to face: retail clerks, delivery men, route salespersons. His goal was modest enough: he wanted everyone to be friendly to customers, to listen to their complaints, and to try to solve their problems. Exerting this type of influence through the management hierarchy, he said, was too slow and unreliable.

My answer, mercifully forgotten, did not impress him, and I did not get the consulting assignment. He made a strong impression on me, however. It was an unusual question for the time, and I later realized that, at least implicitly, he recognized that there was no "standard" management solution to his dilemma. Later, when I began to occupy executive positions, I came to realize that the answer had more to do with leadership than with good management.

This chapter addresses the same question from the point of view of the practicing executive: "What can I do that will affect the way others, who may be several levels or thousands of miles away, conduct our business?" It focuses on the balance of energy in

Note: The thoughts expressed in this chapter have been strongly influenced by conversations with Roger Harrison, Warren Bennis, Charles Kiefer, Alex Moore, and Irwin Rubin. I am indebted to them all.

organizations, on the executive's role as organizational energy manager, and on "common-vision leadership."

Organizational Energy Balance

We use our energy to exercise influence in two major ways: we move against or PUSH people, and we move with or PULL people.

At the organizational level, PUSH energy and influence strategies are manifest in organizational structure and management systems. The structure of an organization is based on a set of logical assumptions and prescriptions regarding the way in which work should be divided among individuals and groups, the distribution of authority, and the approved communication channels. Management systems are also manifestations of PUSH energy in that they prescribe procedures to be followed, control the flow of information and resources, and specify the rewards and penalties associated with various types and levels of performance.

PULL energy and influence strategies are usually manifest in the style and spirit of an organization, rarely in structure or systems. A shared belief in the organization's mission and a commitment to nonmaterialistic values that guide members' behavior are manifestations of PULL energy. When managers routinely involve their subordinates in decisions, and employees recognize what needs to be done and do it without being directed, that is a reflection of PULL energy.

The overriding objective in managing organizational energy is to maximize energy alignment without wasting human energy or stifling initiative and creativity. From our perspective, this means achieving the appropriate balance of PUSH and PULL energy in the organization. A simple analogy will help to illustrate the relationships between alignment, PUSH energy, and PULL energy in organizations. At the one extreme, we have water flowing from an open faucet. The water spills out of the faucet helter-skelter and floods. Its level and direction are a function of the terrain around the faucet, its destination relatively unpredictable. The organizational equivalent of the open faucet is unbridled activity based purely on individual inclination and choice. The results are unpredictable. Individuals may expend great amounts of energy, but it is directed toward doing what they want to do, not necessarily what needs to be done for the organization to survive.

At the other extreme, we have a steel pipe attached to the faucet, which channels the water to a specific point or objective. The direction is fixed; there is very little flexibility. The organizational parallel to the steel pipe is a tightly controlled bureaucracy with no room for individual initiative or variation and very little adaptability. The structure of the organization and the policies, procedures, and systems push people into doing what needs to be done. But what needs to be done is not what people want to do, so they use their energy to resist the pressure or they lose interest and just collect their pay checks.

Somewhere between the two extremes, we have a rather delicate rubber hose. The water is pulled or sucked through the hose, and the hose shifts position, expands, and contracts to find the best path to the source of the PULL energy or suction. This is equivalent to an organization in which people are attracted to a common goal and want to do what must be done to achieve it. Systems facilitate and guide work rather than serving a control function. Energy and activities are coordinated, but there is room for individual initiative and variation.

U.S. Peace Corps: Strong PULL, Weak PUSH Energy. An examination of the Peace Corps in the 1960s will help to clarify this difficult balancing act. Most Americans who joined the Peace Corps during this period were attracted by John F. Kennedy's vision of the United States as a nation that shares its abundance of resources with poorer nations and works to reduce the gap between the "have" and "have-not" nations. The Peace Corps' mission was to make JFK's vision a reality, and thousands of Americans, young and old alike, left their families and careers and volunteered to go abroad to live and work with the people of developing nations. It was an organization founded on inspiration, and there was an extraordinary degree of energy alignment resulting from the strong PULL of a common vision. Most members of the organization wanted to do what had to be done, no matter how difficult, dangerous, or uncomfortable.

During the early days of the Peace Corps, however, the structure and systems were not always adequate to the task of facilitating and coordinating work. As an overseas Peace Corps director during those years, I would often pass through Washington D.C. Friends who lived in Washington would comment that, no matter how late at night they passed the Peace Corps building, the lights were always on. They meant it as a tribute to the ability of JFK and Sargent Shriver to inspire young people. Peace Corps Washington staff, on the other hand, would maintain that they worked into the early morning hours because it took sixteen hours to do eight hours of work! Although the Peace Corps had a powerful common vision, shared values, and a resulting high degree of energy alignment, its lack of smoothly functioning systems impeded productivity.

Even if people want to do what needs to be done, there must be a way of allocating, coordinating, and evaluating work to ensure that the energy is used efficiently. In contrast to the PULL energy created by a common vision and shared values, this concern with organization, systems, and procedures is a manifestation of PUSH energy.

Sargent Shriver and his deputy, Warren Wiggins, the "energy managers" during the early years of the Peace Corps, perceived clearly the danger that the Peace Corps might become "just another government bureaucracy" staffed by veteran bureaucrats doing things as they had always been done. Shriver and Wiggins wanted new ideas and new approaches and were apparently willing to risk a certain amount of disorganization, some would say chaos, to get them. They took a number of fairly radical steps to guarantee fresh approaches and avoid standard solutions. They made sure that Peace Corps staff members were not permitted to stay longer than five years. They systematically recruited staff from outside the government, looking for individuals with a record of success in a variety of fields—medicine, academia, business, athletics, and foundations—thus assuring themselves of a number of different styles and approaches, new ideas, and a certain irreverence for government bureaucracy. They gave extraordinary operating authority to directors in the field, most of whom had little relevant experience. The outcome was very little uniformity and results ranging from spectacular to disastrous. Eccentric high achievers were protected, but poor performers were replaced overnight. All this had the effect of preventing the buildup of bureaucratic systems and at the same time encouraging initiative and innovation.

I will never forget Sargent Shriver's telling me that I was the final authority with regard to field operations, except for the ambassador, and that even the ambassador could be overridden if the cause was worthy. Since the Peace Corps was part of the State Department, this was heresy, of course. Still, it was an important message to give to a young field director in his first government and first management job, because as a result I tried to do things I might otherwise have avoided as being too high risk.

Structure, procedures, and systems are manifestations of PUSH energy and can facilitate and coordinate work or push people into alignment. If energy alignment can be achieved through the pull of a strong common vision and shared values, then the only function of structure, procedures, and systems is to facilitate and coordinate work. If this is the case, as it was in the early Peace Corps, structure can be simple and management systems minimal, thus maximizing creativity and innovation with little if any cost in efficiency.

This particular dynamic balance illustrated in the Peace Corps example has been venerated recently in much of the popular management literature. The PULL forces are strong, creating energy alignment. The PUSH forces are relatively weak—strong enough to guide and coordinate the efforts of people who "want to do what must be done" but not so strong that they stifle initiative and innovation or divert energy from productive work to system maintenance.

Let us assume that the PULL energy generated by a strong common vision weakens—something that in fact happened to the Peace Corps over time. As the magnetic attraction of the shared vision becomes weaker, we would expect less commitment to the organization's mission and a lower level of energy alignment. Since there are no effective supervisory or other management systems in place, individual members would begin to divert more time and energy to personal goals, such as advancement, recognition, adventure, vacation, and creature comforts. If we were the executive in charge, what could we do? One obvious possibility would be to generate a new common vision, based on superordinate values shared by the organization's membership, or potential membership, in the 1980s. Such a development, however, is unlikely. The idealism of the Kennedy era is over. Another possibility would be to develop a management hierarchy to provide closer supervision and more sophisticated management information and control systems. The objective would be to channel energy, to ensure that members would do what needed to be done. The walls of the hose through which the energy flows would be made thicker and more constraining.

To increase PUSH energy, we could develop better methods of selection, training, and indoctrination; increase the amount and quality of supervision to ensure that members concentrate on doing their jobs; develop better ways to measure output; and tie compensation and other rewards to productivity. We could design and implement better systems to control costs and minimize waste. Our more complex structure and systems would continue to guide and facilitate work, but they would serve the additional function of controlling what people do and how they do it, because we can no longer be sure that people will want to do what needs to be done. Stated another way, this buildup of PUSH energy would supplement the partial alignment generated by limited PULL energy and ensure that members pursue the organization's goals.

This is, of course, the real world. Not many executives have the opportunity to lead an organization quite like the Peace Corps or an army that is saving the world for democracy. The price of energy alignment achieved through a balance of PULL and PUSH energy is usually quite tolerable: less individual initiative and creativity but more predictability, fewer extraordinary individual or team achievements but no disasters, less entrepreneurism but more efficient resource management.

The buildup of PUSH energy in the form of structure and systems does not necessarily result from a decline in PULL energy. Suppose that a director of the Peace Corps, a strong inspirational leader, hired as a deputy an equally strong, rational manager who designed and implemented simple but effective systems that made the organization as a whole more efficient *and also* increased the productivity of less committed members. If this balance could be achieved without constraining the energy and creativity of members who are fully committed, we would have an organization that is both well led and well managed. The structure and systems would provide a safety factor that could become important in preserving alignment if something should happen to upset or disturb the PULL energy, such as a change of leadership or, in the case of the Peace Corps, a new administration.

A Textbook Publisher: Weak PULL, Strong PUSH Energy. The elementary and secondary textbook division of a major publishing firm was accepted as the industry leader, both for the quality of its texts and for its role in introducing new educational trends into American schools. Its editorial and sales staffs took great pride in the firm's reputation for quality and innovation, and they worked hard to maintain and build it.

In the mid-1970s, the parent corporation became concerned about a decline in profits and market share and brought in a new division president with a background in marketing to replace the educator who had been president for a number of years. Because costs are heavily front loaded in book publishing, the new president decided that a key leverage point for cost reduction was the selection of titles to be published. Rather than continue to let senior editors select titles on the basis of their nose for quality and intuitive reading of the marketplace, he instituted a new set of publication guidelines. When an editor identified a potential publication, market research was conducted and costs calculated, and the results were fed into a computer to see whether the proposed publication would meet a specific return-on-investment requirement. If it did, the book was published; if not, it was dropped from consideration. Many other systems for analyzing decisions, increasing productivity, controlling costs, and relating compensation more closely to productivity were also introduced, but the change in editorial policy was most visible and controversial.

Within a year or two, the common vision of leading the industry in both quality and innovation, which had gripped the firm for three decades, had lost its hold. Many of the veteran editors and sales staff complained bitterly about the change. Some left or were forced out; others resigned themselves to the situation.

Excitement and commitment disappeared, and employees identified less and less with the company and its educational mission. There were fewer product failures, but overall the product line became less innovative and of only average quality. The employees complained, but they did their jobs, and profits gradually increased to a level acceptable to the parent corporation.

This textbook publisher changed, in a relatively short time, from an organization dominated by PULL energy to one dominated by PUSH energy. Excitement and a sense of mission were replaced by better organization and more complex management systems. The result was a gain in efficiency at the cost of innovation and individual initiative.

For the short term at least, the new version of the textbook publisher may be viable. The choice will be made by officers of the parent corporation, who, we assume, have their own vision of the kind of subsidiary they want to create. We can only speculate about the long-term implications of the changeover. One possibility is that the new division president, or his replacement, will recognize the need and have the leadership skill to develop a new common vision: one that balances excitement about quality and innovation with commitment to building a solid business. A less attractive possibility is that the president will continue to depend on PUSH energy and to focus entirely on his role as rational manager. If so, the PUSH energy, in the form of structure and systems, will have to bear the entire burden of channeling energy; in a sense, people will have to be forced or seduced into doing what needs to be done. Since people are masterful at finding loopholes, or ways to circumvent unwelcome controls, this will lead to more complex control systems, and systems to monitor systems, until the organization is too complex to manage.

It is the illusion of rational managers that complex systems can be managed into alignment. At some point, however, one more system or one more system modification has so many unanticipated consequences that managing becomes little more than tinkering. Management without leadership is, in the longer term, a hopeless position.

Vietnam War: Negative PULL Energy. In certain extreme conditions, an organization's values are in direct conflict with the values of its members. During the Vietnam War, for example, the United States military might have survived the lack of a clear, shared vision of an ideal outcome, compensating for this lack with the strong hierarchical authority and control systems characteristic of military organizations. At the value level, however, members of the military were asked to use highly destructive weapons against peasants with whom they felt no quarrel. If we compare this war with World War II and the PULL energy generated by a common vision of "unconditional surrender" and a shared value of "saving the world for democracy," we should not be surprised that drug abuse, mental disorder, and other forms of pathology are associated with the Vietnam War.

A similar although far less dramatic value conflict occurred in the automobile industry in the mid-1970s. Some employees of large United States automobile manufacturers, personally committed to energy conservation and a clean environment, were very upset when they realized that their employers were resisting environmental legislation for short-term commercial gains. One can at least speculate that this conflict in values contributed to the decline in quality of automobiles during this period.

Asset Management Division: Weak PULL, Weak PUSH Energy. It is possible to have a situation where both PULL and PUSH energy are weak. Our example of this condition is the start-up of a new Asset Management Division within a large bank's Investment Management Group. Formed as a result of bank deregulation, which allowed banks to offer a wide range of investment services to pension fund managers, the new division was expected to compete with entrepreneurial investment counselors. A marketing executive with a consumer-product background was chosen to head the division. Three years after its formation, the Asset Management Division's executives still have not succeeded in creating a common vision that distinguishes their entrepreneurial division from the rest of the bank and gives the staff a sense of mission or purpose. This task is made more difficult by the fact that the division is operating within, and physically surrounded by, a traditional bank culture.

At the same time, the established bank management systems, which the new division inherited, have hindered the development of an innovative, entrepreneurial orientation and the operational flexibility required to compete successfully in such a fast-changing marketplace. Due partly to personal style and partly to frustration, the division's executives have adopted a laissez-faire, sink-or-swim management approach. As a result—except for the bank's general orientation and indoctrination programs, which have little to do with them—new staff members are left more or less to their own devices, with little division-specific orientation, guidance, or support. The result of this weak PULL, weak PUSH energy balance can, with only slight exaggeration, be described as "lethargic chaos."

Managing Organizational Energy

How does our exploration of energy balance in organizations help to answer the executive's question: "What can I do to affect the way that others, who may be several levels or thousands of miles away, conduct our business?" First, we have identified two major sources of power that he has at his disposal as an executive: (1) the PULL energy that he can generate by creating a common vision based on superordinate values shared by members of his organization and (2) the PUSH energy he can bring to bear through organizational structure and management systems. Second, we know that some PULL and PUSH energy is always desirable; so, regardless of the situation he is in, he will have to be able both to lead and to manage. Third, there seems to be little danger of too much PULL energy, as long as there is enough PUSH energy in the form of simple structures and systems, to organize and channel the energy into productive work. (We may, of course, see a danger of too much PULL energy if the common vision and superordinate values conflict with our own, as in the case of "leaders" we label fanatics or demagogues.) Finally, it appears that PUSH energy can become overcontrolling and have a negative impact, even when there is PULL energy present.

What our executive does not know but needs to know if this discussion is going to be helpful to him, is: (1) How can he increase PULL energy? (2) How can he reduce the negative effects of PUSH energy? (3) How can he determine the best balance for any given situation?

Creating a Common Vision. As manager of human energy, the executive must develop or sustain a common vision for the organization. The first step is for the executive to look inward, to ask himself or herself: What do I want to create? What excites me to the point that it could become a personal cause or mission? Fairness? Honesty? Quality? Excellence? Contribution? Service to others?

I remember an evening with a group of community leaders on the island of Curaçao in 1969, just after riots had split the community into several factions. They were struggling with their personal visions of the future, to see whether they shared any aspirations and values that might bring them closer together. The business leaders talked about business goals, minority leaders about minority goals, government leaders about government goals. In a final effort to get them to go beyond goals to values and dreams, we asked them to close their eyes and to envision the island community they would create for their sons and daughters if their every wish could come true. As each one began to describe his vision of the community he wanted to create for his children—the Black Power leader in his fatigues, the Dutch refinery manager, the banker whose ancestors had come to Curaçao from Portugal in the seventeenth century—their common aspirations and values became apparent to all. With this beginning, they went on to develop a truly common vision and to lead their island toward recovery. (See Berlew and Le-Clere, 1974.)

Other executives who have gone through a similar process, as a first step toward developing a common vision for their organization, are invariably surprised and pleased at the overlap of their basic values.

However, one or several executives' vision of the future does not make a common vision. The executive also must listen carefully to the dreams, aspirations, and frustrations of the organization's members. This may require getting through an outer layer of cynicism or preoccupation with material rewards. The values that can become the basis for a common vision are not simply the membership's lowest common denominators; the fact that everyone complains of slow promotions does not necessarily translate into a compelling vision of a fast-growing organization. If the executive has come up through the ranks of the organization, finding shared values may be easier, although the values of an hourly wage earner may be quite different from those of someone making an executive's salary, even if they come from the same roots. The challenge, as in Curaçao, is to find superordinate values—that is, higher-level human values common to all members of an organization or community, which cut across economic, racial, and cultural boundaries. Financial goals are insufficient; they benefit some members more than others. The possibility of a higher return on investment is a more compelling vision to senior executives and stockholders than to union wage earners. However, financial success can play a role as one yardstick for demonstrating progress toward a superordinate goal. An increase in repeat sales, for example, can demonstrate a dramatic improvement in customer service or product quality or a quantum leap in teamwork among functions.

In many cases the superordinate values that members share may be dormant. It is not unusual in my experience to listen to a litany of complaints from members of an organization and then to return six months or a year later and find the same people excited about their mission. The same idealism and desire to do something meaningful and important were present on the first visit, but they needed to be aroused and engaged by a new or renewed common vision.

There is a story of a man traveling through the countryside who came upon three men using sledgehammers to break up a mountain of rocks. "Why are you doing such work?" the traveler asked the first workman. "Because my boss told me to," he replied. The traveler asked the same question of the second man, who replied: "I am earning a wage so I can feed and shelter my family." The traveler turned to the third workman and asked: "Why are you doing this work?" And the man replied: "I am building a cathedral."

The executive must find a way to communicate the vision in a way that attracts and excites members of the organization, so that they will want to do what needs to be done to make the vision a reality (Berlew, 1974). Some executives may have the oratorical powers of a Martin Luther King, Jr., or a John F. Kennedy, but only a few are so lucky. Fortunately for most of us, there are other ways to communicate a vision, to make it a common vision. One is for the executive to interact with members one on one or in small groups. In such settings the executive's personal conviction and credibility are far more important than his or her speaking ability. Another approach is to create heroes out of respected members, past and present, who clearly reflect the values implicit in the common vision. Past heroes, of course, can manifest these values and attributes without the human frailties of present heroes and current leaders. Most of us are comfortable telling stories about people we respect and admire; it is a simple but powerful way of communicating a common vision.

Many of the "mundane methods" described by Peters and Waterman (1982) in their book *In Search of Excellence* are useful for spreading a common vision. For example, if the executive is trying to inculcate a commitment to quality, he or she will have an item related to quality at the top of every meeting agenda, talk constantly to managers about quality improvements, and make a point of asking hourly workers on the shop floor how quality might be improved. The executive will seek out and reward efforts to improve quality throughout the organization. Regardless of how cynical individuals may be, public recognition from a respected leader is powerful magic. Another method of seeding a common vision is to involve members of the organization in its development, as in the Curaçao example. It is easier to imagine doing this in a small organization, where all the key managers and individual contributors can become involved. However, the same thing can be done in a larger organization if the guidelines outlined below are followed.

First, it is desirable but not essential to begin with the top-management team: the most senior executives meeting to share basic beliefs and values, find common ground, and create a vision of the future to which they can commit themselves, individually and as a group. This procedure sets an example for lower-level managers to emulate and broadcasts to the organization that idealism and discussions of superordinate values are not only legitimate but highly appropriate.

Second, teams at other levels should not be required to follow the same process as the top team. Senior executives can set an example and encourage idealism, but they cannot legislate it. A manager at any level can meet with his or her team to create a common vision that has meaning and inspirational value for those involved.

Third, the process of sharing basic values and forging a shared vision in a group should be recognized as more important than the output or product. What is critical is that members of the team make their basic values explicit and public and that they go on record as standing for something that will attract others.

Finally, most teams will need the help of a facilitator or consultant who is not a member of the team to create a meaningful common vision. People who work together daily on concrete tasks usually have difficulty focusing on a subject that not only is nebulous and elusive but that also can be threatening. Personal beliefs, values, and dreams of the future are not easy to talk about, and discomfort can be avoided by changing the topic to something more concrete. Although in my personal consulting practice I help client organizations clarify basic values and a shared vision of the future, I retain the services of an outside consultant when addressing the same issues within my own firm.

Up to this point, developing a common vision sounds almost mechanical, a matter of good technique. Good technique helps, but it is not enough. In order to provide common-vision leadership, the executive must exhibit three fundamental qualities: a preoccupation with quality, integrity, and the ability to "walk the talk." If the executive is not consistent and persistent in pursuing quality in all things—relationships, product, service—there is no solid foundation on which to build a common vision. Individuals who expect and are expected to do their best come to love their work and their organization. Quality is the basis of pride. Individuals will not commit themselves to an organization and its mission if they are not proud of the work that they do.

The second quality, integrity, is simple to talk about but not so easy to practice. In the late 1960s, I managed a consulting firm that had a number of contracts with the Office of Economic Opportunity (OEO) in Washington, D.C. One of these was for a very avant garde community and economic development project in a depressed area. A key resource was a university professor, a national authority in the field. Legislation passed after we obtained the contract limited the daily consulting rate that OEO could pay for a consultant to half of what we had contracted to pay this consultant to work on the project. OEO asked for an exception but was refused. Our OEO contact suggested that—since this consultant was important to the project, and since the project was important to the community involved and perhaps to many others—we bill two days for every day that the consultant worked. To me, at that time, it seemed a reasonable solution to a difficult problem. Only later did I realize that it was merely expedient and lacking in integrity.

Common-vision leadership is a close relative to spiritual leadership. One cannot very well exercise common-vision leadership if one feels, or is perceived as, lacking in integrity. It is easy to have disdain for those executives in government and business who cut corners and make compromises to save their careers, their organizations, or people they care about. We would do better to study how they went wrong and to use our increased awareness to avoid making similar mistakes. If we believe that we are immune, we are as vulnerable as they.

Finally, the executive must "walk the talk." That is, he or she must be in alignment with the common vision and superordinate values. Always. "Do what I say, not what I do" never works. If an executive does not believe in the common vision, he or she should not even try to articulate it. "Walking the talk" reflects a concern with both quality and integrity in one's own life.

Judging Structures and Systems. The positive advantages of management systems and practices that facilitate work are well documented, as is the negative impact when they are poorly designed or implemented. In both cases they are reflections of PUSH energy. As an energy manager, the executive does not have to be an expert designer of structures and systems; he or she does, however, need to be a wise judge of them. The criteria for judging are straightforward:

> Does it facilitate and coordinate work?
> Does it control more than necessary? Is it being misused for control purposes?
> Does it confuse rather than clarify? Does it allow things to be hidden?

The filing system is a suitable metaphor. The basic file is an excellent system for facilitating and coordinating work. In the beginning, all employees kept their own files and shared them with others whom they wanted to help or with whom they needed to coordinate. In time, keeping and managing access to files became a specialty—first for secretaries and eventually for entire departments. All of us have experienced the power of a secretary who is the only person who knows where something is located and can decide whether or not to let us see it. But the power of a secretary is nothing compared to that of a data-processing department that not only keeps the files but indexes and organizes them according to its perception of what is important. Perhaps you can get your questions answered, perhaps not. The answers to some questions may be lost—or at least inaccessible. The point is that an effective facilitative system can become inefficient if it is used for control purposes.

Many systems, such as files, serve a primary purpose of facilitating and coordinating work. It is the executive's job to make sure that they serve that purpose, rather than obfuscating or controlling. Other systems, such as time clocks and travel-and-expense reports, have a rather obvious function of controlling behavior. If these controls are not needed because energy is aligned through PULL power, then other methods of gathering information—methods that do not have the possible negative consequences of encouraging people to work only the required number of hours or to misrepresent their expenses—should be considered. It is up to the executive to make these judgments.

The executive as energy manager, then, is chief systems judge and ombudsman. To have credibility in this role, the executive must follow a personal practice of keeping things simple and not surreptitiously or unintentionally use systems to control, avoid, or obfuscate. Above all, the executive must not make him- or herself exempt or design special executive systems. There is nothing better than a personal test: If the system does not work for the executive, it probably does not work for other members of the organization.

Finding a Balance. We have already concluded that some PUSH and some PULL energy is always required, that an executive should expect to lead and to manage in any situation. We have also suggested that, while the executive cannot err on the side of too much PULL energy, too much PUSH energy—in the form of complex, control-oriented structures and systems—can have negative effects. What else can we suggest to our executive?

First of all, he or she should be aware, if he or she is not already, that it is easier to create a powerful common vision in some situations than in others. It helps, for example, when there is an obvious external threat: foreign manufacturers invading one's domestic market, possible death of the firm and loss of jobs, a competitor's improved technology. Second, it is easier to provide common-vision leadership if the organization's mission is obviously exciting or idealistic and the jobs inherently interesting. Third, it is easier to lead during a start-up or growth stage than during a period of consolidation or reduction in force. Even Japanese companies are finding that employees are less enthusiastic now that opportunities for advancement are more limited.

But when is common-vision leadership most important? It is essential in situations where hierarchical structures and management systems are difficult to implement—for example, in guerrilla armies and the Peace Corps, where individual members or work units are widely dispersed, logistics complex, and communications difficult. Some multinational corporations are beginning to take on this character. Common-vision leadership is equally important in situations where key tasks are carried out at the far-flung peripheries of an organization and the style with which they are carried out is critical to success. Strong PULL energy is especially important in entrepreneurial or fast-changing situations, where individual members have to make quick decisions on behalf of the organization. Alignment is essential to ensure that the right decisions are made at the periphery or boundaries of the organization. A strong common vision and commitment to shared values also are important if members of the organization are asked to tolerate physical discomfort and danger. Many more people die for causes than to fill an organizational requirement. Most challenging of all, common-vision leadership is especially important when it is most difficult: when the mission appears mundane and the tasks dull, when employees are cynical and alienated, and when members of the organization are being asked to pull in their belts. There is no management solution to this type of situation—only a leadership solution.

Conclusion

Now perhaps we can answer the executive's question about how to influence the behavior of thousands of people whom he could never hope to meet face to face. His priority task is to create a high degree of energy alignment so that people want to do what needs to be done. His conclusion that he cannot do this through management systems is sound; there are too many widely dispersed people to be influenced—people who are neither subject to nor probably amenable to close supervision or other forms of control. He will have to devote himself to the leadership task of developing a common vision based on superordinate values that are important to him and to those whom he must influence.

THREE

Leadership
as Empowering Others

W. Warner Burke

In telling the story of the Chrysler Corporation's dramatic turnaround and progress to date, Harold Sperlich, president and chief operating officer of the corporation, emphasizes a program that he calls the "enablers." This program defines "the actions that must take place if productivity and quality can, in fact, happen. . . . As managers, our job is not to make people do something. Our job is to make the process of their doing it possible" (Burke, 1984, pp. 28-29). In discussing this program, Sperlich stresses the importance of common goals between supervisor and subordinate, between suppliers and the corporation, and between management and the union. Thus, enabling provides subordinates with the necessary resources to perform their jobs properly, so that the common goal can be achieved. Essentially, Sperlich is talking about more than just enabling. He is also talking about empowerment. Both empower and enable mean "to increase another's ability to do something." To empower, however, implies the granting of power—delegation of authority; to enable implies providing the means or opportunity to do something. In this chapter we will primarily consider empowerment.

For an organization as steeped in a traditional (some would say primitive) form of management as Chrysler was to change so rapidly and significantly is noteworthy. Auto workers have been

Note: The sections "Having Power" and "Not Having Power" are adapted from Burke, 1982, chap. 7.

paid well, and those who are still employed in the industry continue to enjoy comparatively high wages. Until recently, however, we could not use the term "high" meaning positive, good, a plus, to describe the way in which these auto workers were supervised and managed. Traditionally, they have been told what to do, how to do it, and when to do it; if they did not do as they were instructed, they were verbally abused, or laid off for a period, or summarily fired. The only positive reward was the pay check. For an auto executive to talk about common goals and enabling people is a change indeed.

Yet there is clearly a movement in our country's corporations toward greater delegation of authority and participative management—that is, subordinates, at least to some extent, influencing decisions that directly affect them and their work. Witness the incredible sales records of *The One Minute Manager* (Blanchard and Johnson, 1982), which to a great degree is about delegation; and *In Search of Excellence* (Peters and Waterman, 1982), which concerns not only letting subordinates do more on their own but a more humane form of leadership as well; and the books on Japanese management, which describe a more participative process of management (Ouchi, 1981; Pascale and Athos, 1981). So perhaps the Chrysler story is not all that dramatic after all. Perhaps Chrysler, like many other corporations, is simply caught up in the sweep of this movement. Lee Iacocca, on the other hand, the chief executive officer of Chrysler, would not likely be described as a paragon of participative management. Thus, there is more to this corporate change than simply declaring that it is part of a trend. But a trend exists in any case. We shall therefore briefly consider this trend. Then, and more to the point and purpose of this chapter, we shall explore specifically and behaviorally just what empowerment means.

Toward Participative Management: More Sharing of Power

Harold Sperlich of Chrysler implies that the autocratic form of management is now history, at least in his corporation, and, in any case, he believes that it must be over and done with if one as an executive of an organization wants increased productivity and high quality. He further believes that the turnaround at Chrysler proves the point. For him there is no turning back. To do so would be foolish.

Some executives would not agree with Sperlich, perhaps because the kind of turnaround he has experienced at Chrysler is atypical. But evidence from other sources suggests that his enthusiasm for participative approaches is warranted. Hall (1976), for example, has shown that 9,9 (a participative approach) managers are higher achievers, achievement in this case being defined as moving rapidly up the managerial hierarchy. Sashkin (1982), in a summary of participative management, including research and case studies, shows that there is reasonable evidence of a linkage between this approach to management and higher productivity and quality of work. In a later article, Sashkin (1984) goes much further and argues that "participative management is an ethical imperative." His argument is based on the premise that a participative approach to managing subordinates, as contrasted with an autocratic approach, is more likely to respond to central human work needs (autonomy, wholeness of task, and interpersonal contact). Not to do so—that is, to be autocratic and therefore to disregard these human work needs—runs the risk of harming workers both psychologically and physically. Managerially, then, this practice reflects unethical behavior. Sashkin points to research that shows linkages between employee health and managerial approach.

There are different forms of participation, as Sashkin (1982) has outlined: participation in goal setting, participation in decision making, participation in problem solving, and participation in change. All forms, to one degree or another, provide for involvement of others, and all forms include some amount of power sharing. The sharing of power, then, creates conditions whereby people involved may be empowered. Participation as such does not mean empowerment. Participation may create or lead to empowerment.

In attempting clearly to understand empowerment, we must have a context. That context will consist of an exploration of the holding of power: one's need for power; one's sources of power; and having a great deal of power, having some power, or having none.

This exploration is important and relevant because managers and leaders exercise power, and recent evidence has shown that the more successful managers (and no doubt leaders as well) are those who have an above average need for having and exercising power. Following this coverage of power holding and its implications, we shall then consider the practice of empowerment. This latter consideration, empowering others, will be based on the important distinction of manager versus leader. The empowering process, at least the more effective practice thereof, must be different depending on whether one is a leader or a manager.

Having Power

Need for Power. Is having a need for power a prerequisite for successful management and leadership? Apparently so. In any case, having such a need helps, at least according to the findings of David McClelland. In this section we shall summarize McClelland's work regarding the need for power and conclude with some implications.

McClelland, noted earlier for his research on need for achievement, devoted much of his work during the decade of the 1970s to a better understanding of a person's need for power (McClelland, 1975). Relating his work theoretically to Freud's and Erikson's theories of ego development, McClelland has postulated, with research support, that there are four distinct stages in the development of a person's orientation to power.

Stage I, which is experienced even in infancy, involves incorporating power from another person—that is, from a source of power outside oneself. Early in life this feeling of strength comes from parents; later in life it may come from friends, a spouse, or an admired leader or mentor. Thus, by experiencing the power of a stronger person, the individual self feels powerful.

Stage II, "Independent Powerfulness," involves independence of the self. As McClelland (1975, p. 15) puts it, "I can strengthen myself." As the person learns self-control, a certain amount of powerful feeling typically occurs. A major expression of this stage later in life is through possession of objects, which one experiences as part of the self. These possessions are usually power related, such as a powerful and/or high-status automobile, guns, and even credit cards. The possession of powerful things, as an extension of self in a sense, facilitates the feeling of power.

The primary form of behavior evident in Stage III, "Power as an Impact on Others," is competitive behavior that is intended to win. Another less readily apparent form is helping behavior, for "in accepting . . . help, the receiver can be perceived as acknowledging that he is weaker, at least in this respect, than the person who is giving him help" (McClelland, 1975, p. 18). Research by McClelland and by Winter (1973) shows that a significant number of teachers behave predominantly according to this Stage III helping orientation; many therapists and consultants also may operate extensively at this stage.

Stage IV is called "Deriving Power from a Higher Authority." McClelland has found that a number of people satisfy their power motivation by "joining organizations in which they subordinate personal goals to a higher authority" (McClelland, 1975, p. 20). In this stage the need for power, while not exclusively altruistic in nature, is largely socialized and institutionalized rather than personal. In contrast, the motivation for power at Stages II and III is largely for purposes of self-aggrandizement.

Each stage has an implied relationship to maturity, and pathological behavior may be manifested at any of the stages. In Stage I the person may feel totally controlled by outside forces; in Stage II the person may be compulsive about trying to control everything, particularly with respect to self; in Stage III the person may try to control others regardless of values or ethics; and in Stage IV the person may have a martyr or messianic delusion.

In other works McClelland relates his theory and research more directly to management (McClelland and Burnham, 1976). He documents what most of us have no doubt suspected all along, that more successful managers have a stronger need for power than less successful managers do. A popular misconception is that a good manager has a high need to achieve. This may be so, but power motives are probably more important for explaining management behavior than are achievement motives. To have a high need to achieve means that one wants to do things by oneself. Self-accomplishment is paramount. To be able to do something better than others, or better than one did it before, is the most gratifying.

In contrast, effective management means that a person's needs are typically satisfied by empowering others to achieve. The greatest satisfaction comes from influencing others to achieve, not necessarily from achieving the task(s) for oneself.

Entrepreneurs typically have a high need to accomplish, but when this high need for achievement is coupled with a low need for power, delegation comes slowly, if at all—a situation that causes many of the problems in a growing family business. Conversely, managers with a high need for power and a low need for accomplishment may spend their time politicking and plotting rather than achieving.

Using subordinates' ratings of their organizations' degree of clarity and the amount of team spirit as indices of successful management, McClelland and Burnham found that an organization's degree of clarity was greater (subordinates knew the goals and what was expected of them) and the team spirit was higher when a given manager was high in power motivation, low in need for affiliation, and high in inhibition. That is, the individual's power need was socialized, mature, and not expressed for purposes of self-aggrandizement—a condition most likely to occur at McClelland's Stage IV of development. There are good reasons for this outcome. Managers who have a high need for affiliation usually want to be liked and popular. As a result, their decision making tends to be impulsive, done to please someone at the moment, rather than in rational support of the overall good of the organization. Managers with a high need for power that is *personally* oriented (typically, Stage III of power orientation) are not builders of the institution, according to McClelland and Burnham. They tend to demand personal loyalty from their subordinates, loyalty to them as individuals rather than to the organization. The institutional managers (high need for power at Stage IV) are the most successful because they encourage loyalty to the institution rather than to themselves. As a result, the successful Stage IV manager creates a climate with clarity, team spirit, and opportunities for accomplishment.

In addition, successful institutional managers like and are oriented toward organizations, like the discipline of work and have a preference for getting things done in an orderly fashion, place the good of the organization over self-interest, have a strong sense of fairness, are generally mature (not ego centered or defensive) and willing to seek advice from experts, and have a broad vision regarding the future.

Finally, McClelland and Burnham (1976), corroborating the research of Hall (1976) and others, point out that successful managers tend to have a style of management characterized by participative and coaching behavior; that is, they are concerned with the needs and development of their subordinates. In summary, to quote McClelland and Burnham (1976, p. 101): "The general conclusion of these studies is that the top manager of a company must possess a high need for power; that is, a concern for influencing people. However, this need must be disciplined and controlled so that it is directed toward the benefit of the institution as a whole and not toward the manager's personal aggrandizement. Moreover, the top manager's need for power ought to be greater than his need for being liked by people."

Sources of Power and Compliance. Social psychologists who theorize and conduct research tend to define power in fairly restrictive terms. French and Raven (1959), perhaps the most influential theorists in this group, define power in terms of behavioral acts. Thus, when person A causes person B to do something that B would not have done ordinarily, power has been exercised by A. Although their definition of power may be restrictive, French and Raven have been remarkably instructive in their identification of the primary sources of power, at least within the context of interpersonal and person-to-group relationships. In their terms a person with power is one who holds resources that others desire. The relationship is therefore a matter of reciprocity. According to French and Raven, there are five primary sources or bases of power:

Reward power—having rewards that others want and will do something to obtain.

Coercive power—having resources that can be used to punish and that others will do something to avoid.

Expert power—having information or knowledge that others wish for themselves or wish to benefit from and that they will do something to acquire or benefit from.

Legitimate power—having authority associated with a position or role which others accept as the person's right by the very (legitimate) act of holding such a position or role; because of values they deem important, others will do something in obedience to this acknowledged power.

Referent power—having power because of personal attraction, commonly termed charisma; the person has power because others not only admire him or her but wish to be like and identified with that person. Power is exercised as a result of others' wishing to please the "power holder," to use Kipnis's (1976) term.

To be the chief executive officer of an organization and simultaneously to be viewed as an expert *and* as charismatic is to be *very* powerful indeed. This combination, though very attractive to those with high power motivation, is rare. People may have two or three or perhaps even four of these bases of power but almost never all five, although a current example may be Lee Iacocca. Moreover, the five differ with respect to how wide ranging the base is. Stated differently, a person who operates from a referent base of power typically draws more compliance from others than does, for instance, a person who operates predominantly from a legitimate base. For each of these five sources of power, we can also ask whether the power holder is liked by the recipient(s) of his or her power and whether private compliance is likely to occur. With respect to compliance, we can easily see that any base of power can induce public compliance; that is, if a person desires the reward that the power holder can provide, the person will comply with what the power holder wants. It is not so obvious, however, whether the person will comply privately—whether he or she will internalize the desire to do what the power holder wants without constant monitoring and rewarding. The relationship of these dimensions to the five bases is shown in Table 1. As the table shows, referent power has the strongest base of the five because it is more psychological and emotional in nature.

Table 1. Source of Power, Attractiveness of Power Holder, and Compliance of Recipient.

Source of Power	Personal Attractiveness of Power Holder for Others	Private Compliance?
Reward	May be liked by others, though not necessarily	No (perhaps yes in the long run)
Coercive	Will be disliked by others	No
Legitimate	Will typically be treated with indifference by others	Tends to be yes
Expert	Will typically be treated with indifference by others	Tends to be yes
Referent	Will be liked very much by others	Definite yes

In short, the exercise of power involves a reciprocal relationship. One holds power when he or she controls resources that others desire, and a power holder can exercise power only to the degree that the receiving person allows it. It is difficult to provide examples of absolute power. Perhaps a judge who can determine the death penalty for someone who does not wish to die is an example. As long as the recipient has choice, however, power is reciprocal and limited.

Amount of Power. Having a need for power contributes to success as an executive. Having multiple sources of power responds to this need. How much is needed and required for success as an executive? The more the better? Or does too much power corrupt? One must exercise care and perspective in responding to these questions. The most definitive research providing some answers, or, in any case, providing serious food for thought, is that of David Kipnis. Power corrupts, according to Kipnis (1976), in the sense that it causes people who acquire it to develop exalted views of themselves, and they tend to believe that they are above common moral standards. Kipnis has developed a model of change that describes this effect of power on the power holder.

According to Kipnis, people who have a strong need for power and who have gained control of certain resources then experience a desire to influence others. If these power holders use strong methods of influence—especially via rewards or coercion—to satisfy their personal wants, and if these methods work, then the power holders begin to believe that the behavior of those being influenced is not self-controlled but, rather, is *caused* by the power holders themselves. As a consequence, the persons being influenced are gradually devalued, and the power holders prefer to maintain social and psychological distance. And, finally, power holders' evaluations of themselves change to the point where they view themselves more favorably than they view the persons who were influenced. Kipnis provides considerable background and research data to support his model. In one study, for example, Kipnis compared two groups of managers, one group having less power than the other group. The managers with *less* power tended to attribute their workers' performance to the workers' own motivation to do well, whereas the other managers emphasized their own power to influence, even though the workers were the same people in each case.

Other relevant findings from Kipnis's research include the following:

> Managers who control a broad range of ways of influencing are more assertive and demanding than managers who control fewer ways.
>
> Power holders will be more coercive and less benevolent in situations where they can only punish, or only reward, than when they can do both.
>
> When subordinates lack the ability to perform a desired act and also resist influence, power holders are more likely to use coercion.
>
> Persons who view themselves as weak and powerless are more likely to use punitive means of influence than persons who see themselves as powerful.

The more organizational executives wish to maintain a nonunionized work force, the more they must operate in a participative mode, decentralizing and sharing power.

Summary. Having a need for power seems to be important to success as a manager and as an executive. The broader the base of one's power—that is, the more one's source of power stems from multiple bases—the more powerful one is. This is especially true if the bases include referent or charismatic power. And the more there are multiple sources for the power holder, the more he or she is likely to exercise power but with less reliance on coercion. Yet, according to the change model developed by Kipnis (1976), having power and exercising it successfully over time can lead to corruption. Having no power, as we shall see in the section to follow, may lead to corruption of another sort.

We are therefore faced with an ageless paradox. In a social setting, someone must have and exercise power in order to get anything accomplished. While some of us have greater needs for power than others, and some of us, due to our sources of power, are more powerful than others, with too much power and too much success we all may be vulnerable to becoming immoral. Thus, regardless of one's need and amount or sources of power, how that power is used is the significant consideration of this chapter. Before dealing with this use, let us briefly consider the consequences of not having power.

Not Having Power

Kanter's (1977) coverage of the concept of powerlessness is instructive for two reasons. She furthers our understanding of power itself, and she explains in clear and objective ways the problems of integrating women and minorities into the ranks of management. To be powerless in an organization is to have responsibility without system power. According to Kanter (1977, p. 186), "People held accountable for the results produced by others, whose formal role gives them the right to command but who lack informal political influence, access to resources, outside status, sponsorship, or mobility prospects, are rendered powerless in the organization. . . . They lack control over their own fate and are dependent on others above them." Examples include first-line supervisors, occupants of certain staff jobs, and frequently women and minorities. What is essential to emphasize here are the behavioral responses to powerlessness and their consequences for the organization. When a person feels powerless, the natural response is to attempt to rid him- or herself of the emotion. Powerlessness does not feel good. Frequently, to protect and defend him- or herself, the powerless person will attempt to control others. This response often manifests itself via bossy and critical behavior. In citing a study by Hetzler (1955), Kanter points out that organizational members who are low in status and advancement potential prefer leadership that is highly directive, rigid, and authoritarian. Moreover, "If managers or supervisors who encounter resistance from those they are trying to direct tend to become more coercive in their power tactics, it is a vicious cycle: Powerless authority figures who use coercive tactics provoke resistance and aggression, which prompts them to become even more coercive, controlling, and behaviorally restrictive" (p. 190). Further manifestations of powerlessness include (1) rule-mindedness (controlling rules may represent one of the few avenues—or perhaps the only avenue—a powerless person has for exercising power) and (2) territoriality, sometimes referred to as "turfmanship" (protecting one's domain can provide a sense of exercising power).

Obviously, the consequences of powerlessness do not afford for the organization the kind of efficiency and effective management that is desirable. Rollo May takes the consequences of powerlessness even further. Using the flip side of Lord Acton's famous words, May (1972) contends that powerlessness corrupts. In other words, extreme powerlessness frequently leads to madness and violence. One loses his or her ability to perceive personal boundaries accurately. Plainly, the solution to problems involving powerless-ness is to create conditions whereby people can be empowered. This means providing people with more opportunity for exercising authority on their own and/or in groups, especially for those who are held accountable for results produced by others and who have little or no access to resources. Organizations with significant numbers of powerless members will have difficulty in achieving high performance. To be more explicit, there is likely a direct relationship between degree of experienced powerlessness by organizational members and the degree of overall organizational performance.

Empowering

The antidote to powerlessness is obviously empowerment. For a number of reasons, however, empowering is not a simple process. Many, perhaps most, people believe that power is a zero-sum quantity; to share power, to empower others, is to lose a certain amount of it. This sharing of a precious commodity, especially for those who have a strong need for power, is a difficult act. Some would say that such an act takes courage. But, as Sashkin (1984) points out, it is an ethical imperative. For a Machiavellian, on the other hand, such an act is foolish. For many executives who have labored hard in climbing the corporate ladder, so that more and more organizational power may be obtained, to share this earned reward must indeed seem absurd.

Another reason why the empowering process is not an easy matter or a common occurrence has to do with the complexity of the process itself. One is not born with the skill, or perhaps art, of empowerment. The process must be learned. No doubt the learning comes easier for some than for others, but learning is necessary nevertheless. Moreover, my central thesis is that one's effectiveness in empowering others depends on whether one is a manager or a leader. The two processes differ significantly. A working assumption for this chapter is that an executive is more leader than manager. Organizational size is an important variable, of course. The hypothesis of differences between managers and leaders for effective empowerment holds for medium to large organizations, not a local supermarket (although perhaps it holds true for the corporation that owns the local store among others) or a local YMCA (although perhaps it holds true for the national organization of the YMCA).

Distinguishing between a manager and a leader is not unique to this chapter. Others in the recent past have made such a distinction—most notably, Abraham Zaleznik and James McGregor

Burns. We shall now consider their respective writings as a prerequisite to understanding how the empowering process differs for managers and leaders.

Managers Versus Leaders. Before you proceed with the reading of this section and the remainder of this chapter, a request. Please answer the Leadership Questionnaire at the end of this chapter. There are two purposes for this request: (1) to involve you directly and actively in the subject matter presented in this chapter and (2) to summarize the primary subject matter in a form that may be easier to understand. After you have answered the questionnaire, continue with your reading of the chapter before "scoring" your answers. (The code for scoring the questionnaire appears after the questionnaire itself at the end of the chapter.)

Since Zaleznik's (1977) award-winning paper in the *Harvard Business Review,* in which he contrasted leaders and managers, there has been a gradually increasing interest in the notion that fundamental differences may indeed exist between leaders and managers, between leaders and administrators. For example, most recently Wortman (1982) has distinguished between operating and strategic managers in corporations. His thesis is that top managers, executives, should think and act strategically (that is, long range), whereas managers must be more concerned with daily operations. He laments that executives in United States corporations have acted entirely too managerially; that is, they are overconcerned with short-range operations. This shortsightedness, he contends, has contributed to the decrease in productivity in our country. Others have made arguments similar to Wortman's, yet Wortman casts his points within the context of leader-follower roles. Executives (that is, leaders), as opposed to managers, exercise strategic management not only via the more obvious dimensions of analysis, policy formulation, evaluation, and planning but also in their behavior. Leaders must be more charismatic, inspiring, and flexible. They must have the skills to inspire followers to accept change, to take initiative and risks. Moreover, Wortman argues that leaders must take a highly participative approach to their management of subordinates. Wortman implies that there may be basic differences in personal characteristics between those who rise to executive, leader status and those who remain in the middle ranks.

This implication of Wortman's is Zaleznik's primary premise. In his 1977 paper, Zaleznik argues that leaders and managers do indeed differ in fundamental ways. Not only do leaders behave differently; they also differ in personality, needs, and attitudes. Zaleznik draws his differences between leaders and managers across four dimensions: attitudes toward goals, conceptions of work, relations with others, and senses of self (see Table 2). In short, then, managers enjoy relating with people, attain much of their sense of self from such activities, and work to maintain order. Leaders are loners, risk takers, and visionaries.

In his Pulitzer prize-winning book, Burns (1978) distinguishes between two kinds of leadership: transformational and transactional. There are similarities between Burns's transformational leader and Zaleznik's leader and between the transactional leader and Zaleznik's manager. More specifically, for Burns (p. 4) a

Table 2. A Comparison of Leaders and Managers According to Zaleznik (1977).

Dimensions for Comparison	Leaders	Managers
Attitude toward goals	Personal, active	Impersonal, reactive, passive
Conceptions of work	Projecting ideas into images that excite people; developing options	An enabling process of coordinating and balancing; limiting options
Relations with others	Prefer solitary activities; relate intuitively and empathetically	Prefer to work with people; relate according to roles
Senses of self	Feel separate from their environment; depend on personal mastery of events for identity	Belong to their environment; depend on memberships, roles, and so on, for identity

transformational leader "recognizes and exploits an existing need or demand of a potential follower. But, beyond that, the transforming leader looks for potential motives in followers, seeks to satisfy higher needs, and engages the full person of the follower. The result of transforming leadership is a relationship of mutual stimulation and elevation that converts followers into leaders and may convert leaders into moral agents." A transactional leader, on the other hand, is one who views the leader-follower relationship as a process of exchange: rewards for work, jobs for votes, favor for favor. Burns contends that most leader-follower relationships are transactional.

Table 3 is a summary comparison of transformational leaders and transactional leaders (managers) according to Burns. Some of Zaleznik's views are included also, to provide a fuller range of comparison. It should be noted that Table 3 represents an interpretation of what Burns and Zaleznik mean and does not reflect their exact words. Moreover, the dimensions for comparison are selective and arbitrary.

Leaders—that is, the transformational types—are visionary, solitary, inspirational figures consumed with certain ideals and goals; they engender intense emotions in their followers. In a word, they are charismatic. These transformational leaders, Burns contends, know what their followers' needs are, even when the followers themselves are not aware of their needs. It may be that transformational leaders have stronger empathy skills than the average person. They may be much more accurate in their perceptions of others.

Transformational leaders accurately assess and provide a mission and goals that, when achieved, respond to the followers' needs. The leaders expect the followers to be as dedicated as the leaders themselves are to their joint purpose and mission; when this expectation is not met, leaders will often act in such a way that followers may experience guilt feelings. Mahatma Gandhi, for example, when his followers continued to fight among themselves and did not cooperate with one another as he wished, would fast until near death. Gandhi's act would usually and eventually cause the followers to meet his expectations. Such behavior, although less drastic and dramatic than Gandhi's, is not unusual for transformational leaders. Rather than fasting, a leader might express

Table 3. A Comparison of Transformational Leaders and Transactional Leaders (Managers).

Dimensions for Comparison	Leaders	Managers
Emotional involvement	With the institution and with ideals/vision	With the task and the people associated with the task
Personal life	Work and personal life not that distinguishable	Work is separate from personal, private life
Achieves commitment via	Inspiration	Involvement
Holds people accountable via	Guilt induction; want whole person	Contractual transactions; want task accomplishment
Value emphasis	Terminal; end state	Instrumental; means
Problems	Create them	Fix them
Plans	Long range	Short range
Appreciates from followers/subordinates	Contrariness	Conformity
Engenders in followers/subordinates	Intense feelings—love, sometimes hate; desire to identify with; turbulent	Feelings not intense but relations smoother and steadier

disappointment and remind the followers of the mission, purpose, or goals and of their responsibility to work toward those goals.

Transformational leaders, by definition perhaps, never leave matters as they find them. Change is the rule, not the exception. They usually have a clear change objective, some particular end state in mind, according to Burns. They are far less concerned with how to achieve that end than they are with accomplishing the purpose and mission. They are therefore tolerant of differences of opinion about paths to goals, but they are not tolerant about any equivocation regarding the goals themselves.

Transactional leaders, or managers, with their penchant for teamwork, task accomplishment, and problem solving, and their steadier, less turbulent manner of working with others, complement and supplement transformational leaders. For clarity of goals and direction, managers need leaders. For indispensable help in reaching the goals, leaders need managers.

These comments and Table 3 are meant to provide a flavor of what Burns and Zaleznik have written, not an exhaustive discourse. The work of Burns and Zaleznik is based on their observations of and interactions and experiences with leaders and managers, their understanding and interpretation of the research literature, and their theorizing. Even though Burns particularly uses numerous illustrations to support his points, hard scientific evidence that documents a difference between leaders (transformational) and managers (transactional) is only beginning to materialize (Bass, 1985). Yet the ideas of Burns and Zaleznik are reasonable, coincide with others' observations and views, and, in any case, are provocative. Their ideas, more importantly, represent newer thinking regarding leadership.

Given the assumption that leaders and managers differ in their personal characteristics and in their behavior, the process of empowering others, followers and subordinates, should differ for leaders and managers as well. These hypothesized differences will be contrasted according to five possible empowering processes: (1) providing direction for followers and subordinates, (2) stimulating followers and subordinates, (3) rewarding followers and subordinates, (4) developing followers and subordinates, (5) appealing to follower and subordinate needs. The perspective I am taking is one of effective or successful empowerment—that is, what leaders and managers do that effectively empowers their followers and subordinates.

Providing Direction. Leaders provide direction with their ideals, vision, and purpose. They inspire followers by challenging them to work toward a higher purpose, something that not only is highly worthy of their time and energy but cannot be achieved without a collective effort. Leaders talk and write about superordinate goals. As persons, leaders embody these goals, this purpose, this vision. Direction comes as much from who they are as individuals as from what they say. Successful leaders provide high clarity regarding *what* is to be accomplished and ambiguity about *how* to accomplish the mission. Leaders need managers for the latter activity. Empowerment, then, comes from leaders providing clarity of direction, but not just any direction—a direction that emcompasses a higher purpose, a worthy cause, an idea, and will require collective and concerted effort.

Managers provide direction through clarity of *paths* to the goals, the how or implementation part of the process. Empowerment, however, depends on the degree to which managers involve their subordinates in the determination of that clarity. A participative process increases the likelihood of empowerment among subordinates. Managers therefore are managing a process, not goals or end states. Direction, in this case path direction, evolves. The two critical concepts for success as a manager in providing direction are involvement and evolvement.

Stimulating Followers and Subordinates. Successful leaders are intellectually stimulating; they challenge followers' thinking by suggesting some new direction that the followers had not thought of before, or, at least, not in quite the same way as the leader suggests. Empowerment comes from the stimulation of an intellectually exciting idea. The idea is, of course, cognitive, but the stimulation is emotional and therefore is energizing.

Even more emotionally stimulating is the idea of a higher morality, which, Burns (1978) contends, transformational leaders convey. Mahatma Gandhi stimulated and inspired his people by pointing to the suppression of British rule and by advocating passive resistance to counter that suppression. Passive resistance, Gandhi pointed out, was not only justified under such circumstances but represented a higher morality. Suppression was to be challenged not by violence, exchanging one form of immorality for another, but by a higher form of morality. Perhaps most of the world would agree with Gandhi's ideals and methods. Yet other leaders could claim a higher morality, and most of the world would not agree. For Hitler a super race represented a higher morality, and this ideal clearly stimulated many within his immediate domain; but this position was not considered a higher morality by most of the world. In both instances, however, the appeal to a higher morality was stimulating and emotional and therefore not readily amenable to rational scrutiny and judgment.

For managers stimulation comes from action—from doing things, accomplishing tasks, moving mountains, achieving the impossible. The American attitude or philosophy of "can do" is a significant stimulant for managers. An old U.S. Army adage is "Do something, soldier, even if it's wrong." While most managers, and no doubt most army sergeants, would not go to that extreme, the emphasis nevertheless is on action. Empowerment, again, comes from managers giving their subordinates a piece of this action, providing them with significant and relevant tasks to do that help the action along.

Rewarding Followers and Subordinates. Successful leaders reward their followers primarily through an informal and spontaneous process. They enjoy catching their followers in the act of doing something right and recognizing that act immediately and in a positive manner. Thus, they look for opportunities to reward their followers. Moreover, they reward their followers in a fairly consistent manner. They do not positively reinforce their followers merely for the sake of providing "strokes"; rather, their rewarding is for following behavior that is directed toward accomplishing the leaders' goals. The followers' behavior may not always be completely successful; as long as it represents an attempt to accomplish the leaders' goals, it is likely to be positively recognized. Empowerment, then, comes from being positively recognized by a power figure, the leader; that is, to be recognized by the power holder for doing the right thing is to share, even though perhaps momentarily, that power.

Rewarding by managers is more formal. Their rewarding of subordinates is by way of incentive systems, promotions, merit awards, and the like (extrinsic rewarding). The more managers base their rewarding on individual, subordinate performance, however, and the more they attempt to provide interesting and meaningful jobs for their subordinates to do (intrinsic rewarding), the more likely they will experience success as managers—in other words, the more likely their subordinates will be motivated to put forth effort and to perform quality work. Empowerment, as with the leader, derives from recognition. In the managers' case, this recognition is typically more a function of extrinsic rewards and related more directly to job performance, but even greater effectiveness is likely to be derived from intrinsic rewarding.

Developing Followers and Subordinates. Successful leaders develop their followers by inspiring them to do more than they thought they could. Leaders often set high standards and may even establish goals that seem impossible to achieve. These leaders then challenge their followers to accomplish the seemingly impossible goals by coaxing, cajoling, encouraging ("You can do it!"), and constantly reminding them of what the goals and mission are. Successful leaders work hard to keep their followers focused and directed toward the goals with constant and consistent reminders. Harold Sperlich in his "Conversations" (Burke, 1984) noted that he frequently talked about the three common objectives for all Chrysler employees: objectives that managers and subordinates have in common, objectives that management and the unions have in common, and objectives that Chrysler and its constituents (suppliers, government, and others) have in common. Chrysler employees have been amazed at how much the corporation has been able to accomplish with the unions, with their suppliers, and with the hourly workers in the plants. They seem to say "We have achieved far more than we thought possible." Empowerment comes from accomplishing more than expected.

Managers' development of subordinates differs from that of leaders; at least the process is different, but the outcome is similar— personal growth. And the managers' approach is based on the same participative and involvement processes mentioned before. Successful managers involve their subordinates in important and relevant decision making and, as a part of the process, help them to learn about (1) the consequences of their decisions and actions (managers providing feedback) and (2) management itself (managers providing modeling behavior, especially concerning the act of decision making). Empowerment comes from participation in important and relevant decisions and activities, and individual development comes from the consequent learning.

Appealing to Follower and Subordinate Needs. Perhaps the greatest difference between leaders and managers regarding empowerment is the type of follower and subordinate need to which each appeals. Leaders appeal to a dependency need. Managers appeal to an independency need. Followers need to have direction. Subordinates need *not* to be cast in the role of subordinate for every aspect of their work. Yet followers and subordinates are usually the same individuals. The point is that successful leaders appeal to one need that most people have, and successful managers appeal to quite another need that these same people have.

Even though adults have outgrown their need to be dependent on more powerful people in their past (parents, teachers, coaches, and the like), this earlier and quite basic need may not have been fully satisfied. It may have changed in nature and thus becomes fulfilled via slightly different forms. But the basic need remains. Some adults accept this dependency need fairly readily; others deny it. The Japanese regard it as an appropriate adult need, and it is highly indigenous to their culture. (See Doi, 1973, for a thorough analysis of this phenomenon, called *amae* by the Japanese.) Americans, however, often equate dependency with powerlessness. And, in fact, being too dependent can lead to a follower's being subsumed completely within and under the power of the leader; as a consequence, feelings of powerlessness may emerge and gradually replace the feelings of empowerment. Jim Jones's religious cult of a few years ago, where his followers at his command committed suicide, might illustrate this point—that is, the replacement of earlier feelings of empowerment with complete submergence and submission.

But the successful leader is one who is sensitive to what the group wants and what is good for the system. By being in tune with the group's desires and by conceptualizing and envisioning these desires, the leader is responding. This leader response to real desires on the part of the followers is empowering. A typical follower reaction might be: "Thank goodness, someone has finally provided the direction we need, and we can get on with it!" Dependency, in this case, is the need for that clarity of direction.

And let us not overlook the fact that followers have power. Leadership, after all, is a reciprocal process. By definition, no follower, no leader. The followers' power is manifested when the leader does not respond to their desires. Most experienced leaders and managers at one time or other have faced passive resistance from followers. This resistance may take a variety of forms—"Gee, I forgot" or "I didn't really understand that you wanted it that way"—and is often a reaction to the leader's lack of response to follower desires and needs.

People have needs for autonomy too. Like dependency, these needs vary in intensity from one individual to another. For Americans this is a strong need, deeply embedded in their culture. The cultural term is individualism, "standing on one's own feet." Managers are in the best position to respond to this need, and they can best respond to it via a participative process.

Table 4 summarizes this discussion of the empowering process.

Summary and Conclusions

Although leaders and managers may differ in personal characteristics, in role, and in behavior, the outcomes of their acts

Table 4. Differences in the Empowering Process as a Function of Role: Leaders Compared with Managers.

Empowering Process	Leaders	Managers
Providing direction for followers/ subordinates	Via ideals, vision, a higher purpose, superordinate goals	Via involvement of subordinates in determining paths toward goal accomplishment
Stimulating followers/subordinates	With ideas	With action; things to accomplish
Rewarding followers/subordinates	Informal; personal recognition	Formal; incentive systems
Developing followers/subordinates	By inspiring them to do more than they thought they could do	By involving them in important decision-making activities and providing feedback for potential learning
Appealing to follower/subordinate needs	Appeal to needs of followership and dependency	Appeal to needs for autonomy and independency

can be the same. People can grow and develop with either one or both. Feelings of empowerment can come from both leaders and managers. The primary position of this chapter, however, is that the empowering process must differ as a function of whether one is in a leadership or a management role—even if some *perceive* themselves as leaders rather than managers regardless of formal role. Recent research in executive competence has shown, for example, that the highly competent executives in a federal agency tend to perceive themselves more as leaders than comparatively less competent executives do (Burke and Myers, 1982).

For organizational effectiveness, of course, both leaders and managers are necessary. To refer again to the Chrysler example, Harold Sperlich conceived of himself as both a leader and a manager but said that his role was more managerial and Lee Iacocca's role was more one of leadership. To use Sperlich's words:

> The dramatic leadership that Iacocca provided was in the classic leadership mode—a guy you believe in, you'd follow into battle. He was so strong that, at the worst time, knowing his hand was on the helm, a dealer would keep his money in the business; a supplier would bankroll us; a man would stay with us; a guy would come over from Ford. His personal strength, or the perception of his personal strength, was crucial. . . . [He] provides leadership in battle, his fundamentals are right, and he behaves consistently. . . . My own leadership style is a little bit like his, but on a smaller scale. I'm not big enough and I'm not supposed to be. . . . I'm more actively involved in trying to promote results through common goals and an enabling style. . . . But as chairman and chief executive officer, he's got to establish the fundamental values [Burke, 1984, pp. 35-36].

A further role distinction—or, perhaps more accurately, a personality difference—is that Iacocca is more of an entrepreneur, a term I have not used in this chapter. Iacocca is marketing oriented, promotes the company and the business, and is more external—

dealing with car and truck dealers, government, and suppliers. Frequently entrepreneurs are more leader in nature than manager. Their typically strong achievement needs are met by building a business, a company. They usually have a clear idea of what they want their business and company to be. But as managers they are often less effective, especially as the business grows and when delegation on their part is needed. They like to hold on, to continue to do what they enjoyed in the first place.

The Iacocca-Sperlich combination—leader/entrepreneur and manager—seems to be highly productive. In any case, their example highlights the two distinctive roles that the two men play and the differences in their personal characteristics.

In large, complex organizations, it is not always clear when one is a leader and when one is a manager. Executives serve in both capacities. But those executives who lean more naturally toward leader behavior and desires and have more leadership responsibility need capable managers to help them implement their goals. Those executives who lean more naturally toward manager behavior and inclinations and have more management responsibility need capable leaders to help them by providing clarity of mission, purpose, and goals. Thus, leaders and managers are interdependent. While managers are bosses, they are at the same time followers. They need overall direction and inspiration, but leaders cannot function successfully without managers.

At the risk of oversimplification but nevertheless to summarize the main thesis of this chapter as succinctly as possible, leaders empower via direction and inspiration and managers via action and participation.

Leadership Questionnaire

For each of the following ten pairs of statements, divide 5 points between the two according to your beliefs, perceptions of yourself, or according to which of the two statements characterizes you better. The 5 points may be divided between the A and B statements in any one of the following ways— 5 A, 0 B; 4 A, 1 B; 3 A, 2 B; 1 A, 4 B; 0 A, 5 B—but not equally (2½) between the two. Weigh your choices between the two according to which one characterizes you or your beliefs better.

1. _____ A   As leader I have a primary mission of maintaining stability.

   _____ B   As leader I have a primary mission of change.

2. _____ A   As leader I must cause events.

   _____ B   As leader I must facilitate events.

3. _____ A   I am concerned that my followers are rewarded equitably for their work.

   _____ B   I am concerned about what my followers want in life.

4. _____ A   A primary value I hold is equal justice for all.

   _____ B   A primary value I hold is honesty in all matters.

5. _____ A   As a leader I spend considerable energy in managing separate but related goals.

   _____ B   As a leader I spend considerable energy in arousing hopes, expectations, and aspirations among my followers.

6. _____ A   While not in formal classroom sense, I believe that a significant part of my leadership is that of teacher.

   _____ B   I believe that a significant part of my leadership is that of facilitator.

7. _____ A   As leader I must engage with followers at an equal level of morality.

   _____ B   As leader I must represent a higher morality.

8. _____ A   I enjoy stimulating followers to want to do more.

   _____ B   I enjoy rewarding followers for a job well done.

9. _____ A   I am more social than a loner.

   _____ B   I am more of a loner than social.

10. _____ A   What power I have to influence others comes primarily from my ability to get people to identify with me and my ideas.

    _____ B   What power I have to influence others comes primarily from my status and position.

Code for Leadership Questionnaire

Leader / Transformational		*Manager / Transactional*	
	Your Point(s)		*Your Point(s)*
1. B	_____	1. A	_____
2. A	_____	2. B	_____
3. B	_____	3. A	_____
4. A	_____	4. B	_____
5. B	_____	5. A	_____
6. A	_____	6. B	_____
7. B	_____	7. A	_____
8. A	_____	8. B	_____
9. B	_____	9. A	_____
10. A	_____	10. B	_____

Column Totals

_____   _____

Note: The higher column total indicates that you agree more with, and see yourself as more like, Zaleznik's and Burns's conceptions of a transformational leader or a transactional leader (a manager).

FOUR

Empowerment Strategies:
Balancing Authority and Responsibility

Eric H. Neilsen

Executives today are facing a crisis with respect to the acquisition and use of power—largely because our societal concepts of authority are changing more rapidly than our concepts of responsibility are. Executives throughout the hierarchy in modern organizations are being held responsible to more and more constituencies (Pfeffer and Salancik, 1978; Friedlander and Pickle, 1968), while the authority their followers are willing to grant them is shrinking as a source of power for fulfilling these responsibilities (Quinn and Staines, 1978).

The authority that subordinates are willing to grant their organizational superiors today has become more specialized, more secularized, and more conditional (Kanter, 1979). Several streams of events over the last several decades have contributed to these changes. Many of them revolve around the notion that the average citizen has become more empowered, more imbued with a sense of self-worth and autonomy, than ever before, thereby making blind deference to any hierarchy less palatable and substituting demands for inclusion and influence in decision making in its place (Yankelovich, 1978). For example, welfare capitalism since the 1930s has provided baseline protection from the threat of poverty for much of the population, making deference for the sake of survival less critical. General economic affluence and modern technology have broadened people's career choices and their capacity to move from one organization to another, increasing in turn their ability to negotiate for more influence. Our culture is rapidly developing more diverse, differentiated, and democratic concepts of life-style. The civil rights movement of the late 1960s taught us the positive effects of social activism, which has spread from racial issues to consumer advocacy to women's rights to rights to privacy to due process in the workplace.

Simultaneously, mass communication and the mass media have demystified life in the executive ranks. Models of idealized authority based on childhood experience are no longer easily transferable to formal authority figures, given a constant flow of contradictory data suggesting that authority figures are corruptable, egocentric, and, in general, all too human. The information explosion has also led to greater scrutiny of executive behavior, resulting in stronger corrective measures in response to deviance within the executive ranks and greater willingness by subordinates to respond to an executive according to his track record instead of his formal position. Thus, as the average citizen has been empowered, the executive has been downgraded to the ranks of normal citizenry.

While our concepts of executive authority have changed, our concepts of responsibility have not. If anything, activism and legislation in areas such as social responsibility, equal opportunity, safety and health, ecology, and consumer rights have made executives more comprehensively responsible for their subordinates' behavior. And advances in information technology have increased the number of performance parameters to be accounted for at almost any organizational level. Consequently, executives are getting squeezed between the rock of increased responsibility and the hard place of attenuated formal authority.

Two strategies are available for dealing with this situation. On the one hand, an executive can attempt to accumulate more power from other sources until his power is enough to match his responsibilities. Following Kotter, we define power as "a measure of a person's potential to get others to do what he or she wants them to do, as well as to avoid being forced to do what he or she does not want to do" (Kotter, 1979, preface). And, as many authors have noted, formal authority is only one kind of power. It can be complemented by a wide variety of other types of power that an executive can accumulate on the job—for example, power derived from friendship, personal obligation, perceived expertise, professional reputation, others' perceived dependence on one's actions, and control over information. On the other hand, the executive can close the gap between his or her authority and responsibilities by empowering subordinates to a point where they voluntarily share the responsibilities of the executive's office and delegate their shared power upward to help the executive fulfill this responsibility for the welfare of the larger organization. Empowerment involves giving subordinates the resources, both psychological and technical, to discover the varieties of power they themselves have and/or can accumulate, and therefore which they can use in another's behalf.

The first strategy seems very popular today. It resonates with Western individualism; that is, it implies that an individual actor is the master of his or her own fate and that power can be acquired and managed in the service of this mastery. The second strategy, while less popular, is the substance of what David McClelland has called "the ultimate paradox of social leadership and social power: to be an effective leader, one must turn all his so-called followers into leaders" (Lorsch and Barnes, 1972, p. 170). It resonates with the alternative sentiment that every individual's fate is enmeshed in the larger fate of the groups to which he or she belongs. While this collective sentiment surfaces continuously in the literature, few would deny that the empowerment strategy it supports is the less practiced and accepted alternative among executives. Nonetheless, I believe that it is the underdeveloped but inevitable and necessary polarity of the first.

This chapter is devoted to an exploration of this second alternative. While other writers have begun to address the structural implications of its use in modern organizations (Kanter, 1977, 1979), we will focus on the interpersonal dynamics involved in empowering others; and we will begin by reviewing a model of group development and a series of guidelines for inducing such development. This is an excellent place to start, because a major objective of group development technologies, as they have evolved over the past three decades, has been the empowerment of group members. Consequently, the model and its leadership guidelines can be used in a Weberian sense as an ideal typical strategy of empowerment.

Subsequent sections of the chapter will examine the problems and opportunities that might be encountered in applying such a strategy to the day-to-day activities of the modern executive. This, in turn, will lead to a more general discussion of the empowerment strategy when juxtaposed against the first alternative, personal power accumulation. Finally, we will address the implications of the comparison and posit an emerging need for executives to assume collective responsibility for developing guidelines on how power should be managed in their organizations.

A Group Development Model

For several years some of my colleagues and I have been refining a model of group development designed to help group leaders and members understand and enhance their interactions as they move from being a set of isolated actors to a collaborative and highly interdependent work team. The model has proven especially helpful in team-building meetings, where groups of executives and senior professionals get together for several days to assess the current state of their working relationships with each other and try to improve on them. When successful, such events are typically experienced by the participants as highly transformative, changing their own perspectives on their personal behavior, their relationships with their colleagues, and the behavior of their management teams as a whole in significant ways. What has become apparent to us over the years is that such meetings are successful for the very reason that they involve a process of psychological empowerment. Specifically, as a group progresses, more and more of its members develop more robust, differentiated, and powerful identities in each other's eyes. The leader, while losing some of the deference and awe that goes with his or her formal position, also becomes recognized as a more rounded human being. Moreover, sometimes with the help of a consultant but often without, this person discovers new ways to respond to individual members' empowerment needs as well as to those of the group as a whole.

In the sections that follow, I will describe the various elements in the model and, in the process, detail the relationship between particular stages of group development and the kinds of strategies leaders can use to empower their followers to deal with the personal dilemmas and crises inherent in each stage. My belief is that these kinds of behaviors are representative of what executives in general need to do to empower their subordinates psychologically on an ongoing basis.

Background Assumptions. The model is based on a number of assumptions that will be reviewed only briefly here, since a more detailed treatment is available elsewhere (see Srivastva, Obert, and Neilsen, 1977). First, interaction within any group is meaningful to its members because of their possession of a common language. This language is both social and technical, verbal and nonverbal, and includes shared images of each member's identity, roles, rights, prerogatives, and potentials, as well as the technical terms and symbols used for doing tasks. Such language is based initially on common patterns of socialization that members have gone through outside the group and is gradually modified and elaborated through shared experience within the group (Berger and Luckman, 1967). Second, the evolution of the group's language goes hand in hand with the resocialization of its members. Specifically, the creation of meaning through shared experience not only makes the group language more complex and unique but also changes members' concepts of themselves and their capacities to function both within and outside the group.

The resocialization process revolves around three basic issues, derived from Schutz's (1958) treatment of group development: inclusion, influence, and intimacy. Inclusion, the process of gaining an acceptable identity in the eyes of other members, involves reconciling the identity one wants to have in a group with the one that other members actually develop of oneself, based on their responses to one's actual behavior and societal credentials. The influence process refers to one's own and other members' attempts to mold each other's behavior so that it is consistent with their assumptions about what is appropriate in light of the identities thus established. Finally, the intimacy process involves the expression of affect among members—denoting closeness or distance, jealousy, warmth, love, hate, friendship, enmity—which leads to the merging of one's identity with that of other members, so that, for some purposes, the members of a dyad or clique are considered a single unit.

A third assumption behind the model has to do with the amount of attention a group as a whole gives to each of these issues. On a general level, all three processes—inclusion, influence, and intimacy—are highly interdependent in the life of the group, and issues related to each of them surface continuously. However, again following Schutz (1958), inclusion issues tend to dominate the earlier stages of a group's existence and are followed by preoccupation with influence issues, with intimacy becoming a primary concern only in well-developed groups whose inclusion and influence issues have been, for the most part, resolved.

Fourth, the model assumes that "working through these general issues causes a group to focus on a series of [five] basic dilemmas, reminiscent of Erikson's (1963) stage-based dilemmas of individual development, whose resolutions (or the lack thereof) cause the group to progress or regress along the path of member socialization" (Neilsen, 1979, p. 10). Besides revolving around a different focal dilemma or group-wide concern, each stage is marked by differences in members' concerns about themselves and about each other and by differences in informal structure, the quality of communication among members, their capacity to help each other, and their attitudes toward authority figures and rules.

Fifth, again paralleling Erikson's treatment of individual development, all five dilemmas surface to some degree in each stage. They simply become focal for group members at different times in a group's life and therefore are most amenable to concerted treatment at those times. Moreover, groups progress and regress along the developmental sequence as members' lives change outside the group and the group context itself changes.

While these are the assumptions on which the original model was based, three others need to be added to undergird our more recent thinking about appropriate leadership behavior within particular stages, especially in team-building efforts.

The first additional assumption is that a leader's immediate task is to engage in behaviors that empower other members—that is, that provide them with ways of thinking and acting, that enable them to deal more effectively with the stage-based dilemma they are facing at a given time. The second is that, just as each stage is marked by different dilemmas and group characteristics, the requisite behaviors for empowering members to resolve each stage-based dilemma are different, overlapping somewhat among adjacent stages but clearly having different emphases. These behaviors include both different procedural strategies and operating agendas for the leader and different influence behaviors.

Finally, while resolution of a particular dilemma can be facilitated by a leader's behavior, it is only one of many factors involved and may not always lead to success. The nature of external demands on the group, the personalities of particular members, and the experiences of members outside the group can all contribute to the group's progress through or fixation at a particular stage.

With these underlying assumptions in mind, we will now review each of the stages and discuss the kinds of empowering behaviors that leaders can engage in to help members resolve the stage-based dilemmas. Table 1 outlines the salient characteristics of each stage and the leadership style and influence behaviors necessary for empowering members who are experiencing it. For each stage we will (1) elaborate on each of these issues, (2) discuss the attendant states of members' concerns about themselves and each other, their capacity for mutual help, and their attitudes toward the formal leader(s), and (3) describe the appropriate empowerment strategy for this stage, both in general terms and with respect to specific influence behaviors.

Stage 1: Safety Versus Anxiety. People experiencing the dilemma of safety versus anxiety, no matter how proactive and mature they might be in other arenas, are faced with the fact that in the setting at hand they simply do not know the rules of the game, specifically as they are defined by the powerful authority figure with whom they must deal. Thus, it is only natural for them to be self-protective and

Table 1. Five Stages of Group Development and the Leadership Style and Influence Behaviors Needed at Each Stage for Empowering Members Psychologically.

Stage	Nascent Structure of Group	Relational Issue	Core Dilemma	Needed Leadership Style	Needed Influence Behaviors
1	Each person for him- or herself	Inclusion	Safety versus anxiety	Directive	Commanding, prescribing, legitimizing
2	Dyads	Inclusion and influence	Similarity versus dissimilarity	Coaching	Instructing, debating, bargaining
3	Coalitions and cliques	Influence	Support versus panic	Participative	Involving, committing
4	Connected coalitions and cliques	Influence and intimacy	Concern versus isolation	Appreciative	Nurturing, applauding
5	A single integrated group	Intimacy	Interdependence versus withdrawal	Inspirational	Innovating, challenging

preoccupied with their own welfare until they gain access to this information.

Behavior centers around expressions of anxiety over efforts to establish an acceptable identity and/or efforts to protect the self and gain safety by avoiding exploration of what membership requires. The focal question is "Who must I be to gain membership in this group?"

In this context the (formal) leader has the only clearly differentiated identity. He or she becomes the reference point for others to use in establishing their own identities. Interaction focuses on this person, and dependency is high. Attributions of omnipotence often develop. The emotional valence toward the leader may be positive or negative (savior or tyrant). The key point is that this person is totally in charge.

Intermember relations are superficial. The focus is on the self. Energy is expended on either providing information about the self—one's preferred identity and position with respect to the issues at hand—or hiding these data if their acceptance seems unlikely. Only things that are most relevant to the listener's personal concerns appear to be heard or understood.

Discussion of goals and procedures is self-oriented rather than intended to clarify a shared task. Member-to-member feedback on task performance is low and is designed to enhance the self rather than help the other [adapted from Neilsen, 1979, pp. 10–11].

One important way for a leader to empower the group members at this stage is to give them what they need with a minimum of fanfare and simultaneously to avoid reinforcing or generating more self-protective behavior. That is, the leader tells members what they have to do to satisfy the demands of the larger environment; the leader clearly explains the rewards for conformity and punishments for failure to conform; and the leader refrains from taking advantage of his or her position to satisfy personal needs.

The dimensions of such *directive* leadership include:

- Justifying directives in terms of organization strategy and policies.
- Being direct and unconditional in stating the rules of the game.
- Being friendly but formal.
- Being consistent.
- Being careful to follow one's own rules.

In training managers to lead from this perspective, we have found it useful, moreover, for them to practice a particular kind of interpersonal influence style. Specifically, following the dictates of directive leadership requires leaders to engage in *commanding* (making direct commands to others), *prescribing* (stating goals, roles, decision-making procedures, punishments, and rewards), and *legitimizing* (referring directly or indirectly to higher authority in justifying commands; implying that others must/should/ought to do as he or she says). For many managers this kind of behavior comes close to being punitive toward the people one is trying to empower. Paradoxically, a certain amount of emotional intensity is often appropriate in "laying down the law." The rules are meant to be taken seriously, and conveying one's seriousness through tone of voice, facial expression, and eye contact is an important way to get this message across.

Stage 2: Similarity Versus Dissimilarity. Helping a group to develop is not always a pleasant experience for the leader. Development comes at a price, and in the transition between the first and second stages, the leader is quietly paid back for his or her earlier directiveness. Paradoxically, one can argue that this directiveness, combined with the leader's self-discipline, helps to give the group the psychological security to pursue greater autonomy. People now know what is expected of them; they also know that, as long as they operate within these expectations, they will not be threatened. This awareness gives them the freedom to look around and discover who else is in the room and to begin to form alliances that provide them with additional security. As a result, they can begin to shift their posture from one of self-protection to one of proactivity: "If I am a member of this group, how can I make it serve my interests?" The biggest roadblock, of course, is the powerful leader, whose boundaries are now ripe for testing. Thus, counterdependence sets in.

This stage is transitional between preoccupation with inclusion and preoccupation with influence. While still concerned with their own identities, members start to turn toward definition of the other.

Exploration of the other is begun, but only in the context of the degree of similarity or difference from the self. The central question becomes "If I am who the others say I am, then is the other like or unlike me?" Structurally, individuals tend to form into supportive dyads with others who are more like themselves than the other group members.

Interaction within dyads starts superficially but leads to fuller explorations of interests, skills, and values and mutual help. The dissimilar other is not actively rejected but simply ignored.

The relationship with the leader shifts toward counterdependency. Members now have enough security to be passively aggressive but not enough to confront the leader openly (for example, assigned tasks are not quite done, commands are slightly misinterpreted to avoid tough issues, members grumble among themselves about work loads and directives). Norms begin to be stated and tested. Members begin to test the boundaries of their influence [adapted from Neilsen, 1979, pp. 11-12].

The counterdependent group needs a leader with a *coaching* style, who—through direct example, positive reinforcement, exhortation toward more challenging goals with greater rewards, and constructive critique—can help members overcome their discomfort with depending on a leader by teaching them how to gain greater independence.

Dimensions of *coaching* leadership include:

- Physically demonstrating the roles one expects followers to play, so that they can learn through observation—then coaching them step by step.
- In the face of passive resistance, emphasizing the rewards of meeting the standards one has set and being direct about baseline requirements.
- Praising desired behavior, criticizing undesired behavior, but avoiding attacking individuals directly.
- Being ready and willing to argue the merits of one's own position vis-à-vis others'.
- Being sensitive to people's desire not to be dependent on the leader and loosening the reins as quickly as they learn.
- Making the work as interesting as possible, so that people are enticed into getting involved.

Following the dictates of coaching leadership requires one to engage in interpersonal influence tactics such as *instructing* (responding to requests for expert advice; praising others' conformity to one's suggestions; critiquing others' behavior against a standard of excellence or professionalism, but with a positive, caring tone; giving demonstrations, showing how to do things), *debating* (offering logical arguments in support of a direction or position, asking for information and justification of others' positions), and *bargaining* (negotiating, with a neutral or positive tone, for commitment to a position).

Stage 3: Support Versus Panic. A typically important test of whether a group has reached the third stage is that its members develop the capacity to confront the leader. Members experience support when—typically after articulating their concerns in subgroups away from the leader and planning a confrontation—one member actually voices the group's concerns to the leader in a formal meeting and the other members reinforce the message. Panic is experienced when such support is not forthcoming.

The dominant issue at this stage is influence.

Attention moves to the dissimilar other. The central question is "Given that I am who I appear to be, who must the other be or become to support my identity as a member of this group?"

Structurally, dyads are no longer essential for supporting one's identity. The task now is to get others to accept one's identity as it has unfolded in the context of the dyad. For instance, if A and B agree that A is an expert on a given issue, then both will work together to support this definition of A in their relations with other group members.

Relationships with the leader become less counterdependent. Members willingly accept responsibility for baseline requirements but simultaneously hold the leader responsible for facilitating their needs.

Intermember relations are often characterized by confrontation. The choice to take on greater responsibility for the group's tasks leads to clarification of roles and expectations and much negotiation. More active listening and more helpful feedback develop to influence the dissimilar other. The group begins to become an operating entity [adapted from Neilsen, 1979, p. 13].

Some managers with whom we have shared this description find it more aggressive in tone than their own experiences indicate, since they evidently have been able to move into this stage without bloodshed. We agree that the transition need not involve much open expression of anger. The key ingredient in our view is members' internalization of a set of norms that they are willing to enforce with each other, instead of waiting for the leader to do so. Such proactivity and self-regulation tend to go hand in hand, however, with the development of a more realistic view of the leader's own strengths and weaknesses and, concomitantly, the felt need to address what members regard as undesirable or unfair behavior by the leader. The leader's capacity, in turn, to acknowledge the value of a shared set of norms to which he or she is also beholden, to be willing to apologize for past transgressions, and to work through differences of opinion according to mutually shared ground rules empowers the group to continue in this vein.

The group at this stage needs a *participative* leader, who can teach members how to resolve differences with the leader, with each other, and with other groups and individuals.

Dimensions of *participative* leadership include:

- When difficulties arise, focusing on *what* is the problem, not *who* is the problem.
- Facilitating confrontation by being candid oneself and by asking for feedback and listening nondefensively.
- Suggesting problem-solving procedures for defining goals and strategies for pursuing them and for settling equity issues.
- Leaning toward consensus decision making.
- Acknowledging individual contributions of expertise, data, and support that one could not have obtained alone.

Leading participatively, in turn, invites the use of influence behaviors such as *including* (inviting others' opinions, suggestions, ideas; acknowledging the importance of others' contributions to the task at hand; suggesting ways of addressing a problem that involves broad participation), *committing* (showing willingness to go along with the sentiment of the larger group, building on others' ideas, declaring one's own commitment to resolving a problem to everyone's satisfaction, referring to the welfare and needs of the whole group when justifying a position), and *being open* (asking for feedback on one's own behavior, listening nondefensively, sharing feelings about self and others and about what is happening).

Stage 4: Concern Versus Isolation. Perhaps the most important requisite for reaching the fourth stage is the development of fairly stable resolutions to major influence issues or, more simply, the establishment of a firm, mutually agreed-on set of boundaries concerning who can control whom and in what ways. Such boundaries provide members with the security needed to let them be themselves more fully, rather than stick to the specific roles that have bounded their participation thus far. Letting go allows for greater mutual support, more opportunities for expanding one's skills, more frequent discoveries of untapped resources within the group, and more finely tuned coordination around tasks. When the group is success oriented, however, it also induces people to stretch themselves to their limits and occasionally to experience the consequences of trying to go beyond them.

Stage 4 is another transitional stage; the group moves from issues of influence to those of intimacy. As issues of influence become resolved, attention turns to a fuller exploration of what it means to be a member of a particular clique or dyad within the group. The focal question is "Who are we—our dyad, clique—in the context of the larger group?"

Since personal identities and influence boundaries have already been established, subgroups are no longer necessary for maintaining them. On a personal level, the authority figure is accepted more and more as just another member of the group.

Intermember relations shift from issues of influence to interdependency. Concern arises for making meaningful space for dissimilar others; for instance, the values of deviant members are accepted on their own merits. The attitude develops that everyone has something to offer. Members view their group as cohesive and supportive.

Task behavior is more results oriented. There is less emphasis on rights and prerogatives for their own sakes. There is also greater appreciation of the complexity of the task. Realistic pessimism often develops over the group's capacity to reach its goals and over each member's capacity to fulfill his or her potential [adapted from Neilsen, 1979, p. 14].

Groups in the collaborative mode—that is, at Stage 4—need a leader who can appreciate members' accomplishments and simultaneously the demands of continued excellence. Often a critical ingredient is being, or having been, in the same situation oneself. Groups in this mode tend to need more affirmation, confident assurance, wise counsel, and personal insight than technical direction.

Dimensions of *appreciative* leadership include:

- Getting to know the group members as whole individuals and enabling them to know the leader in that way.
- Keeping an eye on people's breaking points and being there to reassure them when they need support.
- Sharing one's own experience as it coincides with others'.
- Avoiding additional direction, expertise, and advice when the group is performing well already.
- Providing opportunities for the group to play and "regroup."

Leading appreciatively involves the use of influence tactics such as *nurturing* (listening actively, empathizing with others' experience, assuring others of their strengths and competence, offering trust in others' decisions about their own choices) and, *applauding* (acknowledging ways in which other members have helped one personally; praising members as individuals, not just their performance, in front of their colleagues; using terms of friendship).

Stage 5: Interdependence Versus Withdrawal. The group at Stage 5 has achieved a high level of performance on many fronts.

Intimacy is the underlying theme. There is a major incentive to make the most out of everyone's capabilities while accepting and appreciating each person's unique circumstances, goals, and needs. The overall thrust is toward a state of complex interdependency.

The focal question is "Who are we to each other in all our overlapping relationships?" But alongside of this is a dilemma of interdependence versus withdrawal: "Do I keep putting in the energy that is necessary to maintain my connectedness with others—as each of us, as well as our tasks and environment, grow and change—or do I let our relationships obsolesce and focus on new ones elsewhere?"

Structurally, the group is both highly differentiated and tightly integrated around the task issues which are the raison d'être of the group and its entire resocialization process.

The leader is now a fully functioning member, contributing according to his or her expertise; this person's authority and the rights and obligations that go with it are taken at face value, without excess emotional baggage from past authority relationships being tied to it.

Intermember relationships are reality oriented, placing top priority on task accomplishment. Conflict is dealt with openly and constructively. Members can evaluate themselves and task demands realistically and act in behalf of their own and the group interests [adapted from Neilsen, 1979, p. 15].

The biggest problem at this stage is the threat of stagnation. Therefore, the group needs an *inspirational* leader, who can provide members with new challenges and opportunities when they think they already know what needs to be done, how to do it, and the likely limits of their own contributions, and, frankly, who may be beginning to get bored or complacent. The challenge is to get people reinvolved and engaged in new learning activities while giving due credence to current demands and personal choices.

Dimensions of *inspirational* leadership include:

- Working with each member to develop an ongoing learning agenda.
- Scanning the environment for new opportunities, challenges, and threats to the group's current mode of operation.
- Inviting other members to help one develop one's own learning agenda.
- Rotating leadership, where feasible, to allow others the opportunity to develop their own leadership skills.
- Creating opportunities for leaves of absence and personal learning adventures.
- Being a heretic in one's own house, in an attempt to keep others from becoming complacent—exploring unusual options, playing devil's advocate, challenging one's own status quo.

Leading in this way involves the use of influence tactics that include *innovating* (offering unusual ideas, tactics, or strategies that depart from what the group is currently doing; encouraging others' exploration of unusual ideas, tactics, or strategies; playing prophet, seer—identifying new challenges, possibilities for the group to address) and *challenging* (asking the group to shift gears in the way it is approaching a topic or problem; playing devil's advocate, with positive enthusiasm, on a position held by most of the group).

Implications of the Model. This, then, is our theory of empowerment for group development efforts and of the leadership necessary for developing members to a point where they are willing to share responsibility for the welfare of the group. As one can see, the theory's orientation is interpersonal. The central assumption is that willingness to share responsibility derives from psychological empowerment—that is, from being given the support and guidance necessary to accomplish the tasks of gaining membership, influence, and emotional connectedness with both colleagues and people with higher formal status. Such psychological empowerment, in turn, enables members to discover and use with confidence the organizational power they have in the service of the group. Structural shifts in the distribution of power can facilitate such development, but there is no guarantee that gaining access to resources that make one powerful will lead to a change in one's psychological orientation. On the contrary, much needs to be accomplished on an interpersonal level as well if such shifts are to have the desired results.

At the same time, our theory assumes that the leader must also pay a price. With every successive stage, the leader is obliged to rely less publicly on his or her formal prerogatives, to command less of the interpersonal deference that typically accrues with a position of formal superiority, to be judged more as a peer, and to accept subordinates' influence in the articulation and fulfillment of the leader's office.

Many leaders may not be equipped psychologically to engage in this kind of empowerment, especially if they have yet to work through their own issues with authority figures. But by the same token, many leaders also may not be equipped psychologically to engage in the alternative strategy of personal power accumulation (Kotter, 1979). Let us assume, however, that such individual capacities would be sufficiently distributed throughout the leadership population, or that they could be developed through a modest amount of training (McClelland, Rhinesmith, and Kristensen, 1975), to make this strategy a viable option, provided that psychological factors were the only relevant forces at work. More important for our agenda is to consider what other factors might help or hinder the strategy's use in day-to-day management.

Applying the Model to a Typical Executive

As we noted earlier, the dynamics of group development and the kinds of empowerment they involve are most apparent in team-building efforts. In such activities the stated purpose of meeting is to examine current working relationships and improve on them. The group usually meets for several days in an isolated setting. Outside interruptions are kept to a minimum, and there is usually a consultant to facilitate the development process. Most executives, however, face different incentives in management settings, the continuity of group life takes on a different form, the surrounding culture often varies in its supportiveness, and competing patterns of socialization among subgroups—for instance, members' ongoing experience in different functions—can affect the developmental process.

Each of these differences places potential constraints on the general use of the model as an empowerment strategy in its pure form, and in this section we will begin by elaborating on these differences. We will then discuss the strategies for overcoming these constraints and point to the model's alignment with the current cultural press toward greater egalitarianism in the workplace and the kinds of changes in organizational functioning that might support its use. This, in turn, will set the stage for a more general discussion of the model's utility when compared to self-empowerment strategies.

Empowerment as One of Many Objectives Competing for Similar Resources. The preceding sections have posited that the empowerment process involves a wide array of influence tactics. Comparison of this group of tactics with other influence typologies (Etzioni, 1975; French and Raven, 1959; Kipnis, Schmidt, and Wilkinson, 1980; Kotter, 1979) suggests that one need only add tactics such as coercion and threat to create a fairly complete list of how all of us attempt to influence each other on a day-to-day basis. This brings home the basic fact that the behavioral tactics themselves can be used in the service of many objectives and not just empowering others. For example, one can be highly directive in order personally to experience psychological dominance over someone else as well as to empower a particular group facing the dilemma of safety versus anxiety (see the discussion of Alfred Adler's work in Ansbacher and Ansbacher, 1956; see also Zaleznik and Kets de Vries, 1975). One can coach others in order to get a task accomplished that will create personal rewards, as well as to help people learn to be less dependent on oneself. One can invite participation in the problem-solving process in order to respond to a demand for participative behavior by top management, as well as to empower a group to deal with the dilemma of support versus panic, and so on. Likewise, the organizational resources that allow one to succeed in these influence activities are the same, regardless of one's objective. For instance, positional rank facilitates at least short-term control over the use of time and over interaction of any variety, regardless of the purposes one has in mind.

What makes the empowerment strategy different is not the influence tactics themselves or the organizational supports for using them, but the intent and attention of the leader in using them. When the leader's goal is empowering others psychologically, this person's attention is on generating a particular kind of experience in the other, as opposed to generating a particular experience in him- or herself, or accomplishing a technical task, or responding to a behavioral command.

In a team-building session, the implications of all this for the leader are minimal. The leader is typically assisted by a professional human resource consultant, whose calling places high value on empowerment. This person's primary task with respect to the group in question is empowerment. The setting and the activity itself are bounded; that is, they are set apart from the rest of the organization by time and, often, locale.

In the typical organization, however, the settings in which an executive may have the opportunity to empower others are likely to be far less bounded, and his or her own incentives, both internal and external, far more mixed. Using influence tactics for self-empowerment, responding to commands from above, getting a task done that might not be experienced as empowering by the doers, enacting rituals, or combinations of all of these objectives and others are all quite legitimate. Consequently, empowerment as an objective competes with these other objectives for the same resources of time and interaction style and is bounded by the organizational and personal priorities that determine their relative importance.

Intermittent Nature of Group Life. As noted above, unlike team-building activities, the day-to-day life of the executive is not segmented into long periods of intense interaction with a single group, whose activities are often separated symbolically as well as temporally from other events (Mintzberg, 1980). Instead, executives fill their days with meetings—sometimes with individuals, sometimes with groups. Sometimes the memberships of these groups overlap, but often they do not.

As a consultant who moves back and forth between team-building activities and facilitating daily management meetings, I have found that this condition has an important effect on the developmental process as portrayed by the model. On the one hand, because the same general group of managers interact frequently for months, sometimes years, at a time, they develop a capacity to engage with each other in ways that are in tune with each of the developmental stages. Thus, a typical management team will tend to operate momentarily as if it were in a particular stage of group development and to display momentarily many of the qualities associated with that stage: particular intrapsychic and interpersonal concerns among members, shared dilemmas concerning the risks of particular kinds of participation, different capacities for effective communication and mutual assistance, and different attitudes toward formal authority figures.

However, in daily management meetings, as opposed to team-building sessions, whole patterns of behavior seem to shift rapidly from one moment to the next, and from one meeting to the next, as if the group were progressing or regressing instantaneously up and down the developmental sequence. My hunch is that the key to understanding this phenomenon is the kind of topic being discussed. Specifically, the sensitivity of the topic in members' lives, as well as the degree to which they consider other members potential threats to creating the outcomes they want, seems to determine the stage-related behavior of the group as it discusses the topic. The more touchy the issue, the more a group resorts to early-stage kinds of behavior to deal with it.

This hypothesis makes sense if one remembers that the types of influence strategies used by both leaders and followers in the earlier stages of group development are more subject to unilateral control by the wielders, while later stages of group development involve influence strategies that are more mutual and that are apt to change the behavior and thinking of their users as well as the thinking and behavior of those the users are attempting to influence. For example, the managers of an engineering department I worked with had two topics on their biweekly meeting agenda: (1) a proposal for revising compensation practices that would affect each member and (2) the development of a long-term plan for a product improvement. These people had been working moderately well together for a couple of years. Nonetheless, discussion of the first topic started cautiously. Several members requested a clarification of ground rules from the formal leader, while others said very little. To the consultant the conversation had a "testing" quality to it, and the group's behavior was easy to characterize as consistent with Stage 1 or 2, perhaps moving into Stage 3 after people had reestablished a sense of personal security or at least clarity regarding their own fates. Typical influence strategies noted were commanding, prescribing, pressuring, instructing by the leader, and ignoring, misinterpreting, and debating by both leader and subordinates. Note that all these tactics involved unilateral forms of influence. None of the managers were willing to allow the others to gain entry into their thinking to a degree that might reveal or confirm their personal motives or their responses to particular decisions. The conversation ended inconclusively, with an agreement to continue it at the next meeting.

After a ten-minute coffee break, the group reconvened to discuss the second agenda item—long-term product development. The conversation began with invitations by several members, and not just the leader, for opinions, suggestions, and ideas, and it developed rapidly into appreciative explorations of past development efforts by the team as a whole and by individual members. In other words, Stage 3 and 4 behavior predominated from the beginning, as if the prior tension had been either completely resolved or was being consciously ignored. This second conversation involved types of influence that were mutual almost by definition. Inviting someone else's ideas encouraged sharing one's own in return.

In summary, I am suggesting that when a management group made up of members who have been working together for some time encounters an issue around which many members (including the leader) feel sensitive, the group retreats to early-stage behavior and may become stuck there for lack of time to work through the developmental issues necessary for resolving the issue in a way that is mutually empowering. In contrast, when the topic to be addressed is less threatening, later-stage behavior often begins immediately, and mutual influence can predominate.

Even when such development does take place for some members within the allotted time, it may not occur for all of them. Those for whom it does not may remain uncomfortable and either become silent or deviate from the pattern of the rest of the group. An important consequence is that empowerment needs in a typical management group at any given time can become quite idiosyncratic, making the leader's task even more difficult if his or her objective is empowerment and, in turn, encouraging the use of influence for more expedient objectives that ignore member needs and thereby reinforce early-stage behavior. By contrast, in a team-building session, the continuity of interaction, the immediately shared history of the group, is a much more potent force in determining the quality of the current dialogue. Consequently, more members are likely to be empowered from the experience of either working through personally or witnessing the more general resolution of each developmental stage.

Unpredictable Support from Organizational Superiors. A third difference between the contexts of day-to-day management and team-building efforts has to do with the support for empowering others that managers get from their own superiors. In team-building efforts, whether they are conducted by consulting organizations, universities, or in-house human resource groups, such support is taken for granted. However, it may not be available to the typical line manager. In multilevel organizations the same kinds of developmental problems that occur in the top-management group often seem to surface again and again in successively lower levels of the hierarchy (Kanter, 1977). This is easily understood as a consequence of the fact that executives operate as vertical linking pins among different groups, where they are members of some groups but simultaneously leaders of groups lower in the hierarchy. As a result, the level of development in groups where they are only members can limit their own psychological freedom to empower groups in which they are the leaders.

For example, top-management groups that revolve around an owner/entrepreneur who prefers directive leadership can make it extremely difficult for second-level executives to operate participatively with their own subordinates. Neither the emotional support and encouragement nor the raw positional power may be available to them to create firm boundaries around baseline directives that allow subordinates reporting to them to move beyond preoccupation with their dependence on those above them and begin to assume responsibility for a larger share of the decision making in their groups. Consequently, even if a manager has the skills and internal motivation to pursue an empowerment strategy, the press of his membership in groups higher up in the hierarchy can drain him of both the emotional and the positional support necessary to make this strategy work. The same might be said as well for unusually stressful conditions under which an executive might operate. Such conditions might encourage spontaneous obedience to authority (Milgram, 1974) or scapegoating and abortive decision-making strategies (Janis, 1972).

Functional Specialization of Resources. Different groups in a large organization tend to control different types of resources for influencing others. For instance, line managers may have more positional control than staff personnel have; as a result, line managers may be able to use more directive influence strategies. In contrast, staff personnel may have greater access to expert power, which bolsters participative problem solving. Thus, executives may tend to specialize in the kinds of influence they use and to lose sight of their own and others' developmental needs. For example, production hierarchies preoccupied with the strategic movement of people and materials according to centralized plans may gradually specialize in authoritative influence styles. Staff personnel in human resource functions, for instance, may have little line control but considerable skill in participative problem-solving techniques and appreciative influence tactics. In fact, they may gain entry into the thinking of their important clients primarily through their use of these skills. Consequently, over time, they may lose touch with the need for directiveness in the earlier stages of the empowerment process, just as their line counterparts may lose sight of the need for participation in later stages. Such specialization can be interpreted as healthy from the viewpoint of contingency theories of organization design (Lawrence and Lorsch, 1967; Lorsch and Morse, 1974). But, by the same token, it may hamper the development of a group operating within a single function and pose yet another constraint on the use of the empowerment model.

Overcoming Constraints on Empowerment in Day-to-Day Management

One might be tempted, in light of the constraints noted in the preceding section, to discard the empowerment model as an unworkable option for the practicing manager. However, we have yet to consider what the model has to offer managers in a positive view. In fact, each of the constraints we have discussed can be viewed, under the right conditions, as an opportunity.

1. *Intermittent groups can facilitate episodic development.* On the one hand, the intermittent nature of group life in the executive ranks can lead different people to be in different places developmentally with respect to the empowerment process and tie stage-related behavior more to agenda issues than to shared and immediate experience. On the other hand, it facilitates the proactive scheduling and bounding off of more intense group activities, where more continuous patterns of development can be experienced. The same intermittent nature of group life in the executive ranks is indeed what makes team-building workshops fit more or less naturally into the ongoing management of an organization. The same flexibility in daily routines that allows executives to meet in constantly changing configurations makes an off-site workshop a normal event. In such settings, moreover, team members and their leaders can take the time to begin, as it were, at the beginning.

Not surprisingly, we have found the empowerment model an especially useful technique for helping to design such workshops. Meeting off site at a motel or retreat center, especially after preparatory work such as sensing meetings or interviews, signals the presence of a new and potentially threatening agenda. Thus, the first session tends to start with an "each person for him- or herself" tone. How well the group develops thereafter depends on the capacity of the leader to manage the empowerment process. For instance, they can set effective ground rules for discussion that provide people with a maximum of psychological safety (helping the group move beyond Stage 1), show how dialogue on important issues in the context of these guidelines can lead to successful outcomes (helping the group move through Stage 2), work with the group to evolve collaborative decision-making methods that facilitate treatment of even more important tasks (helping the group move through Stage 3), and so on.

Moreover, while team-building activities have been criticized for leaving members with an unrealistic sense of euphoria, which is often dampened when people return to their normal work settings (Gottshalk and Davidson, 1972), successful team-building workshops can go beyond the stage of warm cohesiveness (Stage 4 in our model) by addressing directly the problems of interdependence versus withdrawal and contracting for new ground rules for interaction on the job.

The total experience, then, represents a prototype for empowerment that members can hold in their minds and use in their daily activities. While day-to-day meeting patterns may continue to be intermittent, diversely attended, and strongly affected by the threat content of particular agenda items, periodic episodes of team development can create baseline agreements and shared perspectives that facilitate the rapid reestablishment of trust and the recognition of what needs to be done to move the group to an advanced stage.

2. *Linking-pin membership configurations can help as well as hinder.* We noted earlier that the linking-pin nature of the typical executive's role set may hinder his or her practice of empowerment strategies with subordinates, if this person in turn is a subordinate in groups whose leaders foster early-stage behavior. On the positive side, executives whose superiors practice empowerment strategies can just as easily gain the emotional support for fostering similar development down through the ranks. This point has long been implicit in the organization development literature, where support from the top is identified as a critical success criterion (French, Bell, and Zawacki, 1978).

3. *Functional specialization in the use of stage-related influence tactics can also be viewed as an important resource.* While the task environment of a given group may promote the constant use of particular kinds of influence tactics and therefore stifle its development, the presence of a diversity of functional specialties, each focusing on different influence strategies, can serve as a resource to the organization as a whole. What needs to be done to make use of this resource is to engage in empowerment-oriented

team building across functions. This may not always be convenient, but it is clearly a possibility given the intermittent nature of managerial group work and the increasing frequency of cross-functional efforts in modern organizations.

In my own work, empowerment activities with different kinds of specialists has often proved to be easier than with groups comprised of people from the same functional specialty. While it is easy to exaggerate this point, my colleagues and I have found that, on the whole, production and administrative managers are best at modeling directiveness and coaching tactics; marketers, engineers, and other technical specialists are best at problem solving; and human resource specialists tend to know somewhat more than their colleagues about appreciative tactics. Progress can be made without having the appropriate experts in the room, but more modeling on the part of the leader and/or the consultants is then required.

4. *Competing priorities around the use of influence can be discussed openly and complementary objectives identified.* We began our critique of the applicability of the empowerment model to day-to-day management with the argument that the use of influence tactics to empower others competes with other priorities, such as self-empowerment, technical expedience, and compliance to directives from above. Of all the constraints surrounding the strategy's use, this probably is the most important. And yet it too is not insurmountable. What is required is that managers openly share their priorities and, in essence, agree on the game to be played before they play it. Sometimes a fortunate convergence of forces makes such agreement relatively easy. For instance, the start-up stage of a new organization tends to require both directive and coaching strategies by the leadership, for technical reasons as well as social; and the group as a whole cannot survive, nor can any individual within it succeed, without the evolution of shared ground rules and help in mastering basic competencies. Subsequent stages in an organization's evolution might require different leadership demands in ways that suggest interesting parallels with the group development model as well (Greiner, 1974; Neilsen, 1979).

Likewise, it is occasionally possible to order priorities rationally according to the logic of some superordinate goal. For instance, the long-term development of a particular team in a new product or service area might warrant its being buffered for a specific period of time, and within specific cost constraints, from near-term performance criteria and/or adherence to prevailing behavioral norms. More often than not, however, the conflicts among priorities are less easily settled by external forces and rational economic criteria. Substantive rationality, the conscious weighing of competing alternatives that cannot be linked neatly through a complex series of means/ends chains, is the only way out. Paradoxically, this is the kind of collective reasoning that is most strongly affected by the stage of a group's development. Given the nature of the influence process—specifically, the multiple utilities inherent in any behavioral act—the only criterion for deciding whether a priority is really being carried out is the reported experience of those acting and of those acted upon. A group's stage of development, in turn, indicates whose experience is reported, listened to, and believed; and this stage, in turn, depends on the predispositions of the leadership.

In summary, while there are important constraints to applying the empowerment model to day-to-day management life, none of them are insurmountable. The intermittent nature of management group life can be dealt with through off-site workshops where group continuity is temporarily established. The potential lack of emotional support from above for empowerment can be avoided by the use of empowerment strategies at the top of the hierarchy. Cross-functional participation can overcome the effects of functional specialization in the use of influence, and substantive dialogue can make empowerment a high-level priority.

Egalitarianism in the Workplace as the Wave of the Future

At the beginning of this chapter, we posited a growing gap between the responsibilities of the typical executive and the authority granted by this person's subordinates. In brief, societal expectations and legislative demands have increased, and advances in information and administrative technology have allowed these demands to be made specific and measurable. Simultaneously, the concept of authority has become more specialized, secularized, and conditional, making the executive's capacity to respond unilaterally more difficult. Two strategies were identified as potential ways of closing this gap: (1) self-empowerment, or accumulating the necessary personal power to match increased responsibilities; and (2) empowering subordinates interpersonally, so that they are willing to share the executive's increased responsibilities and use their own power in his or her behalf.

This second strategy is rapidly increasing in popularity among today's executives. To begin with, one can point to the proliferation of experiments in empowerment of all sorts— autonomous work groups, quality-of-life experiments, quality circles, sociotechnical design efforts, worker buy-outs, worker collectives, and other attempts at workplace democracy—and to the increasing popularity of subordinate-centered theories of leadership. Some authors have argued that the momentum is shifting back toward greater preoccupation with the welfare of the organization, to the detriment of the individual (Hart and Scott, 1975). Our position, however, is that, while the intensity of the movement may vary from year to year, the trend toward egalitarianism is here to stay.

Our reasoning is not that egalitarianism is necessarily a more effective form of organizational governance in the economic sector but, rather, that the modern corporation is gradually being subordinated to sociopolitical concerns of society in general. In his modern classic on social forecasting, *The Coming of Post-Industrial Society*, Bell (1973, p. 373) comments: "The decisive social change taking place in our time—because of the interdependence of men and the aggregative character of economic actions, the rise of externalities and social costs, and the need to control the effects of technical change—is the subordination of the economic function to the political order." In other words, the economic sector has become so potent in modern life and its functioning so interdependent with other societal objectives—such as the determination of personal worth, the creation of meaningful careers, increases in minority employment, maintenance of a healthy ecology, community responsibility, and morality—that its independent functioning according to the dictates of economic logic is no longer tenable. Society must intervene for the welfare of the larger system, and this leads to the politicization of decision making with regard to the pursuit of economic ends.

In different societies this politicization may have different consequences, but in the United States egalitarianism is a major and enduring organizing principle. Thus, along with the press for specific responses to community demands—levels of minority employment that reflect community demographics, the use of technology to minimize pollution—the politicization of economic policy is also likely to support and promote egalitarian forms of management. Ultimately, such support may result in the institutionalization of many of the structural changes now being experimented with.

For the typical private or professional enterprise, however, we suspect that the greater near-term impact will be on organization culture and, in particular, on the personal comportment of people in vertical relationships. The empowerment strategy presented in this chapter is consistent with this trend and embodies a clear strategy on an interpersonal level for making the transition from hierarchical to more egalitarian forms of organization.

Empowering Others Versus Self-Empowerment

One final question needs to be addressed in order for us to conclude this chapter with a clear conscience. That is the question of how far this strategy can be pursued. What are the prospects for the unalloyed pursuit of collective empowerment in the large organization? Our prognosis in this regard is less sanguine. From a sociological perspective, one need only point to the fact that individualism, a sentiment that supports self-empowerment, is just as strong in modern society, especially in the United States, as egalitarianism and that modern enterprise has been one of its strongest supporters.

From a social/psychological perspective, a quote from *The Coming Crisis of Western Sociology* (Gouldner, 1970, p. 509) is especially telling: "Individual men do live out the cycle of their existence, pursue their careers, and establish their families within encompassing civilizations, cultures, and societies. The concerns and interests of men do, in large part, derive from and coincide with these larger entities; but they do so, however, only in part and never *in toto*. However deep men's identification with and dependence upon a larger cause or group, there are always points in the lives of men when they must go their own ways, when it becomes painfully evident that their cause and their group do not constitute the totality of their personal existence."

Moreover, if there is one thing that history has taught us, it is that every strategy for organizing has its limits. From an organizational perspective, both self-empowerment and collective empowerment are subject to this truth. Research has already shown us that too much preoccupation with self-empowerment can lead eventually to collective retaliation, which often takes the form of stifling bureaucracy that shields an organization from the data it needs to survive (Crozier, 1964). Parallel to this pattern, we suspect that too much preoccupation with collective empowerment leads to the retaliation of individuals who simply refuse to meld their language, their goals, and their life-styles with the larger organization. One is reminded of the old saw that 90 percent of a manager's (group leader's, parent's) time is devoted to dealing with the deviance of 10 percent of an organization's members. Individual retaliation in turn leads to exclusion and factionalism, and thus the organization's loss of access to some of its members as resources.

What we are left with, then, is the problem of balance—a problem for which there is no permanent solution. Empowering others may well be the theoretical and practical task of the next decade or longer, but ultimately it will have to be weighed against the merits and the human need for self-empowerment. Our hope is that as executives begin to address the need to order their priorities substantively, regarding which strategy to sanction and under what conditions, they will refrain from idealizing either strategy and accept the fact that the decision they arrive at is nothing more than the beginning of a collective experiment, born out of dialogue that is in itself a mixture of collective interest and self-interest, and therefore a microcosm of the very tensions they are trying to resolve.

This kind of self-consciousness, especially if it is acknowledged publicly, addresses the problem of empowerment head on and—by obliging each person to take responsibility for his or her own decisions and to share responsibility for the results of others' decisions as well—represents a first step toward empowering everyone.

 **FIVE**

Putting Executive Action in Context:
An Alternative View of Power
Meryl Reis Louis

Power is commonly considered to be the capacity to influence others. Individuals exercise power through their actions. Power is the abstract capacity; action, the immediate reality. In one sense, then, action is the "doing," while power is the "being." This chapter focuses more directly on action than on power. A premise of the argument presented here is that the effectiveness of one's action can be enhanced if one takes into account the context in which the action will take place; more effective action, in turn, enhances one's demonstrated power.

This should not seem surprising. In fact, it is reminiscent of past arguments for situational or contingent views of managing. Yet when one reviews literature relevant to executive action or power, it is clear that the phenomenological context in which executive action takes place has been overlooked to a surprising extent. Managerial and organizational contingencies have been investigated, but experiential continuities have been overlooked. That is, the day-to-day experience of life at work among

Note: I would like to thank Jean Bartunek, Frank Friedlander, Philip Mirvis, and Walter Nord for helpful comments on an earlier draft of this chapter.

nonexecutives has not been reflected in guidance to executives. For instance, neither scholarly nor practical writings have derived executives' roles or activities from the nature of everyday work situations or the characteristics of meaningful work. Yet the sum of such experiential continuities constitutes the phenomenological context of executive action. If we subscribe to the notions that action occurs in context and that actions appreciative of their contexts are more effective, then we must rejoin executive action with its phenomenological context. The link needs to be made. Hence, this chapter proposes an action-in-context approach to executive power.

The aim here is to link context to action by deriving executive roles from characteristics of various phenomenological domains attendent to work settings. The process is to capture what it is like at work for the nonexecutive when things are going well. Questions that will guide our inquiry include: What is the experience of going to work and working? What is the experience of one's relationship to task, setting, and organization in a fairly healthy work environment?

Executive roles of interpreter, integrator, enabler, and creator of high-performance conditions are derived as we identify how executive action can support a healthy work environment. The context examined here is one of organizational effectiveness—"a fairly healthy work environment"—rather than ineffectiveness. Future inquiry into the role of executives in unhealthy work contexts would be useful for understanding how their actions help transform ineffective to effective work settings.

The Executive as Interpreter

Executive action takes place in a context of everyday life in work settings. Several features of work settings converge to create a gap that may quite naturally be filled by executive action. This gap is revealed as we develop an appreciation of the phenomenological domain of the individual in relation to everyday life in the work setting.

Imagine standing on a busy street corner. Listen first for a siren, then for a car horn, and finally for someone yelling. When we are listening for the siren, human voices blend into the background, as sirens do when we listen for someone yelling. Our decision to listen for sirens, rather than babies crying, orders the ongoing stream of stimuli, targets our attention, and provides categories of meaning through which we experience the street corner. And as Thomas (1971) has noted, we respond to situations on the basis of the meanings we associate with them; the definition of the situation is real in its consequences. Such processes take place in work settings as well—but with a few twists. Work settings differ from street corners in that the same set of people convene regularly, they experience subsets of common interests and stakes, and they are connected through structured task interdependencies (Louis, 1985). As a result, workers come to listen for the same categories of sounds against the daily din of life at work.

This convergence in categories listened for, or in meaning making among organizational members, is being studied under the rubric of organizational culture. Such work has documented the presence of shared meanings and their effects on employees' organizational commitment, among other things. But the nature of the situation that allows for common meanings to be constructed needs to be appreciated in more detail if we are to realize the potential contributions of executive action.

Consider first the feature of ongoingness. Almost any interaction among members of a work setting is nested in thick history and future's promise. Although the true beginnings of today's interaction may be long forgotten, they may shape and screen the parties' actions in the current moment. Previous encounters between the parties over resources, territory, influence, access, information are joined to the configuration of the immediate situation and its anticipated consequences as each party experiences the interaction. Thus, the past and future contribute as meaning is made in ways different in work settings than on the street corner.

But the present itself is problematic as well. Situations and events do not arise well packaged and bound into discrete time and space portions. Instead, the actors on the scene pronounce this experiential moment to be an event or a situation marking beginning, middle, and end, bounding and naming some portion of the ongoing flow of sensory input. Weick (1969) refers to the human act of packaging the ongoing stream of stimuli into events as parsing, a task encumbent on the actor whether at work or on a street corner.

Additionally, much of daily life at work is automatic and insignificant, a backdrop against which one particular scene becomes figure. There is a sorting of the significant from the insignificant and an assignment of appropriate actions for each. Actions for insignificant events are likely to be automatic, as in the case of turning on lights. To some extent, what is automatic and insignificant is common across work settings—for example, turning on the lights or hanging up one's coat. But a large portion of what passes for insignificant is given in and by the setting, just as a large portion of what is significant is locally given.

Another feature is the equivocality of meaning. Alternative meanings are possible as interpretations of any behavior or event. Meanings are attributed to events rather than being prepackaged with their very emergence in our experiential awareness. The particular meanings assigned to significant events come in part from the actor's immersion in and habituation to that setting. A moment's recognition of the presence of something precedes our appreciation of what it represents, its significance. Some meanings gain consensus in organizational situations; in current terms, they become part of the local culture.

For example, the members of an academic department at one institution might agree tacitly that administration actions are "often" devious, designed to squeeze the school for the sake of the university, while members of a department at another university agree that the administration is an ally. Although there probably is some basis in fact for the difference across these two institutions, it is unlikely that fresh reality testing will take place; other meanings for new administrative action are unlikely to be entertained. Thus, the organizational member paints a picture of daily life at work from an ongoing stream of stimuli: categories of significance are applied to package stimuli into events and situations; systems of meaning are used as lenses through which situations at hand are interpreted. And actions are taken in response to the meanings that organizational members give in and to the moment.

Enter the executive. Meaning-making processes of such prevalence and consequence ought not to be left to the vagaries of social influence or idiosyncrasy. Instead, what is needed is the guidance of the executive in interpreting current reality. One recent instance of the power of doing so is illustrated in the 1984 reelection of Ronald Reagan over Walter Mondale. Reagan emphasized descriptions of our current economic situation in vivid word pictures, crisp images, interpretations. Mondale presented detailed information, facts and figures, and supporting evidence, but with insufficient summary interpretation or description in terms that "the average man" could easily pick out and take away.

By extension, we can see that part of the effective executive's role is to help others construct a definition of the workplace situation. The worker's sense of "who we are" and "what we represent" as an organization ought to be shaped in part by inputs from the executive. How can the executive shape such interpretations? The answer has less to do with what the executive does than with the way in which it is done. For instance, recall that both Reagan and Mondale engaged in speech making and debates, press conferences, and pep rallies. But, because of the content of his speeches, the emphasis in his press conferences, Reagan was far more effective than Mondale in this interpretive role. Effectiveness in the interpretive role requires an emphasis on summary images, on digests of details, on vivid word pictures that can serve others as handles for grasping otherwise complex and highly nuanced situations. When the interpretive role is well performed, the executive has helped shape a shared definition of the situation. Framing and naming of present workplace realities in turn shape the reality experienced and individuals' responses to it. Whereas Pfeffer (1981a) and Peters (1978) have noted that effective leaders perform an interpretive or symbolic or interpretive role, the discussion in this section should have demonstrated that that role is necessitated by the nature of the day-to-day experience of life at work.

The Executive as Creator of High-Performance Conditions

It seems clear that executives should aim to create work environments that stimulate high levels of performance among organizational members. However, it is not clear what constitutes high performance, what kinds of environments might stimulate it, or how executives might help create such environments. These are the issues addressed in this section as we develop an appreciation of the phenomenological domain of the individual in relation to work.

Performance Defined. In traditional organizational science formulations, individual performance has referred to by-products, residuals, or remote consequences of an individual's efforts rather than to those efforts as such or to the individual's experience of performing. However, the phenomenology of performance does not support traditional academic formulations. In organizational settings workers experience their performances directly; they do not experience the tangible by-products of performance, nor do they experience the abstract categories of measurement into which productive efforts are translated for organizational (ac)counting purposes. They do, however, experience themselves working and themselves in the work situation.

Let us consider this experience in a fairly healthy work situation. Mirvis (1980, pp 474–475) has written: "Workers know how it feels to be absorbed in work, to be swept along by it, and to have their efforts in harmony with their endeavors. . . . This feeling, irreducible as it is to core characteristics, is an integral and fundamental element of the quality of a job. . . . Harmony with the job . . . is a reaction to the job experienced within its social and historical context." Csikszentmihalyi and Graef (1979) refer to this quality as flow. I want to suggest that a sense of harmony or flow constitutes the individual's experience of high performance. Vaill's (1978) work on "high-performing systems" captures parallel qualities at the organizational level.

Let us move from an appreciation of the experience of high performance toward an understanding of environments that might stimulate it. Sarason's (1977, pp. 29–30) distinction between work and labor provides a crucial building block in this regard: "To labor is to be imprisoned in activity in which outcome or product has no personally meaningful relationship to the person's capacities and individuality. . . . To work is to have one's outcome and product bear the stamp of one's capacities and individuality." The crux of this distinction lies in the presence or absence of a "meaningful relationship" between task outcomes and person. The experience of working represents a joining or union. It requires at least a partial intersection of person and product, of effort, capability, and task. The nature of the activity is one of relatedness.

If the experience of working versus laboring is associated with an experience of harmony or flow, and if harmony is associated with high performance at the level of the individual, what aspects of a work situation are likely to precipitate the experience of work versus labor, and thus of harmony?

Past relevant research has sought to identify aspects of the job itself (Hackman and Oldham, 1975) that have the potential to motivate. Although such work has generated a modest yield of variance explained in job satisfaction, it has been criticized as not capturing important motivating forces in the work setting. For instance, Salancik and Pfeffer (1978) have suggested that workers' ratings of job characteristics are products of the work group's influence. Further, Katz (1980) has shown that particular job characteristics are salient at different times during one's early career (for example, feedback from others is most salient early on and then recedes as autonomy becomes salient). Finally, Katz (1980) has demonstrated that the relationship between job characteristics and performance weakens as workers' organizational tenure increases, suggesting that the job is too narrow an arena in which to examine aspects of the work environment that stimulate performance. The larger social and technical setting and situation in which an individual works needs to be considered in appreciating what stimulates performance. So, too, must the match of a person's needs with what is available in the situation.

Conditions of Performance. Four conditions for high performance are proposed as aspects of work situations that support the experience of work versus labor and help generate a sense of harmony or flow. (These conditions are drawn from examination of longitudinal data on the work experience of MBA graduates, from interviews with academics and naval officers, and from more casual observations of professionals at work.)

First, the job situation needs to afford the worker a sense of making a contribution, of "making a difference," as MBAs are prone to say. Bennis's (1983) phrase is that "people feel significant." There are several components to this condition. First, the work situation needs to provoke a sense that there is a contribution to be made, in whatever terms the worker finds compelling. The individual may experience "making a difference" in any of a number of arenas—for example, when giving a co-worker advice on child rearing or when pointing out product features to customers. In part, this condition is met as individuals carve out their own opportunities to contribute, even before the actual contribution is made. Thus, the organizational objective is to develop an atmosphere in which individuals find it easy and inviting to create opportunities to contribute. This is not something that should be done for the individual. Another component is that workers need to feel that they have the ability to make a difference. When one realizes that the opportunity to contribute is there but feels ill equipped or incapable, frustration or inadequacy is likely to be experienced. The sense of contributing, of participating in something larger and worthwhile, addresses basic existential issues. It enhances the sense that one's life and efforts are meaningful and that one is a member of a community. In the absence of a match between one's need to make a difference and one's sense of the situation affording such an opportunity, workers may become cynical.

The second condition for high performance is a quality of pleasurableness. A job situation that is experienced as enjoyable, as intrinsically pleasurable, is self-reinforcing. As long as no extrinsic rewards come into play to undermine the self-reinforcement, the situation will continue in a mutually beneficial cycle. When a job situation is experienced as enjoyable, no sense of instrumentalism develops. Work is not simply a means to an end. It is an end in itself. A sense of pleasurableness or fun may come from formal task-related activities and interactions, or it may come from non-task-related experiences that take place in the work setting. For instance, for some people a challenging job is experienced as pleasurable; for others "challenge" is not pleasurable. It is unlikely that any one set of objective job characteristics is universally experienced as pleasurable. In any event, this aspect of one's experience of a work situation is highly energizing.

The third high-performance condition is a match between the worker's need to be stretched and the stretch afforded in the work situation. Work situations that provide appropriate opportunities for growth and development in areas relevant to the worker are revitalizing. People may be stretched in myriad arenas, including cognitive, motor, judgment, interpersonal, and self-assessment competencies. The stimulation and renewal that come from being stretched stave off burnout. Even (or sometimes especially) when one has a sense of making a contribution and having fun, one can become burned out.

The fourth high-performance condition is that the individual must find appropriate support in and through the work situation. Support conditions high performance through its link to each of the other three conditions. Support is related to the third high-performance condition (stretching) in that there are people around with relevant knowledge who are willing to help as the person takes on development challenges. Support also means that other relevant resources (such as information sources or materials) are near at hand. Without support, a stretching work situation could be experienced as overwhelming, defeating, and/or frustrating. Support is related to the second high-performance condition (pleasurableness) in that there are witnesses to one's enjoyment. For some people solitary "fun" is akin to the sound of one hand clapping. The fun may be shared or one's delight may be deepened by the knowledge that others are watching. For many people pleasure is experienced more fully in the presence of others. Witnessing is also a key process through which support is related to a worker's sense of making a difference or a contribution. Witnessing need not involve the active participation or involvement on the part of the witness. Witnessing another's contributions and achievements is fundamental to a sense of community; it reinforces one's sense of having contributed.

Certainly, a portion of the overall quality of work and setting is fundamental to the nature of the task. For instance, high-technology firms in the United States in the 1980s likely offer a more inherent sense of contributing than do steelmaking or automotive firms. Similarly, research-and-development activity in a firm can provide conditions of stretching and contributing more readily than can the production activity. A Ken Olsen or an An Wang in high technology can provide high-performance work conditions more easily than can a Lee Iacocca or a Roger Smith in automaking. Some differences in industry performance can be attributed to differences in the level of high-performance conditions inherent in the fundamental task of the industry. Yet some high-tech executives do a better job than others in creating high-performance work conditions. So do some steel- and automaking executives. Industry and function do not account for all the variance. How, then, can executives influence relevant characteristics of work settings and workers' experiences of these settings?

Creating the Conditions. Executives need to appreciate the phenomenology of individual performance such as has been developed here. We have seen that harmony characterizes an individual's experience of high performance; that harmony results from one's engagement in work, not labor; that high-performance work environments are stretching, pleasurable, and supportive and afford opportunities to contribute to an extent appropriate for the individual. Such appreciations should affect the executive's orientation in a number of areas.

For example, just as quality and quantity characterize the by-product of individual performance, a degree of harmony or flow characterizes the experience of individual performance. Executives need to recognize both the performance experience and its by-products. Traditional performance measurement systems capture aggregated and abstracted information, are remote in time and space from the person whose performance is to be gauged, and are focused on by-products of performance alone. They are not sufficient. Executives also need to gauge the extent to which employees exhibit a sense of harmony—by walking through a work area or noticing workers' affect and energy as they come to work and leave. In their use of reward systems, executives need to recognize the pulling force or intrinsic incentive associated with a sense of harmony and need to avoid undermining it with inappropriate extrinsic rewards.

The phenomenology of individual performance suggests that executives should encourage workers' initiatives across a fairly wide range of activities and arenas. Encouragement may take such forms as modeling of desired behaviors, publicly recognizing as exemplary desired behaviors that others have exhibited, and commenting on the positive effects of such behaviors to the actors, their superiors, and associates.

Task-based initiatives concerning improvement of production processes or product design are normally reinforced in the executive's actions. Initiatives that contribute to the functioning of task groups or the competence or well-being of a co-worker ought to be encouraged as well. These initiatives support high performance in several ways. First, such an initiative constitutes a worker's creation of an opportunity to make a contribution and thus enhances a key condition of high performance for that worker. Second, it may provide the task group or co-worker with a sense of support, thus enhancing conditions associated with high performance that others are experiencing. Third, such an initiative models desired behavior and can serve as an example to others. Initiatives associated with stretching or with developing one's skills also should be encouraged.

So the executive needs to be on the lookout for opportunities to reinforce the enactment of each high-performance condition. At the same time, it is important to recall that no absolute level of each condition is appropriate for all workers. For one person an appropriately stretching situation is highly developmental, while a match to another worker's needs is achieved with very little stretching.

The Executive as Integrator

In turning from the phenomenological domain of the individual in relation to work to that of the individual in relation to the organization and other workers, we also move from a concern with individual performance to a concern with overall organizational performance. Traditionally, we have thought of the executive as responsible for overall organizational performance. But what are the organizational aims toward which executives should direct their actions and otherwise exercise power?

Two main concerns have long been recognized, though they have been framed in various ways. Bales (1955) has distinguished two broad classes of problems that any group or organization must tackle on an ongoing basis: external adaptation and internal maintenance. Attention must be paid to making progress on tasks related to the group's mission, or remaining competitive by adapting to changing conditions, and to working through problems that arise and enhancing the group's capacity to manage problems in various interpersonal processes. The same tasks are noted as universal requirements for survival of groups, organizations, and societies. In general systems theory, these dual challenges to any system's survival are termed adaptation and continuity/ stability (Miller, 1978).

Although past approaches have considered the need for a balance between the primary organizational tasks of adaptation and maintenance, they have not adequately integrated the tasks across individual and organizational levels of analysis. A recent work by Roger Harrison begins to do this. Introducing the organizational processes of alignment and attunement, he emphasizes the way in which experiences of an organization's members figure into organizational purposes. Alignment can be interpreted as serving the organizational function of adaptation: "Alignment occurs when organization members act as parts of an integrated whole, each finding the opportunity to express his or her true purpose through the organization's purpose. [It is] the expansion of the individual's identity and sense of purpose to include the organization and its purpose" (Harrison, 1983, p. 211). Bennis (1983, p. 18) has identified a related competency of effective leaders: "the capacity to create and communicate a compelling vision of a desired state of affairs . . . and induce commitment to it . . . to gain the support of their multiple constituencies." This he labels vision and alignment.

Thus, the executive provides input to the alignment process by articulating an organizational purpose and vision. The vision is a vehicle for integrating individuals into the organization. Vision differs from the executive's intepretive input to the definition of the situation or day-to-day meaning making that was discussed early in the chapter. Vision describes some desired future state; it captures collective aspirations. The definition of the situation describes the experiential landscape in which we find ourselves at present; it mediates how we experience the present.

Recent work on organizational culture calls attention to the power of a common theme, image, identity, assumption, or vision. That it can energize and harmonize the efforts of members has been well documented (Peters and Waterman, 1982). It has been discussed as a substitute for traditional rational control systems (Ouchi, 1981).

Several qualities of an executive's vision contribute to its potential functioning in the service of organizational adaptation. In an aligned situation, organizational members become energized when an organizational purpose is clear, compelling, and incomplete. This last characteristic of incompleteness is the enabling condition, yet it has not been mentioned before. When a vision is incomplete, there is room for elaboration and refinement; the openness provides a vehicle for the worker's self-expression. Expression is the individual-level process associated with the organizational process of alignment. Through the act of expression associated with filling out and beyond the barebones vision, the individual gains a sense of making a contribution; this in turn links back into providing a condition of high performance. The individual's engagement and expression help to serve the existential function of giving meaning to one's being and efforts.

It has recently been noted that participation in goal setting influences performance by enhancing the individual's acceptance of the goal selected (Erez, Earley, and Hulin, 1985). Not surprisingly, researchers have demonstrated that individuals are more likely to accept goals that they have selected than those they have been assigned. Researchers have speculated that participation enhances acceptance by increasing the individual's perception of control over the goal. The ambiguity of an incomplete vision invites participation. It requires that the individual help define a specific end to pursue within the broader but incomplete vision. An experience of choice and volition is produced at the initial stage in the performance cycle of selecting ends. But participation in selecting ends is unlikely to produce significant acceptance in the absence of a sense of selecting means as well. (This point is taken up in the next section.)

As co-workers witness one another's expression or individual interpretation of the vision, the link is made to the second of Harrison's organizational processes. In well-functioning systems, alignment is coupled with attunement. Whereas alignment refers to a connection between member and mission, attunement calls attention to a connection among members and serves the organizational function of maintenance. In Harrison's terms, attunement refers to "a resonance or harmony among the parts of a system, and between the parts and the whole. When we are attuned, we become more receptive to the subtle energies that connect us with one another. We become open to one another's needs and to our own sense of what is worthy of reverence in the work we do. Where alignment channels high energy and creates excitement and drive, attunement tames and balances the daimonic qualities of our quest by opening us to each other and to the messages from our hearts" (1983, p. 219).

In this context harmony refers to an interpersonal experience. While the process of expression seems fundamental to Harrison's notion of alignment, the process of witnessing seems to underlie attunement. In witnessing, someone notices and acknowledges another's expression. The expression conveys the person's experience; in the noticing, the experience is affirmed. Sarason's notion of a "psychological sense of community" points to the general state resulting from attunement and the complementary interpersonal process of witnessing. It suggests that attunement is manifest in the individual's experience of life in the work setting. Through attunement the existential function of community is served. An integration among organizational members is produced, just as alignment facilitates an integration of individual and organization. (See Table 1 for a summary of the relationships.)

Inadequate attention to the maintenance function will undermine the adaptive capability and task performance of the organization over time. Whereas the executive plays a major role in facilitating alignment by providing an incomplete vision, the

Table 1. Relationships Among Processes.

Link Facilitated	Process of Interest		Function Served	
	Individual	Organizational	Strategic	Existential
Individual to organization	Expression	Alignment	Adaptation	Meaning
Individual to others	Witnessing	Attunement	Maintenance	Community

executive's role in attunement is to take care not to disrupt the development of natural connections among members. Some structural features, such as incentives for cooperation versus competition at individual and group levels, can be monitored. But basically it is a matter of recognizing the value of emergent interpersonal connections and not undermining them or the social processes through which they emerge. On balance, the executive in the integrator role is more active in linking individual to organization by effecting alignment than in linking individuals to one another through attunement. Yet both must be facilitated to achieve organizational effectiveness.

The Executive as Enabler

In the 1960s social science presaged developments in the larger society. It offered organizing models, value bases, and a pragmatic rationale linking the models to societal improvement. In the 1980s, by contrast, society leads social science. Innovations are burgeoning in practical settings, with social scientists scurrying to describe and interpret them. In this section social science prescriptions of the 1960s will be contrasted with present societal practices toward understanding what participation means in the healthy organization of today. Along the way, we will develop a view of the phenomenological domain of the individual in relation to self in the work setting.

To begin, consider the basis for organizational membership and the form of worker participation. As Etzioni (1975) among others has noted, work organizations traditionally have drawn and retained members on an instrumental or contractual basis. Occasionally membership has been based on some identification producing a moral or normative involvement. Seldom has membership been based on pure coercion—for instance, when members have no options for work elsewhere. For decades the industrial plant of the United States functioned adequately on the instrumental involvement of its employees. Times have changed. Instrumental involvement is no longer competitive in the international marketplace. Nor is it adaptive within organizations in mastering new and complex work technologies. There are as well pressures for change from workers. A new activism, a search for community, distinctions among money and meaning as sources of motivation invoked by new waves of graduates entering the work force (Yankelovich, 1978)—these and other trends call into question the sufficiency of instrumentalism as a predominant work orientation.

In the 1960s normative leadership "theories" urged executives to employ participative management techniques. Conclusions one might draw from examining the Japanese experience (Ouchi, 1981; Pascale and Athos, 1981) or excellent firms in the United States (Peters and Waterman, 1982) sound a familiar participative refrain. Is it the same participative message? Have we come full circle?

There are at least three fundamental differences between the call for participative management of the 1960s and current instances of effective "participative" practice. In the prescriptions of the 1960s and their translation into practice, occurrences of participation were initiated in most instances by the superior. Participation "at will" was not supported. Subordinates were invited to contribute their ideas or react to alternatives if and when the superior determined that their participation was advantageous in some way. Participation was solicited. In contrast, actual observations indicate that in effective organizational situations subordinates initiate participation (Ouchi, 1981; Pascale and Athos, 1981). They do not wait for an invitation. If they notice something that could be improved, they take action, involving appropriate others. Whereas in the 1960s passive participation was implied, in the 1980s active participation is the practice. Prerequisite to these practices must be the development of an atmosphere of support for such participation. The executive serves as an enabler by creating and maintaining such an atmosphere.

In the 1960s participation was bounded in time and space to a particular instance. The instance was identified and framed by the superior. Thus, participation occurred in an immediate, preframed, and well-bounded context. For example, in pursuit of an operator's input on the layout for a new line, the supervisor would have sought the worker out with narrowly focused, directed questions. Today an operator might be a member of the design team.

In current exemplary practices, no preframed context provides the primary stimulus for worker participation. In fact, the quality circles movement illustrates a means by which workers can consider alternative time, space, and frame parameters in systematically looking for potential improvement areas. Thus, there has been a shift in the context of participation vis-à-vis time, space, and frame from immediate and circumscribed to open-ended, ongoing, and flexible.

In addition to shifts in the context and initiation of participation, a boundary internal to the participant has shifted. In the 1960s role-based participation prevailed. The notion of role-based views is rooted in the theory of bureaucracy and trends in the 1960s toward increased professionalism; the "Organization Man" type of thinking epitomizes it. Even the local versus cosmopolitan distinction is made within a role-based framework; it is merely the role context that shifts. In contrast, today people increasingly bring many non-work-related parts of themselves into work situations. They come as people rather than as narrowly defined role holders. The so-called excellent companies represent settings in and through which members may pursue a variety of activities not directly related to their work roles, including social, recreational, existential, community involvement, and/or intellectual, skill, and personal development activities. Expression of extrarole talents and sentiments takes place not only as part of "after-hours" activities or as fringe benefits. Concurrently, there is less compartmentalization and/or role bounding by workers while doing the job. One might characterize this as a move from the workplace professionalization of the 1960s to a workplace personalization in the late 1980s.

Common to all three trends is a broadened base for worker expression. Past boundaries of time, space, subject matter, and personhood have eroded. Participation in current exemplary practice is participant initiated, open ended, participant frameable, and person (versus role) based.

Recent efforts to understand why Japanese industry has outperformed United States industry have pointed up differences in corporate practices relevant to the point here. In Japanese society, education, and business, there is not a separate managerial class. An "up through the ranks" system prevails. Thus, people who become managers have an in-depth and firsthand appreciation of the tasks, products, and personnel associated with the particular business that the firm is in. In addition, demonstrated competence appears to be the basis for promotion, whereas demonstrated loyalty is the basis for employment security. In contrast, the United States system has for most purposes imposed ceilings for those moving up through the ranks, drawing from separate labor pools those who will manage and those who will do the work. As Reich (1981, p. 29) notes: "This bifurcated way of viewing production—separating thinkers from doers, corporate mind from corporate body, white collar from blue collar—has had disastrous results in America and Britain. . . . The costs of this artificial distinction between corporate thinkers and doers are by now obvious. White-collar thinkers and planners often don't comprehend life on the production line, and in consequence their schemes are either impractical or irrelevant, either sabotaged or ignored by the work force. Meanwhile, workers who understand production and could improve it in countless ways don't give a damn. They have no institutional voice."

The more open practices contribute to the adaptiveness of the organization and the fulfillment of the worker. Workers who act out of a sense that their voices would be heard and their observations valued are more likely to take serious interest in the effectiveness of production processes. Workers' inputs can reduce downtime, highlight product refinements, and otherwise enhance the firm's competitiveness. The overhead of internal controls can be trimmed as self-control toward common ends is exercised.

A worker's sense that "my ideas matter" translates over time into the experience that "I matter." This can generate commitment, or a belief that "it matters." The individual develops a feeling of being involved, of taking responsibility, of ownership. Thus, an orientation of attentiveness and care, of commitment and ownership, goes together with a sense of mattering. At its base this type of participation requires conveyance of a sense of potential influence. The seeming tautology is really more paradox. To the extent that one has a sense of being able to influence in those instances where one determines the need to do so, one is more likely to be on the lookout for improvement opportunities.

In the previous section, we saw that an incomplete vision provides workers with a sense of control or choice over ends or goals pursued. We propose here that an experience of institutional voice or potential influence contributes a sense of choice or control over available means. For participation in goal setting to affect performance, the individual must have a choice of ends and means; an incomplete vision and influence potential must both be present.

So participation in the 1980s is more open ended, participant initiated, and person based than in the 1960s; it is advantageous to organization and worker alike; and it flows from a belief in one's potential to influence events beyond the domain of a narrowly specified work role. The task of the executive in the enabling role is to create an atmosphere that engenders a sense of influence potential or institutional voice.

Conclusion

A final aspect of the context of executive action is a powerlessness that many executives experience—notwithstanding a rather macho stereotype held by those not "in power." Organization is an act of structured reliance on others. The deeper the hierarchy, the more dependent are those at the top, and the more people on whom they are dependent. Organization arises as individuals cannot "do it all" alone. Rule by the "consent of the governed" captures much the same quality of the context of power. Leaders' positions are maintained by virtue of the ongoing acceptance of the followers or subordinates. Mutiny occurs literally or figuratively when followers no longer accept the leader as leader, when they stop acting in the role of followers. Similarly, Barnard's (1938) "zone of indifference" suggests that the wise executive is careful not to request followers to behave in ways that cause them to feel that carrying out the request would compromise their personal beliefs or values in some way.

The talk of corporate and government executives conveys this sense of powerlessness in phrases such as "My hands are tied," "I am merely a caretaker/coordinator, with no real decision power," "I have too many masters to answer to." Yet in reading the organizational literature, one would never know that an essential reliance on others characterizes the context in which executives exercise power. Perhaps it is time to recognize that the setting in which the executive acts powerfully constrains the bounds of executive influence. We can have no better guidance on this point than that of Shakespeare:

Glendower: I can call spirits from the vasty deep.

Hotspur: Why so can I, or so can any man; But will they come when you do call for them?

[Henry IV, Part 1, III.I.53]

I have argued in this chapter that we can neither understand nor provide guidance in the use of executive power without a more thorough appreciation of the context in which executives act. The process has been to describe facets of the context—such as the relationship with task, setting, and organization that workers experience—and to derive executive roles from them. Together these facets or phenomenological domains make up the context of executive action. The several executive roles and the domains of experience with which they are associated are summarized in Table 2.

Executives who consider the experiential realities of those whom they wish to influence can expect to be more influential and to accrue more power than can executives who overlook that

Table 2. Executive Roles and Phenomenological Domains.

Domain	Executive Role	Aim Is to Foster:
Daily life in the work setting	Interpreter: Shape meanings made	Shared definition of the situation
Relation of worker to work	Creator of high-performance conditions	Harmony as the experience of high performance
Relation of worker to organization	Integrator: Impart incomplete vision	Alignment
Relation of worker to others at work	Integrator	Attunement
Relation of self to work	Enabler: Ensure institutional voice	Ownership

context. Though this is merely stating the obvious, it has heretofore not been made explicit in guidance to executives. Nor have descriptions of such experiential realities been developed or used to suggest appropriate roles for executives. It was toward those ends that this chapter was undertaken.

SIX

Some Limits of Executive Power in Creating Strategic Change

Andrew M. Pettigrew

At the Battle of Waterloo on Sunday, June 18, 1815, the armies of Wellington and Blücher finally and comprehensively defeated the Napoleonic quest for military and economic power over continental Europe. Wellington's envoy, Major Henry Percy, arrived in London on June 21, expecting to be the first man to tell the British government the joyous news. Apparently, Percy was the first man whom the British government chose to believe about the outcome of the Battle of Waterloo. However, very early on the morning of June 20, Nathan Rothschild told Lord Castlereagh that Napoleon had been defeated. Faced with Castlereagh's skepticism, "Nathan Rothschild took his leave with no further ado and went straight to the Stock Exchange, where he bought large quantities of British bonds. This fact is recorded in the *London Courier* of June 20 with the laconic statement: 'Rothschild has made great purchases of stock,'" (Cowles, 1973, p. 49).

There are a dozen or more accounts of how Nathan Rothschild received this critical piece of information and what he

Note: The research reported in this chapter was partly supported by a Personal Research Grant awarded by the Economic and Social Research Council.

did with it. In some versions carrier pigeons were used; in others Nathan is said to have been on the battlefield, and in many versions there is the implication that Nathan delayed imparting the news and then pretended all was lost in order to depress the market and make a fortune for himself. Corti's (1928, p. 179) account of the implications of Nathan Rothschild's superb intelligence system seems to be balanced and respected: "Nathan naturally applied the early information that he had obtained to his own profit in his business dealings, but the substantial part of the fortune of the brothers Rothschild had been amassed already; the successful issue of the Battle of Waterloo merely served to increase it, and to open up wider fields for profitable business in the future. This was all the more so as England had been victorious and Nathan had transferred the centre of gravity of the Rothschild business to her side."

This case clearly illustrates the power of timely and apposite information in business dealings, but a quick look behind and beyond the events of June 18–21, 1815, could unravel some broader theories about the acquisition and use of business power. For a decade or more before 1815, the Rothschilds had successfully exploited the "Great Napoleonic Crisis" to satisfy the various needs of the combatants and themselves. At the end of the eighteenth century, the focal point for the Rothschilds had been Frankfurt. By 1815, however, they had broadened their bases: the elder brother, Amschel, was in Frankfurt; Nathan was in London; Solomon alternated between Berlin and France; James linked Paris to the Channel ports and thence to Nathan in England; and Karl was in Vienna. Using and building these interlinked networks, the Rothschilds were at various times able to establish an artery of gold to pay for Wellington's campaign in Portugal and Spain, to spirit money from England to France for Louis XVIII's entry into Paris in May 1814, and to transmit subsidy payments from the British government to Russia and Prussia without depressing the English exchange rate. All this was achieved through the trusted and secure relationships among the five brothers, by the brothers' demonstrated financial skill and therefore emerging credibility in their host country, and by the dependency relationships between Britain, Russia, and Prussia and between those countries and the

Rothschilds. Behind all this was the Rothschilds' skill in setting up private courier systems to transmit information and financial resources across land and sea at a time when the normally available mechanisms of communication were primitive. It was, of course, the efficiently running system of couriers between Brussels, Ostend, Dover, and London that got the news of Wellington's victory to Nathan Rothschild before Wellington's own envoy could get this information to the British government.

The rise of the House of Rothschild indicates that the capacity and ability to produce preferred outcomes is grounded in the differential access to material and structural resources. In this view of power, leverage is conferred through dependency relationships. Because resources are scarce, some actors are dependent on others for access to them. Those who successfully possess and control these scarce resources are the powerful. In the more recent literature on organizational power relationships, relevant power resources have been found to include the control of information; access to political arenas; expertise; control over impressions of personal credibility; control of technology: control over rewards and punishments, symbols and systems of meaning; feelings of status; legitimacy; and the ability to cope with uncertainty (see, for example, Mechanic, 1962; Hickson and others, 1971; Pettigrew, 1972, 1973; Pfeffer, 1981b; Hardy and Pettigrew, 1985). These power resources—if possessed, controlled, and successfully mobilized—enable actors to prevail in the face of competition and conflict (Pettigrew, 1973).

However, as Hardy and Pettigrew (1985) argue, the analysis of power cannot and should not be restricted to situations of overt power—that is, to circumstances where power resources are used to produce preferred outcomes in the face of conflict between declared and active opponents. Power can also be used to ensure that conflict does not occur. Political actors may define success not so much as winning in the face of confrontation (where there must always be a risk of losing) but as the ability to section off spheres of influence where domination is perceived as legitimate and thus unchallenged. The use of power in this situation revolves around attempts to create legitimacy and justification for certain arrangements, so that they are never questioned by others. In this way power is mobilized not only to achieve physical outcomes but also to give these outcomes certain meanings—to legitimize and justify them: "Political analysis must then proceed on two levels simultaneously. It must examine how political action gets some groups the tangible things they want from government, and at the same time it must explore what these same actions mean to the mass public and how it is placated or aroused by them. In Himmelstrand's terms, political actions are both instrumental and expressive" (Edelman, 1964, p. 12). Pfeffer (1981b) has distinguished between substantive outcomes of power (outcomes that depend largely on resource-dependency considerations) and sentiment outcomes of power (the way that people feel about these outcomes). Sentiments are mainly influenced by the use of political language, symbols, and rituals.

If outcomes can be legitimized to the point where they are not questioned, even by potential opponents, actors have succeeded in obtaining their desired outcomes by using their power to *prevent* conflict from arising. Specifically, conflict is prevented by the shaping of preferences, perceptions, and cognitions of potential opponents in such a way that they "accept their role in the existing order of things, either because they can see or imagine no alternative, or because they see it as natural and unchangeable, or because they value it as divinely ordained and beneficial" (Lukes, 1974, p. 24). Such processes depend heavily on the use of various symbols (Pfeffer, 1981b) and myths (Cohen, 1975) to manage meaning (Pettigrew, 1977, 1979). These are relatively unexplored aspects of power, although the use of power to prevent conflict has recently been attracting some empirical attention (see, for example, Gaventa, 1980; Saunders, 1980).

This aspect of power has been termed "unobtrusive" (Hardy, 1985), not so much because power is used unobtrusively but because of the circumstances in which it is used and the objectives of its use. *Overt* power is employed in situations of overt confrontation, with the aim of *defeating* opposition. *Unobtrusive* power is used before overt confrontation occurs, with the explicit aim of *preventing* it. Empirical research reported by Hardy (1985) and Hardy and Pettigrew (1985) illustrates why and how managers were success-fully able to use unobtrusive power in factory closures to reduce the likelihood of overt confrontation and industrial action. In the reported cases, managers perceived a threat of industrial action and were anxious to avoid it because of the negative consequences, such as damaged reputations, difficulties in transferring production, or the setting of bad precedents.

A person who uses overt power will tend to rely on resource interdependencies, whereas someone employing unobtrusive power will usually rely on more symbolic sources of power. It is not inconceivable, however, that resources such as expertise and information may be used to prevent opposition from arising, while symbolic power, such as myths, might be used to discredit active opponents. Thus, some power sources at least can be employed both to prevent and to defeat opposition. In fact, both types of power source are derived from the control of (more or less tangible) scarce resources.

Unobtrusive power is important for a number of reasons. First, it incorporates an aspect of power that all too often has been ignored in the literature: the use of power in the absence of conflict. Second, it draws attention to the fact that actors may, if they feel threatened by the consequences of overt confrontation, undertake actions with the explicit objective of reducing the likelihood of confrontation. Third, to assume that the absence of conflict automatically indicates some sort of "genuine" consensus or satisfaction is not theoretically justifiable because, in some situations at least, quiescence may be the result of the use of power: "We may, in other words, be duped, hoodwinked, coerced, cajoled, or manipulated into political inactivity" (Saunders, 1980, p. 22).

The particular concern with unobtrusive power is dependent on a view of organizational life in political-cultural terms (Pettigrew, 1977, 1979; Ranson, Hinings, and Greenwood, 1980; Pfeffer, 1981b; Astley and Rosen, 1983). The political-cultural view of organizational functioning gives emphasis to the propensity of actors and groups in organizations to create and maintain systems of meaning and to articulate broad interpretative schemes, values, and interests. These systems of meaning, belief, and interpretation have been variously labeled as the organization's idea system

(Normann, 1977) or organizational ideology (Brunsson, 1982). Although, at any point in time, an organization may be dominated by a particular group and a particular ideology, structural forces within and outside the organization ensure that alternative and potentially competitive ideologies will develop. The resolution of any tension between an established and an establishing ideology will be a consequence of power dependencies.

In this chapter it is argued that the creation of strategic change often represents a challenge to the core system of meaning, belief, and interpretation in an organization. Because strategic changes can involve the questioning and eventual displacement of an organization's central ideology, such changes usually are not a consequence just of managerial perception, choice, and action. More often they are a result of crisis, environmental pressuring, and then a flurry of executive action. However, although the empirical material reported in this chapter and developed in Pettigrew (1985a), as well as in work by Miller and Friesen (1980), Miller (1982), and Brunsson (1982), has established a relationship between economic and business crisis and strategic change, no simple economic determinism lies behind this work. Any adequate framework for examining strategic change must include not only objective changes in business and economic conditions but also processes of managerial perception, choice, and action. The study of managerial processes of strategic change provides a focus on the role of executive leadership and managerial action. According to this view, executives can intervene in the existing concepts of corporate strategy in the firm; they can use and change the structures, cultures, reward systems, and political processes in the firm to draw attention to performance gaps resulting from environmental change; and they can lead the organization to sense and create a different pattern of alignment between its internal characteristics, strategy, and structure and its emerging concept of its competitive environment. The real problem of strategic change, therefore, is anchoring new perceptions of the environment, new issues for attention, and new ideas for debate. The task is to mobilize energy, concern, and enthusiasm, and this goal is achieved most often in an additive and evolutionary fashion.

Character of Strategic Change Processes

Although one can find contrary examples, both in different societies and in varying fields of inquiry, by and large social scientists have not studied the elite and powerful groups in the societies where they practice their skills. The most often quoted empirical studies of organization power relationships are confined largely to lower operatives and managers (Crozier, 1964) or to specialist or advisory groups in business (Pettigrew, 1973) or are conducted in less central institutions, such as universities (Pfeffer, 1981b). Consequently, some of the key processes of decision making and change, which involve those with high levels of positional power, are shielded and lie unrevealed. A result of this shielding is that myths abound and are perpetuated about rational problem-solving processes of formulating and then, in a linear fashion, implementing strategic change—processes conducted by all-seeing and presumably omnipotent chief executives or general managers.

Thus, strategic planning in organizations has been conceived of as a rational-linear process (Ansoff, 1965; Andrews, 1971; King and Cleland, 1978) dominated by powerful entrepreneurs. As applied to the formulation of strategy, the rational approach describes and prescribes techniques for identifying current strategy; analyzing environments, resources, and gaps; revealing and assessing strategic alternatives; and choosing and implementing carefully analyzed and well-thought-through outcomes. It also assumes that, either explicitly or implicitly, the firm speaks with a unitary voice and is composed of omnipotent, even heroic, general managers or chief executives, looking at known and consistent preferences and assessing them with voluminous and presumably apposite information, which can be organized into clear input-output relationships. Bourgeois and Brodwin (1984) have recently and appropriately labeled this the "commander model" of formulating and implementing strategy.

But does this "commander" view of rational choice and change processes equate with what we know of top-management behavior? Does organizational action derive so singularly from decisions taken at the top, or do many senior executives find that the levers they are pulling are being pushed and pulled in different directions by their peers or subordinates or that, in the task of strategy implementation, the levers they are pulling are not connected to anything or anybody? Indeed, is it the case that, as far as senior executive behavior is concerned, thinking big is not the same as acting big?

In the sphere of politics and government, March and Olsen (1983) have noted the phenomenon of a succession of United States presidents—from Wilson to Johnson to Nixon to Carter—generating and abandoning reorganization plans. Apparently, there is a tendency for presidents to experience cycles of enthusiasm and disappointment, for problems to be identified but not solved and for promises to be made but not kept—with all this reaping a harvest of frustration and disillusionment. On the basis of their review of the literature on politics and government, March and Olsen (1983) derive two important conclusions that are pertinent to the theme of this chapter: (1) Long-run developments of political institutions are less a product of intentions, plans, and consistent decisions than of incremental adaptation to changing problems. (2) Attempts at comprehensive reorganization invariably fail; instead, change often materializes as a product of continuous, incremental processes. In effect, changes often fail whereas changing often succeeds, because changing is not noticed whereas changes most certainly are.

Kotter (1982) and Quinn (1980) also recognize the incremental and often intuitive character of executive behavior and, by implication, some of the limitations of executive power. The agendas that Kotter's general managers generated were often vague, unwritten, only partially connected to implicit and explicit business strategies, and dependent on the availability of wide networks of relationships for implementation. Quinn (1980, 1982) conceives of strategic change as a cautious, step-by-step evolutionary process, a jointly analytical and political process in which executives muddle through with a purpose.

Kanter (1983) contends that innovation in the firm is inhibited by the antichange structures and cultures found in "segmentalist" companies and facilitated by the change-receptive contexts found in "integrative" companies. Kanter's view of the politics of innovation is more explicitly laid out than Quinn's, arguing as she does that would-be innovators have to compete in a marketplace for information and ideas, an economic marketplace for resources, and a political marketplace for legitimacy and support; but her overall characterization of the process of change is very similar to Quinn's treatment of the subject, where building awareness and credibility for new ideas, offering partial solutions, broadening political support, and overcoming opposition are all central activities.

The research published in the 1970s by, for example, Bower (1970) and Mintzberg (1978) and more recently by Quinn (1980) and Kanter (1983) has made a number of descriptive contributions to the understanding of strategic change processes. Strategic processes of change are now more widely accepted as multilevel activities and not just the province of a few or even a single general manager. Outcomes of decisions are no longer assumed to be a product of rational or boundedly rational debates; it is now recognized that these outcomes are also shaped by the interest and commitments of individuals and groups, by forces of bureaucratic momentum, and by the manipulation of the structural context surrounding decisions and changes. With the view that strategy development is a continuous process, strategies are now thought of as reconstructions after the fact, rather than just rationally intended plans. The linear view of the strategic change process has been questioned, and with that questioning has come both an additional awareness of the substantial but limited power of chief executives in implementing strategic change and new attempts to develop models and processes of implementation other than the simple commander model (Bourgeois and Brodwin, 1984).

Strategic Change as a Pattern of Revolution and Incremental Adjustment. Quinn's (1980, 1982) work captures well the additive, evolving, incremental character of strategic changes and thereby clearly demonstrates that, in the management of strategic change, not only cognitive limits but also process limits must be considered. However, Quinn's logical incrementalist approach overemphasizes the continuous incremental nature of change and thereby conceals the major role that environmental disturbance and crisis can play as an enabler and a trigger for significant change. Mintzberg (1978), Miller and Friesen (1982), and Miller (1982), using a mixture of metaphors, all see strategic change occurring in spurts, revolutionary periods, or quantum leaps, each followed by a period of continuity. Although the work conducted at McGill University by Mintzberg and his colleagues usefully identifies the ebb and flow of individual strategic concentrations in the firm and also the existence of periods of revolutionary and evolutionary change (Greiner, 1974), these authors do not clearly develop a process theory that links the periods of high levels of change activity and low levels of change activity and thus begins to explain the timing, content, and relative intensity of those periods. An approach that does have more to say about precrisis, crisis, and stabilization, and thus the linkages between revolutionary and evolutionary periods, is offered by Jonsson and Lundin (1977); Starbuck, Greve, and Hedberg (1978); and Brunsson (1982). By introducing more explicitly into their analysis the importance of organizational ideologies and standard operating procedures—both as inhibitors and, in the case of changing ideologies, as precipitators of change— these authors provide a more satisfactory way of explaining revolutions and evolutions and the links between high levels of change activity and lower levels of change activity. Brunsson (1982), in an elegantly written paper, argues that organizations periodically jump from one predominant ideology to another and that radical changes must be preceded and initiated by ideological shifts. To the question of how ideologies are changed, Brunsson answers that they are changed as a result of externally driven crises, shifts in leadership, and the properties of ideologies themselves. The most stable ideologies are those that are vague and widely applicable; sharp, definite, and particular ideologies are easier to question and eventually debunk in the face of a changing reality. Crucially, Brunsson also argues that the periods when ideological shifts are in process—that is, when the dominant ideology has not yet been debunked and when any aspiring new ideology still lacks a critical mass of support—are poor contexts for action. During such periods ideological inconsistencies increase uncertainty and make it difficult to marshal the strong commitments and high levels of motivation and energy necessary to create radical organizational changes. Thus, Brunsson argues, an ideological shift has to be completed before radical action in the change sphere can begin.

In what follows I shall use an illustrative example from a major study of Imperial Chemical Industries (ICI) to provide confirmatory data of the waxing and waning of particular strategies in the firm and of the tendency for strategic changes to occur in radical packages interspersed with longish periods of absorbing the impact of revolutionary action and then coming to terms with the fact that further changes are eventually necessary. Explicit in the presentation of the ICI data is the point that crucial to the timing of such radical actions are real and constructed crises, changes in leadership and power, and the transformation of organizational ideologies (Pettigrew, 1983, 1985a, 1985b).

The ICI Study of Strategic Change. ICI is one of Britain's largest manufacturing firms and in 1981 ranked the fifth largest of the world's chemical companies in terms of sales in United States dollars (after Du Pont and the big German three of Hoechst, Bayer, and BASF). The study described in this section examines ICI's attempts to change its strategy, structure, technology, organizational culture, and the quality of union-management relationships over the period 1960–1984. An important and unusual feature of the research strategy has been the collection of comparative and longitudinal data. Interview, documentary, and observational data are available from ICI's four largest divisions and the head office of the company. These data have been assembled on a continuous real-time basis since 1975; through retrospective analysis of the period 1960–1974; and, in the case of the divisional chapters, by probing into the traditions and culture of each division established long before the last two decades.

The study explores two linked continuous processes. The initial focus of the research was to examine the birth, evolution, demise, and development of the groups of internal and external organization development consultants employed by ICI in order to help initiate and implement organization change. This analysis of the contributions and limitations of specialist-led attempts to create change prompted an examination of broader processes of continuity and change in ICI as seen through the activities of the main board of the company and the boards of ICI's four largest divisions: Agricultural, Mond, Petrochemicals, and Plastics. The ICI study (Pettigrew, 1985a) contributes to knowledge about the part played by very senior executives in corporate-wide strategic changes; the role of divisional boards and directors in making division-wide changes in structure, organizational culture, and manpower; and the influence of development specialists in making changes happen. Throughout, the emphasis of the study is on describing and analyzing processes of change in the context of the traditions, culture, structure, and business of ICI as a whole and each of its divisions (the inner context) and of the gross changes in the business, economic, and political environment ICI has faced through time (the outer context). In this approach strategic change involves the continuous interplay of ideas about the *context* of change, the *process* of change, and the *content* of change, together with skill in regulating the relations among the three.

The ICI study thus asks questions such as: What kinds of managerial processes inside the firm encouraged continuity and change? How and why and when was the need for change sensed? How also were planning and action in the sphere of strategic change finally justified? What combination of environmental triggering and executive leadership eventually led to the implementation and stabilization of change?

Five cases of strategic change are compared and contrasted in the study (Pettigrew, 1985a). Here it is feasible to discuss only one of those five cases—the one relating to the strategic development of the whole ICI group. In this case, as in all others, there is a clear pattern for the timing and intensity of strategic change to be associated with significant changes in the outer context of ICI. The limitations of the power of those who champion strategic changes appear to require the massive enabling opportunity provided by gross alterations in outer context.

An examination of the corporate development of ICI from the late 1950s until 1984 reveals three periods of high levels of change activity. Two of these three periods, the ones between 1960 and 1964 and between 1980 and 1984, could be sensibly labeled as revolutionary periods in that they featured ideological, structural, and business strategy change; during the third period, between 1970 and 1972, further structural change was made, and elements of the ideological and business strategy changes made ten years earlier were accelerated or deemphasized. The periods between these packages of changes were occasions for implementing and stabilizing changes; most notably, the period between 1973 and 1980 was an era of organizational learning, when ideological justification was prepared for the revolutionary break between 1980 and 1984.

These periods of high levels of change activity were associated with world economic recessions, with their associated effects on world chemical production, markets, and prices, and in turn on ICI's relative level of business performance. Table 1 shows the peaks and troughs in ICI's profits and ratio of trading profit to sales from 1958 to 1982. Since 1958 there have been five years of peak profits followed by downturns of varying severity, with each cycle lasting from four to five years. The improvement from trough to peak has been 82 percent (1958–1960), 74 percent (1961–1964), 92 percent (1966–1969), 255 percent (1971–1974), and 95 percent (1975–1979). The period from 1980 to 1983 evidenced a stepwise change in macroeconomic trends; a sustained recession in the United Kingdom, a dramatic downturn in ICI's profitability; and major structural, manpower, ideological, and business strategy change.

Table 1. ICI Record of Sales, Profits, and Ratio of Trading Profit to Sales in Peak and Trough Years 1958–1982.

	Sales (millions)	Profits (millions)	Ratio of Trading Profit to Sales
1958	$ 463	$ 51	11.0
1960	558	93	16.6
1961	550	65	11.8
1964	720	113	15.7
1966	885	99	11.2
1969	1,355	190	14.0
1971	1,524	130	8.5
1974	2,955	461	15.6
1975	3,129	325	10.4
1979	5,368	634	11.8
1980	5,715	332	5.8
1981	6,581	425	6.4
1983	7,358	366	5.0

The two periods of revolutionary change between 1960 and 1964 and between 1980 and 1984 were preceded by and further reaffirmed ideological shifts and were associated, on the first occasion, with the 1958 and 1961 economic and business downturns and, on the second occasion, with the 1980–1983 recession. They were also occasions when new business leadership was supplied by men who had not spent their whole career at ICI. In 1960 Paul Chambers (later Sir Paul Chambers), a former senior civil servant and the first nontechnical man for some years, was appointed chairman. He began to emphasize financial and commercial management skills in a management culture heavily preoccupied with science and technology. And in November 1981 the announcement was made that a former naval intelligence officer, John Harvey-Jones (now Sir John Harvey-Jones), was to be chairman of ICI. His ideological contribution is emerging as a lessening of bureaucracy and centralization in ICI, sharper business accountabilities, and a greater emphasis on entrepreneurial skills and continuous change into the 1980s.

Both revolutionary change periods witnessed structural and business strategy changes in the organization, with the structural changes occurring in a cumulative way over a relatively short period of time and the business strategy changes emerging and being implemented rather more slowly *after* the ideological and structural changes had been justified and then introduced. One of the contributions of the ICI research is therefore to question Chandler's (1962) dictum that structure follows strategy, by indicating why and how business strategy change follows ideological and structural change.

Leadership Tasks in Creating Strategic Change

The above highly synoptic and partial account of some patterns in ICI's corporate development has revealed an association between environmental change and pressure and internal strategic change. As such, the view so far of strategic change is that real change requires crisis conditions; and, by implication, senior executives who may be pushing for change in precrisis circumstances do not have sufficient leverage to break through the pattern of inertia in their organization. However, although the above brief analysis does reveal periodic eras of high levels of change activity precipitated by crisis, it is not being argued that the process and content of strategic changes can be explained solely by economic and business-related environmental disturbance. Clearly, a potential danger of an analysis that might infer too simply a relation between economic and business crisis and organizational change is that the firm may thus end up being seen just "bobbing on the economic waves, as so many corks on the economic bathtub" (Boswell, 1983, p. 15).

As I have already noted, no such brand of simple economic determinism is intended here. Behind the periodic strategic reorientations in ICI are not just economic and business events but also processes of managerial perception, choice, and action influenced by and influencing perceptions of the operating environment of the firm and its structure, culture, and systems of power and control. Crucial to the character and content of the package of structural and then business strategy changes made at the revolutionary points when those changes are actually delivered are the antecedent factors and processes of the precrisis period. Crucial in the precrisis period is the process through which the dominating ideology nurtured in earlier contexts is first challenged and then changed. Since business strategies are likely to be rooted in the idea systems that are institutionalized in an industry sector at any point of time (Grinyer and Spender, 1979; Huff, 1982) and are represented in the values, structures, and systems of powerful groups who control the firms in any sector, a change in business strategies has to involve a process of ideological and political change, which eventually releases a new concept of strategy that is ideologically acceptable within a newly appreciated context. Because this precrisis era of ideological change represents a fundamental challenge to the dominating ideas and power groups of the organization, such eras of ideological challenge are often thwarted, sidetracked, or otherwise immobilized, leaving many who have attempted to champion new ideas faced with stereotyping as oddballs, moral entrepreneurs, or folk devils. Posed in this way, the development of strategic change in the firm takes on the character of a political learning process, a long-term conditioning and influence process designed to establish the dominating legitimacy of a different pattern of relation between strategic content, context, and process.

But how is this done; indeed, prescriptively, how can it be done? Is it possible to describe and codify the tasks and skills appropriate for such a contextually sensitive activity as managing strategic change without reducing the change process to a mechanical and overdetermined set of phases or stages, and reducing the activities of changing to a set of platitudinous generalities? Quinn (1980, 1982), with his discussion of logical incrementalism, has offered one prescriptive view of strategic change. He describes and prescribes a process of strategic change that is jointly analytical and political and where executives are recommended to proceed flexibly and experimentally from broad concepts to specific commitments: a cautious step-by-step activity of building awareness of the need for change, legitimizing new viewpoints and challenging old assumptions, making tactical shifts and finding partial solutions, overcoming and neutralizing opposition while building political support around particular ideas, and then formalizing commitment for action.

Kanter (1983), on the other hand, sees a prototypical innovation having three waves of activity occurring in sequence or as successful iterations. First, information is acquired, sorted, and exchanged to shape the definition of a problem that may become the focus for change. Then coalitions are built, teams created, and individuals encouraged to buy in or sign on for the change in question. Finally, there is a mobilization and completion phase, in which the boundaries and momentum for the change are maintained, opposition and interference are dealt with, and the change proceeds through periods of secondary and subsequent redesigns until particular pieces of the change are implementable. Kanter (1983) sees champions for change ideas holding together and managing the above three-stage process. These advocates of change will use what she calls power skills to persuade others to invest information, resources, and support in new initiatives; team skills to share information, resolve differences, and generate enthusiasm and commitment to particular solutions; and change-architect skills to design and construct microchanges, which are eventually connectable to macrochanges or strategic orientations.

Both of these prescriptive views of change put their fingers on important aspects of the practice of change, but both also underemphasize or ignore other elements of the management task. Quinn's (1980) view captures well the additive, evolving nature of the task but tends to underplay the role of environmental disturbance and the contribution that changing features of intraorganizational context can play in creating a new pattern of learning, thought, and action as change proceeds. Kanter, on the other hand, clearly emphasizes the power skills required to create change. Moreover, in her discussion of segmented and integrated contexts, she demonstrates that some contexts are more receptive to and enabling of change than others; and she indicates that the career of a change idea might depend not just on power skills as such but on skill in changing a context toward more integrative features while the change idea is being championed. But neither Kanter nor Quinn deals with the key management tasks of stabilizing a change once changes have taken place or are taking place.

An approach that complements both the views of Kanter and Quinn and the empirical findings of the ICI study is propounded by Johnston (1975). Johnston's argument is predicated on three assumptions: (1) that some evolution is occurring in a natural way in most organizations; (2) that this natural evolution is in response to external pressures and is therefore retrospective and remedial, rather than preventive; and (3) that any such change process absorbs a great deal of energy in the firm because it may require power redistribution, role changes, the abandonment of past practices and old ideologies, and restructuring. Building on these assumptions, Johnston makes an assertion highly compatible with the findings of the ICI study—namely, that development or change processes are often dependent on a few people, are reactive to changes in the general world, and can peter out or be reversed. Such regression or reversals might be prevented if one understands the evolution of natural processes of change in organizations and establishes an organization process of change with the necessary internal skills, actions, and systems to maintain development in the direction sought. Prescriptively, this means in the broadest sense that the first step in the change process should be to improve and build on any natural processes of change by tackling questions such as: How can existing processes be speeded up? How can conditions that determine people's interpretations of situations be altered? And how can contexts be mobilized to move the organization in a different strategic direction? Thus, any adequate approach to managing change must be based on the principle of understanding the context, of knowing what one is dealing with, and of choosing as a starting point some area of movement that can be built upon.

For all its oversimplifications, including the tendency to assume both discrete and exclusive categories and linear sequential development, Johnston's (1975) notion of four stages in the natural process of change does usefully capture broad elements of the descriptive findings of change elaborated in the ICI research and allows one to make sensible prescriptive statements about necessary leadership and management tasks at each of the four stages. The four stages are development of concern, acknowledgment and understanding of the problem, planning and acting, and stabilizing change.

In fact, the data from the ICI study, particularly about the contribution of visionary leaders and early adopters in change processes, indicate the importance of an initial problem-sensing stage, which may predate a stage of development of concern. In the sphere of strategic change, signaling problems as worthy of attention is itself a time-consuming and politically very sensitive process. One of the contributions made by Lord Beeching and George Bridge in ICI in the 1960s and by Harvey-Jones and Woodburn throughout the 1970s was to sense and flag key problems worthy of management attention. From a political-process point of view, it is critical not to rush prematurely from problem sensing to planning and action in the change sphere. Actions recommended about problems which themselves are not yet accepted as legitimate topics of debate invariably produce the rejection of the change idea. The essence of the political learning process implied in this view of change is that individual sensing of problems must be complemented with activities that encourage some level of shared problem sensing, spreading of concern about the emerging problem, and eventually broadly based understanding of the problem, if novel ideas for change are not to be imperiled at birth.

The development-of-concern stage assumes the presence of a small group of early adopters or even, as is catalogued in Pettigrew (1985a), the presence of a single visionary change leader, sensing and imprecisely articulating a performance gap between the organization's present condition and some feature or features of its operating environment. The major leadership task here is to educate the organization by building on the perspective, information, and contacts of the early adopters—in effect, to recognize the group doing this early sensing; to broaden the group by helping to connect it to peers, bosses, and subordinates with similar views; and to prepare a critical mass of people to help influence key power figures. This educational process may also involve setting up unusual meetings that cross existing organizational and departmental boundaries and help spread information and views and integrate such data around particular issues or problems. Key line managers or consultants may also be able to set up meetings where power figures receive and test data; or these managers may counsel individuals to act on the emerging views of the problem in parts of the organization where it is legitimate to do so. As the ICI study demonstrates, it can be valuable at this stage in the change process for deviants, even heretics, to think the unthinkable, and say the unsayable, and for key line managers to be persuaded to help break traditional patterns of thought by setting up unconventional meetings where the process of discussing the previously undiscussable can begin.

In the next stage, the process of trying to get acknowledgment and understanding of emerging problems and issues, the main leadership task is to help the early adopters and key power figures maintain and develop any structured dialogue about the problem and avoid a tendency either to escape from the problem—by, for example, projecting it onto others—to rush into action before the present situation has been carefully diagnosed, change objectives clarified and agreed on, and a process plan to move from the present to the desired future developed. This stage is critical not only for perpetuating any ideological change now in process but also for exposing alternative diagnoses of the problem, exploring causes, generating alternative solutions, and developing criteria for choosing a solution.

The ICI data on strategic change suggest that the above processes of problem sensing, educating, and climate and tension building for change are long processes with many iterations, blocks, dead ends, and unpredictable areas of movement. Persistence and patience in championing change seem to be necessary to initiate and perpetuate this process of conditioning and influence; and deliberative attempts to alter the structural and cultural context of decision making and capitalize on environmental disturbances se··m necessary to break out from mere acknowledgment and understand-ing of problems into a stage of executive planning and action. Because radical changes require strong commitments and high motivations, they also presuppose the existence of ideological reorientations, and therefore the unequivocal availability of a new ideology that precisely and enthusiastically endorses the changes. Ideological reorientations can occur through the processes of climate building and education, but major ideological change also requires other deliberate management actions: efforts made to influence patterns of socialization by changing career paths and reward systems; to use the newly promoted as role models to signal behavior required in the new culture; and to use retirement situations to combine portfolios and responsibilities previously divided. Ideological reorientation may also be facilitated by breaking the global problem into actionable bits that reinforce one another or by creating temporary or permanent task forces, coordination committees, and business teams to resolve conflicts and imbue enthusiasms and commitment for action around pieces of the change.

Johnston's (1975) otherwise helpful prescriptive view of change management tends to underemphasize management action to change and thereby restructure the context in which change processes develop; it also underemphasizes the extent to which effective action in managing strategic change is dependent on mobilizing environmental disturbances and crises in order to achieve practical effects. Gross change in the environment of the firm can be orchestrated and capitalized on to create opportunities for organizational learning, to destabilize power structures, and to

connect previously unrelated solutions around now more precisely
stated and more enthusiastically supported organizational
ideologies. But if crises provide ideological closure and therefore
justification for action, it is evident that some organizations are
more likely to be able to capitalize on the "window for change"
provided by environmental disturbances than others. Here, of
course, what has or has not happened in the precrisis circumstances
may determine the quality of planning and action taken to
implement strategic changes. Paradoxically, the delays and
incremental movements in problem sensing, the development of
concern, and the acknowledgment and understanding of a
problem's stages may have sensitized a wider set of people to the
incipient problems and enabled debates to occur around a variety
of solutions; they also may have helped to draw out and test new
leaders who can manage the new circumstances or who at least can
use the temporary structures and administrative mechanisms to
prepare the ground for new patterns of organization. The ICI data
also demonstrate that management training and development
experiences can be used in the precrisis situation to develop a
common language for thinking about change management and to
increase the capability and confidence of managers to carry through
operational change management tasks delegated to them by senior
executives.

The planning and acting tasks in change management have
been well codified and described in the concepts and techniques
reported by Beckhard and Harris (1977) and by Beer (1980). These
tasks include (1) defining the present condition of the organization
in relation to its changing environment; (2) clarifying the desired
future state for the organization; (3) building commitment around
particular change objectives; and (4) appointing transition
managers to move from the present to the desired state. The ICI data
also reveal that this operational process of change management is
greatly facilitated by unity of philosophy and purpose among the
senior executives leading the change process.

If the top leadership role at the action stage in change
management is to put tension into the organization by providing
a clearly articulated rationale for change and some consistently
stated change objectives, the operating management responsibility

is to plan and organize the use of this tension to generate movement. Here agreeing on the targets of change and the form and timing of their publication is important. The publication process is really a contracting-negotiation exercise, which takes into account the different positions of individual units, deals with possible differences in interpretation of the leadership message, and manages apparent conflicts in the implications of the messages. There is clearly a monitoring task to ensure progress and a support task to ensure that problems inhibiting progress are dealt with creatively and ethically and that operating managers are provided with a "political umbrella" for the risks they have to take.

A key to success in these kinds of change activities is the effective management of the links between the senior group leading the change and the operating managers carrying through the details of implementing particular changes. Even in crisis-driven circumstances, the operating management role is like to involve detail and grinding on over time and is very dependent on the leadership role's being consistently maintained. If someone in an operating management role is close to acceptance of hard targets in his or her sphere of negotiated influence, his or her work could be undermined and even destroyed by a weakening of the leadership position.

But the ICI study also indicates that strategic change is not just a question of justification and initial action, of making things happen; it is also a question of making things stick. Making changes stick requires the additional management task of stabilizing changes, of making sure that reward systems, information flows, and power and authority distributions support the newly emerging state. Since changes are often initiated by or otherwise associated with key figures and changes often remain as long as those key figures remain, a critical part of the stabilization process has to do with the development and choice of successors who will want to maintain the new situation and, more idealistically perhaps, who will maintain and then initiate changes themselves when external pressure on the organization makes further change appropriate.

Returning for a moment to our earlier discussion of the generation and use of power in the context of strategic change processes, it is clear that the above process of ideological change is often a long struggle to use overt and unobtrusive power sources to fashion legitimacy for a new order of things. It is a process of using potential power, expertise, information, and political networks, and at the same time exploiting environmental disturbances and incipient and embryonic changes in intraorganizational culture, in order to accelerate the rise of new ideas and delegitimize the idea systems that previously dominated organizational perceptions. As I have argued throughout this chapter, the content of such changes must be remarkably sensitive to process and context considerations. The Rothschild family clearly understood this principle well. The Rothschild brothers were able to generate power in the Napoleonic era not only because of their networks of political contacts, their control over vital information, and their credibility as expert financiers, but also because those power sources were constructed and maintained in a manner appropriate to the political and cultural context of the day and at a time when the Napoleonic crisis offered an opportunity and a need for their services.

SEVEN

Top Management Politics and Organizational Change

Larry E. Greiner

For many years I have puzzled over why even the best-planned change efforts by management consultants and experts in organization development seem to go awry. Despite numerous reports of success in the research literature and in the anecdotes of bravado consultants, I would be willing to wager that the private failures far outnumber the public successes—say, in a ratio of 20 to 1. I base my hunch on several years of serving on the boards of three management consulting firms, my own consulting experience, one daring book on failures in organization development (Mirvis and Berg, 1977), keeping up with my reading in *Fortune* and *Business Week*, and eavesdropping over cocktails to hear close colleagues "tell it like it is." Admittedly, this loose grouping of kibitzers is hardly a scientific sample (and no doubt we need one), but ask yourself the same question about the degree of success and failure in your own attempts at major organizational change.

As you reflect, remember that I am talking about corporate change of a *major organizational and strategic nature, where the goal is to exchange one set of operating practices for a very different set, so that the entire organization takes on a different relationship with itself and its environment.* Be sure to exclude those modest projects that were restricted to a department or subunit level, or those training efforts where the goal was to develop better managerial skills for decision making. These are not major efforts at organization change at the corporate level.

Now, you may say that I have unfairly reduced your sample size by such a demanding definition. And right you are, but isn't that a telling sign in itself? Doesn't the absence of reported attempts at major organizational transformation point to a serious void in our academic consulting experience and in our research literature? Rarely do academic consultants or researchers get near the apex of corporations, except for a guided tour. Nevertheless, such experience with implementing massive organization and strategic change does exist in the world of full-time management consulting, especially among firms such as McKinsey, Boston Consulting Group, and Management Analysis Center. These consultants routinely bid for and receive large-scale change projects of the scope I am discussing. Yet they too, in their private moments, acknowledge not only the frequent rejection of proposals but subsequent failure to achieve change in ongoing projects— although they are still amply rewarded with large fees.

Even if I relax my definition to include organizational changes that are more modest in scope or limited to the subunit level, I think we still could all agree that far too many efforts fail to make headway. And when this happens, we usually point to the "system" as the culprit, although the specific sources of resistance are less clear. Ironically, we are usually quick to point to ourselves when the process goes well.

For my finger pointing in this chapter, I will focus on the entry stage for a consultant coming into an organization at the top-management level. When we talk informally about the consulting process, we usually neglect this early stage in favor of telling anecdotes about dramatic events later in the change process. Our research literature, too, has been neglectful of the entry stage. Yet I view these early-entry steps as critical for determining what happens later. It is not simply a period of "marketing," as professional management consultants might have us believe, or a period of open flexibility for skillful change agents to maneuver, as self-flattering behavioral science consultants might contend. I will argue instead that a certain political dynamic is encountered in the top-management group from the first day of a consulting engagement; moreover, this dynamic is so embedded that it is extremely hard to alter. Depending on the nature of this political dynamic, the subsequent change process can be greatly affected, so much so that, while a large project may be initiated, the project itself can still fail.

The political dynamic that I speak of occurs within the very top management of a corporation (the chief executive officer and his or her immediate subordinates). It refers to the manner in which these key leaders handle their power relationships with each other. An ingrained political pattern has formed among this constellation of senior executives, and it colors all subsequent intervention attempts.

In order to explicate these power relationships and their effects on the change agent, I will refer in this chapter to the power and intervention literature and discuss a case of failed change in a large corporation. On the basis of this material, I will then propose a conceptual model for guiding future interventions at the top-management level.

The Literature Gap

Our research literature on the relationship between change and top-management politics is virtually nonexistent. Yet it is here where a major change effort begins. Popular references to "bottom-up" change, I believe, represent the romantic illusion of humanistic scholars, since I know of no previous research documenting successful organization changes that were not planned and led from the top. The seeds of change may have been sown at lower levels, but organization-wide change does not transpire without active leadership at the top.

The intervention literature, with the exception of Argyris (1970), is also deficient for not being targeted at top management and the entry process. This literature typically contains the following broad streams of intervention advice to change agents:

1. Global interventions—a programmatic focus described in formal terms (for example, laboratory training, team building, and confrontation meetings).

2. One-shot dramatic process interventions—made at a late stage
    in the change process—such as "co-opting" a key leader who
    is a source of resistance.
3. Stylistic interventions of a "one-best-technique" nature—such
    as "9,9" behavior for bringing conflicting parties together to
    reach a creative solution.

These intervention approaches are preoccupied with
technique, devoid of contextual reality, and narrowly restricted to
socioemotional events. The intervention literature does not describe
top management as a unique behavioral context for intervention.
Only one book, *Consultation*, by Blake and Mouton (1976), makes
a stab at defining context in contingency terms, but it too often
lapses into the three universalistic solutions described above.

Among the few authors who link the subject of intervention
with power and politics, Pettigrew (1975) and Schein (1976) strike
a similar theme: building the power of the change agent as a means
for influencing the power structure of an organization. To quote
Pettigrew, "It is suggested that the consultant's ability to influence
clients will be a function of his possession and tactical use of five
power resources: expertise, control over information, political
access and sensitivity, assessed stature, and group support" (p. 191).
And Schein argues, "If one values the merits of organizational
change programs, then political skill acquisition [by the
consultant] would seem far wiser and more realistic than remaining
Little Red Riding Hood and being devoured by the wolf" (p. 12).
While Pettigrew and Schein move closer to what I want to discuss,
their focus is almost exclusively on the change agent's degree of
power and its acquisition, rather than on accepting and working
with the existing political situation. For Pettigrew and Schein, the
consultant must overpower the current power holders in a macho
game of who has the most power.

This chapter will take a contrary position, arguing that
consultants cannot do a great deal to build their own power base
relative to the power of senior executives and that it is very difficult
to change the balance of power as it already exists among senior
executives. Rather, I will contend that consultants must adjust their
overall intervention strategy to recognize and work with the

established political dynamic. Otherwise, the consultant will be treated as an innocent pawn or a threatening knight.

But I am getting ahead of my story; let me first present an in-depth case description of a consultant's intervention in a major corporation, which should illustrate my point of view. From it I will develop a political framework for understanding better not only the fate of the consultants in the case but also that of those in other consulting engagements as well.

Case of the Retiring CEO

Gamma Industries is a Fortune 100 company with a diverse product line and extensive international operations. In early 1983 the company was faced with a third year of declining profits and the possibility of red ink for the first time in its history. The downward trend had continued despite a large infusion of $500 million from a European investor, which had taken a majority position in Gamma.

Prior to 1980 and the period of declining profits, Gamma had been led for ten years by a dynamic and dominating CEO and chairman, John Amato, who had greatly increased profits, sales, and market share. When Amato retired in 1980, he was succeeded by his second in command, Ralph Hines, age sixty-one, who had been a loyal but undistinguished subordinate. In contrast to the charismatic Amato, Hines was seen as a quiet "gentleman" who had emerged from years of obscurity in Gamma's administrative staff.

Shortly after becoming CEO and chairman, Hines divided the company into two major industry groups, one group representing an industry for old-line products, and the other group including new products in a different and rapidly growing industry. Hines promoted Bill Baker, age fifty-one, to be president of Gamma, and gave him responsibility for the old-line group. Harry Katz, age forty-two, was made vice-chairman and assigned the new-products group. Baker had come to Gamma three years before and was seen as a cool intellectual in the company, while Katz, recruited from a competitor in 1979, was known for his aggressive but warm personality. Hines assigned responsibility for daily operations of Gamma jointly to Baker and Katz, while he attended to relationships with the board of directors, the financial community, and the European investor.

In late 1982 Ralph Hines, at the urging of Harry Katz, decided to replace the retiring vice-president of human resources with an outsider, Chris Miller, age fifty, who had been a personnel director at another Fortune 100 company. Miller was made an executive vice-president and member of the executive committee, which included Hines, Baker, Katz, and James Samuels, age sixty, who resided in London as vice-chairman in charge of international operations.

Miller spent his first three months interviewing executives and workers throughout Gamma. In his report of his findings to the executive committee, he stated that "significant morale problems exist at all levels" and that "few people perceive a clear strategic direction for the company." He also noted but did not report to the committee that there seemed to be a "growing feeling that Gamma was being run like two separate companies." The executive committee directed Miller to look into the morale problem and to begin a program to deal with it. He then began a search for an outside consultant to give him assistance. Gamma had long been a heavy user of management consultants in functional areas and strategic planning.

Through various contacts and referrals, Miller phoned me and asked if he could stop by for a visit. We met and discussed the situation for about one hour, at which point I referred Miller to one of my faculty colleagues, who is well known in the motivation and job design field. I did not feel sufficiently qualified to deal with problems of morale at the factory level.

Miller was sufficiently impressed by my colleague to invite him to make a presentation to Gamma's management council, a fifteen-member committee composed of the members of the executive committee and their immediate subordinates. Miller asked my colleague to describe how a "quality-of-working-life" (QWL) program might be introduced in a selected part of Gamma's organization as an experiment to improve morale and performance.

Upon returning from the meeting, my colleague told me that he had never attended a meeting where "so much one-upmanship was going on among the participants." He said that the chairman, Ralph Hines, had remained quiet throughout the meeting and that Harry Katz had been "less than enthusiastic about the presentation." The program described by my colleague was not adopted by the committee.

Two months later Chris Miller phoned me again to arrange a second visit to my office. On this occasion he reported that "political differences made it difficult to agree on a QWL project" and that therefore he was "looking for a consultant who could work more with the top-management group in charting a strategic direction for Gamma." He also felt that an "academic consultant would not be effective because of top management's skepticism toward professors."

Miller went on to describe the political situation as centering around Baker and Katz, the two heads of separate halves of the business. He said that the chairman refused to intervene because, as he told Miller, "competition between key managers is healthy for the profit center concept." Miller went on to tell me what he had not revealed to Hines, that "Baker and Katz were not taking decisions to Hines." They had instead formed a "Thursday-morning group"—composed of themselves, a couple of key subordinates, and Miller—to discuss important operating issues. According to Miller, "Baker and Katz had little respect for the chairman, and each saw himself as the logical successor to the chairman's job." However, he said that Baker and Katz were not fighting publicly or privately with each other. "They simply do not cooperate with each other."

My recommendation to Miller was for him to consider using Strategic Management, Inc. (SMI), a "blue-chip" management consulting firm that had established a strong reputation in strategic planning projects, as well as an ability for bringing greater strategic consensus to a top group. Miller indicated an interest, so I arranged for him to meet with two of SMI's most experienced consultants, who I thought would be well received not only by Miller but also by the two political contestants. Miller had warned me previously that whoever worked on the project from SMI would have to be acceptable to Baker and Katz.

In an initial meeting with the SMI consultants, Miller described at length his perceptions of Gamma's problems, saying that the company was "drifting in the marketplace." He also spent considerable time discussing the personalities of Baker and Katz. The two senior consultants listened intently and asked occasional questions, after which they described SMI's background and clientele and explained how they would likely approach a study of Gamma's problems. Miller liked what he heard and decided to set up a second meeting for the consultants to meet Baker and Katz.

The time and place of the second meeting were changed four times by either Baker or Katz, but finally after one month a one-hour meeting was arranged. During this meeting the SMI consultants did most of the talking in response to an initial question from Katz, who asked about their personal backgrounds and previous clientele. Both Baker and Katz reacted in a friendly manner, although neither spoke to the other during the discussion. They both placed blame for Gamma's problems on "changes in the industry." At the end of the meeting, as they stood shaking hands, Katz invited SMI to submit a written proposal for a first stage of field research to "ascertain the nature of Gamma's strategic problem." Chris Miller was delighted with the outcome.

A proposal was written and submitted by SMI to "determine the nature of the strategic problem facing Gamma through interviews with the top seventy officers and an examination of financial and marketing data." The proposed fee was $100,000, and the proposal concluded with a statement that "if this first stage goes well, a second stage on implementation planning will be proposed."

Two months passed after receipt of the proposal, during which Miller reported to SMI that he had "an easy time in getting agreement from the chairman" but that it had been difficult "to get Baker and Katz together at the same time to sign off on the proposal." Finally, agreement was given and the project began.

The first stage was supposed to be completed over a two-month period, but it took almost four months because of scheduling difficulties. The consultants had intended to meet informally with the Thursday-morning group every two weeks to report on their progress, but these meetings were postponed three times at the last minute; when they did occur, Baker and Katz were rarely present together. The consultants' reports were usually brief, confined to work steps that had been taken, with substantive comments limited to general observations, such as "We're finding a lot of diversity in points of view as to what the strategy of Gamma is and should be." The group listened with interest and encouraged the consultants to continue.

About halfway through the project, one of the senior consultants, Bob Hagen, happened accidentally to meet the chairman, Ralph Hines, at the local airport. Hines invited him to ride into the city with him. The chairman asked Hagen about the project, and the consultant replied with an informal report, highlighting one finding that "a large discrepancy seems to exist between budgeted cost savings and the amount that key executives now actually believe can be saved." Hines expressed surprise but did not inquire further.

Shortly after the airport incident, Chris Miller called SMI to ask that Bob Hagen be removed from the project because Baker and Katz had complained separately to him about Hagen's revealing results of the study before talking with them. Apparently the chairman had returned to his office and called in Baker and Katz separately, asking them to explain the budget discrepancy; each had denied that a shortfall existed. Miller told SMI that Baker and Katz still wanted to complete the consulting project because of its potential value. A different interpretation of these events was given by the remaining senior consultant, who said, "We had learned too much about Gamma, and lower-level executives were too favorable toward the project for us to be fired; so we replaced Bob Hagen, who had a lot of other work to do anyway."

The project continued as before, including sporadic meetings with the Thursday-morning group. Baker usually attended but Katz was seldom present. When the final report was ready, it was given orally with slides to the Thursday-morning group, which reacted favorably. The report called attention to a lack of agreement on corporate strategy among Gamma's senior executives, as well as to a proliferation of formal systems, such as compensation and budgeting, that seemed to be in conflict with each other. The same report was also given to Gamma's management council with Ralph Hines in attendance. Again, the report was well received.

Shortly thereafter, Chris Miller asked SMI to prepare a second proposal on implementation planning. The proposal was immediately written and submitted, with estimated fees of $200,000, which were to cover further investigation and preparation of an action plan. Within two weeks Chris Miller called SMI to say that the proposal had been approved.

The second stage was relatively uneventful for SMI, compared to the first stage. There were fewer meetings with the Thursday-morning group because of continued scheduling difficulties, but Baker and Katz indicated, in separate contacts, that they were pleased with the project to date.

As the final report neared completion, a sudden and unexpected event occurred: the European majority shareholder moved in to take charge of Gamma. It had acted, with agreement of Gamma's board and Ralph Hines, because of a concern for Gamma's deteriorating profit position. The European company arranged for the appointment of one of its senior executives to be acting vice-chairman and chief operating officer of Gamma. The new vice-chairman was to reside at Gamma headquarters, where he was to make a full assessment of the situation and submit recommendations to Gamma's board and its European shareholder.

Gamma's senior management was stunned by the move, as was SMI. Chris Miller told SMI to postpone its final report on implementation for a few weeks until he could become better acquainted with the new vice-chairman. Four weeks later Chris Miller asked SMI to make its report on implementation to the new vice-chairman. SMI gave its report orally with slides to the vice-chairman, Ralph Hines, Chris Miller, and Harry Katz, who requested at the last minute that he be allowed to sit in. The vice-chairman listened thoughtfully, asked questions, and took a few notes. The other parties remained silent. At the conclusion, the new vice-chairman warmly thanked the consultants, saying that he would like to meet privately with them in a few weeks.

SMI heard nothing from Gamma until four weeks later, when an SMI consultant learned from a friend at Gamma that Harry Katz was "rumored to be on his way out." However, one week later the newspapers reported that Bill Baker had resigned as president of Gamma. Three days later the newspapers also reported that a new president had been appointed from outside the company. The new president was placed in charge of the entire company and reported directly to Ralph Hines. The temporary vice-chairman from the European shareholder announced that he was returning to his London base.

The SMI consultants were last seen trying to make an appointment with the new president, but Chris Miller said that it was too early for a report to be made to the president. Three months passed, and still nothing had happened. The consultants had made over $300,000 in fees, but they felt deeply frustrated over the lack of response from Gamma.

Power and Consent

How do we make sense out of this case example? What caused a major change project to be initiated and carried out for several months without anything happening in the way of actual change? Why were the consultants apparently deceived by Gamma's management, which asked for assistance, acted pleased with the work, paid sizable fees, and yet did nothing with the results?

An immediate reaction from the reader might be that "the consultants blew it by their lack of process skills." As this argument goes, "If the consultants had only confronted what was really going on and engaged in an off-site team-building exercise, they might never have found themselves out in the cold." However, I could retort that both senior consultants had been heavily trained in process skills (one was a long-time T-group trainer) and that they had a track record of success at achieving major change in other large corporations.

An alternative explanation might come from the advocates of corporate culture. Their analysis would accuse the consultants of failing to take into account the intractability of a total corporate culture that had produced executives like Hines, Baker, and Katz.

A corporate norm of individual competition had obviously led to political infighting. This explanation, however, is questionable because Baker and Katz had been with the company for only three and four years, respectively. Also, the individual differences in their behavior were great enough to question whether they were clones of a corporate mold.

Other readers might contend that the case is atypical, but a little reflection should reveal that it is a more common occurrence than many of us care to acknowledge. I reviewed the case with several management consultant friends, and they saw little that is unusual about it. In fact, they were ready to contribute many more examples of failed change.

For my personal unraveling of the Gamma case, I would like to turn to the concept of power, beginning with the power literature. While this literature is quite vast, it is relatively undeveloped when it comes to understanding the relationship between power, top-management behavior, and change.

The most sweeping review of the power literature and an attempted integration of it was recently reported by Mintzberg (1983), in his book *Power in and Around Organizations*. The book's scope and macroconceptual development are commendable, but its definition of power, "the capacity to effect organizational outcomes," is too general and abstract for explaining political intrigue among key executives in a top-management group. I prefer returning to the classical definition of power used first by Weber ([1947] 1961), who referred to it as "legitimate authority," and then developed further by French and Raven (1959, p. 159), who define power as "stemming from internalized values which dictate that there is a legitimate right to influence and an obligation to accept this influence." In a similar vein, Dalton, Barnes, and Zaleznik (1968, p. 41) refer to power as "the potential one individual has to direct, guide, control, or alter the behavior of others. . . . Power therefore involves the desire to use authority to influence others." Salancik and Pfeffer (1977, p. 8) summarize the concept succinctly: "Power always depends on other people."

All these scholars clearly go beyond traditional definitions that confine power to a person's formal position, although they accept "authority" as a starting point. They view power as a latent and subjective attitude toward interpersonal influence that is embedded in the relationship between a superior and subordinates. We can see this shared viewpoint rooted in words like "legitimate," "obligation," "internalized," "potential," "desired," and "accept."

Both the "objective" side of power, which is related to formal authority and its command over resources, and the "subjective" side, which is concerned with interpersonal attitudes toward exerting and accepting influence, seem essential in any contemporary definition of power. We cannot deny that a vice-president in an organization can do a lot of nice or nasty things to a foreman, based simply on differences in formal position. But formal authority is often more ambiguous between a supervisor and immediate subordinates, especially in today's organizations, which are not so pyramidal or arbitrary in their decision-making processes.

Mintzberg (1983) contends that the CEO is "inevitably the single most powerful individual in the whole system of power in and around the organization." While he may be correct when considering the CEO from the vantage point of employees several levels removed or of distant shareholders, the degree of a CEO's power can become more tenuous when considered in close proximity with immediate subordinates. The CEO may, in fact, hold ambivalent attitudes toward asserting influence, especially if subordinates also retain a great deal of formal authority. In this intimate setting, we can expect a dynamic juggling act, as each key subordinate assesses his or her own power base and set of personal ambitions, which in turn are weighed off against each other and the CEO.

Missing in all these definitions is the behavioral context of a social group, especially a top-management group, as the unit of analysis for understanding how the balance of power results in political behavior. It would be naive to conceive of power as a discrete and isolated element that only occasionally comes into play between two people, boss and subordinate. Rather, the members of the top-management group build up a series of experiences together as they observe over time how the CEO interacts with them as a group. They have learned through trial-and-error experience what they can get away with and what brings sanction from the CEO.

They have also learned that it is possible, on occasion, to band together as a coalition to subvert or enhance the power of the CEO. Gradually, over time, a social norm emerges in the group as to what is considered "legitimate" influence behavior between the CEO and the rest of the group. A state of quasi-equilibrium has been established that serves the collectivity of individual interests.

Therefore, as a working definition in this chapter, I will define power as *an institutionalized pattern of influence behavior that emerges over time in a top-management group, stemming from (1) the extent that the CEO in a superior authority position is willing to assert influence over his or her immediate subordinates and (2) the extent that these subordinates are willing to accept the CEO's influence.*

A simplified matrix derived from this definition seems to capture not only the political dynamic at Gamma but also other patterns of influence behavior that appear in top-management groups. Figure 1 highlights the two key underlying dimensions of power noted in my definition, along with four alternative manifestations of political behavior that emerge as the two dimensions intersect. As varying degrees of willingness to assert and accept power come together, we find a different balance of power and its accompanying pattern of group behavior.

The lower-left box, labeled "Peer Rivalry," characterizes the situation at Gamma. Here we find two key subordinates, Baker and Katz, who felt a low willingness to accept the CEO's authority. They excluded Ralph Hines from their meetings and neglected to take decisions to him. Hines even tolerated his exclusion and reinforced it by orienting his attention to the board and other external stakeholders. What emerged was rivalrous behavior between Baker and Katz, who avoided contact with each other, seeking only to build their separate business units. Their personal ambitions predominated over a concern for declining corporate performance. As profits worsened, each party likely smiled at the prospect that Hines would be replaced.

In the upper-left box, "Passive Loyalty," we find a group of key subordinates who are willing to accept the CEO's power, but this power is rarely used. It is a laissez-faire situation, where

Figure 1. Different Political Resolutions of Power in Top-Management Groups.

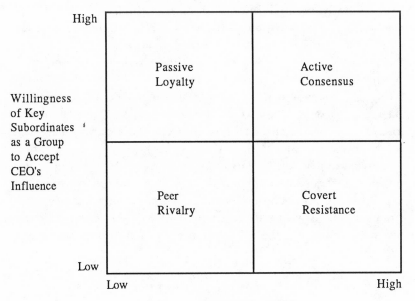

behavior in the group can be described as slow and ponderous as the subordinates wait for the CEO to act; when he does act, they will likely follow. In the meantime, they go on about their jobs within the last mandate given by the CEO. They are dedicated to the CEO and have his best interests at heart, but they move only according to the pace set by the CEO.

The upper-right quadrant, called "Active Consensus," represents a more complete alignment between the CEO and his or her immediate subordinates. Here they accept the CEO's power, and he exercises it. They join together to behave as an active team under the strong leadership of the CEO. Key subordinates are not waiting for the CEO to act, because they already embody the president. What the CEO would do is what they as individuals would do. They have merged their individual interests with the good of the group to create a state of "empowerment" where the group members would climb a mountain together or walk off a cliff arm in arm.

Finally, in the lower-right box, which I call "Covert Resistance," is the consultant's nightmare. Here we find an assertive CEO whose actions are not accepted by the key subordinates. Furthermore, the subordinates are working sub rosa as an active coalition to undercut the CEO's actions. The Gamma group reverted to this box whenever the CEO, on rare occasion, chose to act, such as when Hines questioned Baker and Katz about the discrepancy in budgeted cost savings. This is a group in a state of constant tension, where total energy is expended on playing games to outwit the CEO. The entire organization can be torn apart by mixed signals emanating from the top—the CEO going one way and the subordinates headed in another direction. It is an unstable situation where eventually either the CEO will be removed by the board or, more likely, the CEO will act to remove the subversive subordinates.

Diagnosis and Intervention

The four alternative political behavior patterns indicated in Figure 1 present different challenges to the entering consultant who is concerned with producing major change throughout an organization. Failure to diagnose these patterns at the outset can doom the change effort. Each situation is not intractable but does require carefully tailored actions that stem from a sensitive appraisal of the political condition. Moreover, this diagnosis must be made immediately, beginning upon initial contact with the client organization. Depending on the conclusions reached, the consultant will make several decisions as to who should be the principal client contact and how to conduct himself with this contact and other members of the top-management group.

The consultant's first diagnostic step is to assign the top group to one of the four quadrants of the model I have outlined. Clues essential for this placement arise out of initial observations and interviews by the consultant. The model itself provides a set of general questions to guide the consultant's inquiry: To what extent is the CEO willing to exert influence over the group, and to what extent are key subordinates willing to accept this influence? Of course, specific questions in interviews with subordinates of the CEO will have to be phrased more subtly, such as: "Where do you see the strategic direction of the company headed?" "Has the CEO given much emphasis to this direction?" "To what extent are you in agreement with this strategy?" "To what extent do you see your colleagues in agreement with this direction?" "How often do you meet with the CEO as a group?" "Do you feel that the group is a strong team that is working closely with the CEO?" "Does the CEO get involved in solving conflicts that arise among you?" "Can you tell me about one of these recent conflicts and how the CEO handled it?" The same questions can be rephrased in interviews with the CEO as he or she talks about working with the top group.

Observations by the consultant may be even more revealing. For example, in the Gamma case, the SMI consultants should have been alerted by difficulties in scheduling an initial meeting with the two rivals, Baker and Katz. Also, when they did meet, the fact that neither spoke to the other should have confirmed a hunch that a condition of rivalry existed. Furthermore, the CEO was not invited to this meeting, and his exclusion from the Thursday-morning group added validity to his lack of acceptance.

Once the consultant forms an opinion about which "box" the top group is in, the diagnosis should be refined to determine more specifically where the group is located in the "box." Is the group deeply mired in the lower-right corner of "Covert Resistance," or is it up closer to "Active Consensus," where only a minor issue is causing subordinates to resist? Placing the group in this fashion will aid the consultant in knowing how difficult it will be to move the group toward active consensus.

Next the consultant should develop a clearer picture of the underlying "causes" behind the "box" placement. Here it is useful to classify these "causes" along a continuum from "emotional" to "substantive" differences. In the "emotional" area, there may be deep personality differences of a "chemistry" nature, or several of the subordinates may have written off the CEO as "incompetent." More toward the "substantive" side are differences arising from an understanding of the marketplace or the degree of technological change in the industry. To the extent that a majority of causal factors line up on the "emotional" side, the job facing the consultant is going to be much more difficult, if not impossible. On the other hand, if the differences are largely the result of "substantive" factors, the consultant should have an easier task of gathering additional data to support or refute various positions in the group.

These diagnostic steps cannot be performed in a mechanical sequence, nor can they be time consuming. All three analytical steps must take place simultaneously, and a tentative set of conclusions must be drawn within a few days of beginning a project, preferably before a project is even agreed upon. Knowledge about the political dynamic should allow the consultant to answer such questions as "Should we even attempt this project?" "What are our chances of success?" "Do we have the right person as our client contact?" "Where should we direct the focus of our project?" "Do we need to confront and test certain hunches with the client before proceeding?" "Should our initial agreement with the client contact be renegotiated?"

Let me now illustrate how the above diagnosis leads to alternative consulting strategies and interventions for each of the four political conditions described in Figure 1.

The Gamma situation, which I would place in the deepest left-hand corner of the "Peer Rivalry" quadrant, is a very difficult consulting arena. The CEO is seen as weak and even "incompetent" by his subordinates. They are divided by deep "emotional" differences, not "substantive" conflicts over corporate strategy. More assertive behavior by the CEO over the budget discrepancy threatened to move the political situation into the lower-right box of "Covert Resistance." Overall, at Gamma there is little willingness by the top group to engage in serious collaboration with each other, with the CEO, or with the consultant. They are playing out a political drama that precludes a strong CEO or teamwork.

We can see from this analysis not only why SMI was accepted as a consultant but also why it failed to have any significant effect. The rivalrous parties at Gamma were willing to assign responsibility for worrying about the total firm to an outside party, while they were pursuing their own narrow interests. At the same time, the consultants were co-opted by the political dynamic that existed. They accepted the Thursday-morning group as their client, an amorphous group that paid only lip service to taking concerted action at the firm level. For Baker and Katz, the real value of the consulting study was to provide proof that Hines should not be the CEO.

What might SMI have done differently? I seriously doubt that the consultants could have reformed Ralph Hines, the CEO, into a more assertive and competent leader, and even these actions would probably have been resisted. Team building for the top group would likely have been rejected or engaged in without serious intent. Instead, my recommendation to SMI would have been two-fold: first, advise Hines to remove either Baker or Katz and to place the survivor in charge of both halves of the business; or, second, choose the most powerful peer—namely, Katz—and work with him on his separate organization. A change effort directed at the total organization seems out of the question until the composition of the top group is changed. If it is impossible to get Hines to remove either Baker or Katz, then SMI might be better positioned to focus first on Katz and then work later on total corporate issues, assuming of course that Katz survives and that SMI's work with him has proven effective.

The "Passive Loyalty" box represents a political situation that is more amenable to consulting and organization-wide change. Intervention in this benign situation requires the change agent to build a close advisory relationship with the CEO. The consulting problem is to assess how possible it is to assist the CEO in becoming more assertive. Such an effort does not necessarily require the CEO to change his or her personality; in fact, the consultant may have to become a surrogate CEO who leads the real CEO by the hand. The CEO could sanction a new plan, prepared by the consultant, which would redirect the activities of the key subordinates. However, personal chemistry between the consultant and the CEO will be a determining factor. If the consultant aligns with any of the key subordinates, positive action is not likely to be taken because all eyes are turned upward toward the CEO. They will not act until the CEO acts, or until the CEO sanctions their acts.

As mentioned, the "Covert Resistance" box contains the seeds of a consulting disaster, especially if "emotional" factors are behind the situation. If the assertive CEO is resented as a tyrant, which is often the case in my experience, the consultant will probably get chewed up in the process. The CEO cannot become the client because his subordinates will resist whatever comes down, and none of the subordinates can become constructive clients because they are interested only in actions that will subvert the CEO. Other than withdrawal, one daring intervention might be to go over the head of the CEO to the board and recommend his or her removal. This act would stand little chance, however, if the board is a captive of the CEO. Another naive intervention, in my opinion, would be to initiate a "confrontation meeting" for the top group. I doubt that the proposal would be accepted, but should it be, the personal conflicts seem so deeply rooted that only a more severe crisis would be precipitated.

There is hope in this situation, however, if the "causes" are rooted more in incompetent and obstructive subordinates or if the conflict is due to substantive differences. In the case of obstructive subordinates, the consultant can work with the CEO in recommending that certain subordinates be removed and replaced with more constructive executives. Substantive differences are resolvable through counseling the CEO to seek a new plan or set of policies that both the CEO and the subordinates can reach greater agreement around. Searching for substantive agreement will be difficult because strong differences clearly underlie the present situation. Either side, CEO or subordinates, may have to compromise significantly in order to join together as a united team.

The "Active Consensus" box presents a "good news and bad news" dilemma for the consultant. The "good news" is that the consultant should be able to build an effective relationship with any member of the group, although the most likely client is the CEO and the total team if large-scale corporate change is the issue. In this cohesive setting, the consultant can be assured that concerted action will be taken. Political side trips to satisfy individual agendas will not be a significant problem. If the consultant is working on a subunit issue with any of the key subordinates, the consultant can also assume that actions taken by the subordinate will have the support of the CEO. Unfortunately, this paradise for a consultant rarely is found in a majority of organizations.

As for the "bad news," what if the "active consensus" group is blindly united in committing corporate suicide, such as persisting in manufacturing gas-guzzling cars while being aware that imports are taking over the market? Here we have a case that likely requires major strategic and cultural change in the company, and the top group is unaware of this need. The values and competencies of this group are geared to past successes, not future requirements. Short of wholesale replacement of the entire top team, which is rarely within a consultant's power, what can be done? Here the consultants will have to work intensively over a long period of time with the whole corporation, first with the top group and then with other levels, in unfreezing them from past values and reeducating them in new market demands and managerial practices. This is a job reserved only for a large consulting firm, equipped with an army of multidisciplinary consultants who know as much about behavioral therapy as they know about global competition.

An Overdue Challenge

Top-management politics is a subject about which management scholars have been strangely silent, and only occasionally do we hear about it from political scientists and consultants. We all know Allison's (1971) book on the Cuban Missile crisis, but in the corporate realm there is a rarely cited but insightful article by McKinsey consultant Alonzo McDonald, who states: "If the power center at the top is in chaos, what hope has the rest of the corporation for constructive action? Business cannot go on as usual. Limp, anxious, and vulnerable, the organization is unable to react effectively to new threats. As the contagion spreads, even distant departments are soon infected with pettiness, personal rivalries linked to different leaders, and arbitrary rulings of little logic or importance" (McDonald, 1972, p. 60).

While McDonald goes on to propose a higher moral code for the selection and admission of executives to top management, I am more concerned with pragmatic steps that a consultant can take in working with the political contestants. Too many change attempts with noble aims falter on the rocks of a political dynamic that the consultant fails to understand. Furthermore, the consultant can be misled for months into thinking that all is well and that progress is being made. Only much later, when it is too late for recovery, does the consultant realize that his efforts have been subverted by the power structure at the top—beginning on the first day of the project.

So far the interventionist literature, with its admirable humanistic values, has been blinded to the importance of an astute political diagnosis during the entry process. And the power literature—with few exceptions, such as Pfeffer (1981b) and Kotter (1982)—has neglected the concrete implications for managerial behavior and change in favor of constructing abstract theories on paper.

My immodest hope is that the framework proposed in this chapter, along with its accompanying message, is an initial start in a new direction for research and consultancy at the top-management level. Scholars should seek grounded political theories of the "if-then" type described here—theories that focus on real behavior in a contextual setting. And consultants must begin to incorporate the same systematic approach in tailoring their interventions to a particular political dynamic that cannot be easily altered by a foreign intruder. Senior executives can use such analytical frameworks to gauge their own situations and personal actions, instead of waiting for problematic rescue by a consultant. The overriding message is that universal theories and solutions are relics of the past.

The place to focus our efforts in this search is on the executive suite. Researchers will find only weak explanations for failed strategic and organization change out on the shop floor or in elusive concepts of corporate culture. Likewise, consultants will have to value their political savvy more than big bucks at the end of the rainbow. Future executives, too, will need formal training in power and politics instead of learning the wrong lessons in a corporate jungle.

The stakes are high because organizations must adapt to a new economy based on services, technology, and information. Organization change is an imperative where little slack exists for delay or error. Yet we still remain naive about power and politics, as if science or education cannot be muddied by real-world events. The challenge is waiting for us to accept.

EIGHT

Focusing Executive Power:
Matching Values with Action
Robert T. Golembiewski

This chapter constitutes a kind of worm's-eye-view-of-the-bird, written by a consultant reflecting on a period of intense collaboration with a chief executive. The project was the development of a bus and rapid-rail system by the Metropolitan Atlanta Rapid Transit Authority, or MARTA, and it focused on complex give and take. Both CEO and consultant agreed that the project required degrees of teamwork and transitioning unusual in urban mass transit and that the consultant could provide required technical assistance. Beyond that elemental agreement, a kind of tug-of-war existed. The CEO's dominating interest was in the products of the technical assistance. The consultant emphasized the values underlying that assistance, which derived from what is commonly called OD—that is, organization development (see, for example, Golembiewski, 1979a). For some purposes this difference in emphasis caused no problem; for others it lowered "value complementarities" to such a degree as to warrant dissolving *that* relationship between CEO and consultant.

Ideally, this chapter should be complemented by a bird's-eye view written by the CEO. I even have a title: "Focusing Technical Assistance to Constrain It: Providing Executive Thrust with Time-and-Dollar Targets in Sight." But limited bias it must be, in this case, although other published materials provide useful context (Golembiewski and Kiepper, 1976, 1983a, and 1983b).

CEO Reflects on Costs/Benefits of OD Initiatives

MARTA may be unique in urban mass transit in that its $2 billion-plus program of development (1975–1982) came in on time and within budget, and part of that record can be attributed to the OD program that was begun at start-up and continued in various forms as major system milestones were met. Elements of this experience have been captured in several places, most extensively in a set of seventeen case studies (Golembiewski, 1981). In addition, a set of published articles provide fore-and-aft perspective on the project: start-up activities are described; personal reactions of MARTA executives are assessed after several great leaps forward; and lessons about how to do better the next time around were derived from a project that basically met time-and-dollars targets.

These personal and systemic considerations will only be alluded to here, but they can be reinforced as well as transcended by the recollection of MARTA's chief executive officer, general manager (GM) Alan Kiepper. Four points provide perspective on both the triumph and its limits: (1) four situational goods to beginning MARTA's OD efforts, (2) the focus on the products rather than the processes or values generating them, (3) three critical balances that OD efforts had to serve and/or accommodate, (4) the consciously limited concept of "team." Cumulatively, the points help explain the approaches taken at MARTA, while sketching some of their major costs and benefits, viewed retrospectively. In other words, the discussion focuses on the complex dynamics of constraining/focusing involved in the interplay of executive power and OD values.

Four Situational Goods. MARTA's OD efforts were sharply constrained, even determined, by four powerful situational factors that all but mandated the creation of a "team" of executives, as contrasted with a one-to-one style more congenial to the general manager. First, the immediate past suggested the value of a "lean and mean" central MARTA capability, as described below. The other major alternatives were a thin Authority staff in an organization driven by an external general engineering consortium, as was the initial choice of the Bay Area Rapid Transit (BART) in California; or a large bureaucracy that included its own general engineering capability and hired and managed individual contractors, which approximated the model of Washington's urban transit effort. Soon both moved away from their original model: briefly, BART became meaner and Washington leaner. BART sought a greater set of internal resources to monitor externals; and the Washington property struggled to free internal resources from overwhelming detail, so as to emphasize broad and effective oversight over a general engineering consultant whose basic commitment was to implement rather than make key choices. MARTA sought to go directly to the middle ground—staffing the public agency with (in Kiepper's words) "a cadre of well-trained people who had enough knowledge and experience to make independent judgments on the major choices that had to be made." So "lean and mean" meant a MARTA organization that was relatively small but that had all the major specialties represented by top-flight people who could provide meaningful direction for the consortium of firms hired as general engineers. Initially, the MARTA cadre numbered about 150 managers and professionals, almost all newly assembled.

Second, that cadre of necessity would be very diverse, since it would be composed of people with different employment histories, training, amounts of direct experience in transit, and big-project seasoning. All these contributors to diversity were exacerbated by a uniquely strong commitment to affirmative action, in part because of the central role of the black vote in gaining approval of the MARTA referendum. By that referendum, MARTA had acquired a local bus property and its capable management that could run and expand it. But the basic challenge lay in the proposed rail component of the system. Here local resources did not help much; and the national mass-transit industry—only recently showing early signs of arresting a twenty-year plunge in ridership— also was resource poor, especially as demand had suddenly careened upward. Moreover, blacks and females traditionally had been rarities in the transit industry. In sum, the MARTA team had to be assembled via a series of difficult searches—nationwide, from various nontraditional sources. Because of the contraction of the urban transit industry in the past two or three decades, which resulted in a dearth of manpower, MARTA's search for personnel necessarily was biased toward younger persons of great promise and those near or beyond normal retirement age attracted by "one more project."

Third, rail and bus initiatives not only had to be variously orchestrated into a set of rapid transitions and shifting priorities, starting from a base of little or no common experience, but some argued that it was worse than starting at square 1. The key bus managers had *owned the property*, had become capital-gains rich as a result of the purchase, and had signed long-term contracts as MARTA managers as a condition of the sale. In those senses, the bus management might pose special challenges for integrating a MARTA team and developing a bus/rail system.

To GM Kiepper the basic givens implied a direct conclusion. He recalls the challenge: "We had to make about 150 important personnel selections of first-, second-, and third-level people in a relatively short period of time. It was a variegated group, from all over the country, from various backgrounds—some public, some private, and some military—young and old." The general action plan seemed clear. "I guess," he explains, "the one thing that prompted me to engage in the OD experiences more than anything else was the need to quickly weld this group together into a real team." The times were not propitious. BART and the Washington property had (in Kiepper's words) "been peppered with problems," so much so that there were "strong negative attitudes in the United States toward new rail systems and serious questions in Washington as to whether any new systems ought to be built."

So care in gearing up was paramount and got prime attention for perhaps eighteen months. Kiepper details the prime consequence of "this backdrop of very negative experience": "So we were in a sense running scared. We were the next one on the starting blocks and we were conscious of the fact that we had to be successful, not only for our own sake but probably for the future of rail transit in the United States. So we took a lot of time building a team, and then the OD experience was designed primarily to weld that team into a smooth-working organization."

Fourth, a realistic concern also underlay the multilevel OD activity. Mistakes in recruiting MARTA's cadre were anticipated, and the several OD experiences would help to identify those who might not be "good fits" because they lacked skills or emotional tolerance for a fast-track project. Kiepper observed: "Part of the problem in staffing a new organization is that you make a bunch of initial decisions and then you have to go back later and remedy errors, after helping people settle in. We had probably a 20–25 percent casualty rate, which I think is not bad when you are starting from scratch with a new organization, and given our special recruiting problems."

The emphasis on "fit" had multiple and opposing facets. Thus, all publicly recognized its criticality in a fast-track project, both for individuals and for the employing system. Moreover, prominent cases illustrated that—especially early on—time and resources would be devoted to working toward a "better fit" by changing relationships and work as well as by personnel changes. But the emphasis on building comfortable systems over time became more counterpoint than dominant theme. Efforts to heighten trust, in short, commingled with palpable personal threat. Kiepper put the point directly: "So I think that we were motivated largely by fear—which I have found in my life is a very, very effective motivator." Openly, the trust building sought to constrain the fear and cushion the consequences of most people being severely tested and several having to leave.

Focus on Products Rather Than OD Processes or Values. From Kiepper's point of view, the OD efforts were mostly driven by a desire for "the product"—a cohesive team, knowledgeable about one another's strengths and weaknesses, willing and able to face issues and thus to successfully "push the project." The processes or values leading to those outcomes came to have a distinctly secondary status. To simplify some but not much, GM Kiepper was of two minds concerning the OD activities. He personally nourished and supported them, even relished them, for perhaps two years after start-up. Later, and increasingly as the push to achieve milestones provided the basic momentum, Kiepper transcended or even neglected OD values and processes, his basic commitment being to the project's timetables and the complex agreements underlying them.

So GM Kiepper always luxuriated in those attractive OD values/processes, but he often responded to more compelling necessities. Three stages of this dualism can be distinguished, in fact. They occurred at start-up through the first eighteen months or so, at intermediate phases, and in the midst of meeting milestones.

At start-up through perhaps eighteen months, OD processes and values got major attention. Aspects of the heterogeneous MARTA culture were being quickly formed, catalyzed by standard OD activities: getting to know others, working on values and skills appropriate for regenerative systems, developing less conflictful personal and group relationships, building a managerial credo about how to do business, and so on.

At intermediate phases a two-track model became increasingly prominent—for normal and extraordinary business, respectively. "Normal business" either involved new initiatives mandated in one-on-one settings, characterized by negotiating and politicking, or it focused on implementation of generally accepted agreements and objectives. In largest part, the former kind of "normal business" was encouraged by those individuals who had incompletely accepted OD values regarding owning and openness (characterizing them, for instance, as "charming") or who were "top dog" and hence with variable impunity sought to save time and avoid complexity via closed covenants narrowly arrived at. Then there was "extraordinary business," when "normal business" broke down or was otherwise inadequate, and here OD processes/ values dominated. Typically, the pressure would build, an off-site meeting would be called, ventilation would occur, most attendees would recommit to openness, and (almost always) logjams would be broken by general agreement. An off-site meeting virtually signaled that "the OD lamp is lit." Witness this exchange:

Consultant: I got the strong impression you would call an off-site [meeting] only when things were getting rough, when the pressures had built up to high levels. As long as things were going OK inside, there was not much reliance on "OD technology." But when things went badly, you usually said, "Well, let's bring the troops together . . ."

General Manager: Yes.

Consultant: ". . . and see what we could do."

General Manager: I guess I looked at OD more as a damage repair technique than I did a preventive maintenance technique.

Consultant: Or as opposed to a way of creating a social culture that would persist through time. You had a kind of episodic notion of intervention—kind of a mid-course correction. If things got off track quite a bit, you jammed them back with OD.

General Manager: Yes, that's true.

There was some leakage from off-site to back home, but the flow generally was the other way around. Off-site activities could later influence back-home dynamics, sometimes in dramatic ways (Golembiewski, 1979a). The effects, usually more modest, were, in Kiepper's words, "in making our regular group meetings more effective because experiencing a sharing and a willingness to deal with red-hot subjects off site made us more willing to do it in our regular meetings when we got back to Atlanta." However, most evidence suggests a storing up of back-home concerns to unload at an off-site meeting, particularly by low-power participants. For them OD processes/values remained throughout a vehicle for exerting influence with "less of a chance of getting run over."

In the midst of meeting the milestones, "normal business" of the one-on-one variety came to dominate. The excitement of system openings carried along even the substantially opposed, overall. In this period of over a year, in short, the product was "satisfactory" and OD process/values got scant attention. "Pushes" became the dominant management vehicle.

Three Critical Balances. The costs and benefits of OD at MARTA also can be suggested in terms of three kinds of "balances." These balances involve interdependencies between realms that may roughly be designated personal, political, and technical.

Most immediately the general manager faced tradeoffs between his personal tastes and OD processes/values. From an important perspective, for example, team building suited the general manager's self-description as an "oral executive." He develops that description via a useful contrast: "The way I function is to interact with people on a face-to-face basis. Some people ask for reports and sit down and study those reports and get most of their cognitive knowledge about a problem through reading. I don't do that. My style of operation is to have personal contact and to deal with problems through talking directly with people and looking them in the eye. If I've got a problem, my way of attacking it is to get all the people in the organization who can make a contribution, regardless of what level they may be. I am stimulated by that. That's the way that I am stimulated to think, that's the way that I'm stimulated to make decisions." The connection seems obvious to the general manager: "So I think that the idea of getting people together at MARTA probably was somewhat an outgrowth of that personal style."

Other aspects of the GM's tastes were less congruent with "bringing the troops together." Consider only two features: the GM's "hard-nosed attitude" and a sharp separation of business from social spheres. The former aspect stands out in the general manager's recollection of his basic attitude during start-up: "I hire good people, screen them carefully, recruit them, pay them well— and our salaries and benefits *were good* at MARTA, by comparison with other public agencies. I expect them to do a job, and I don't like crybabies. That was my attitude. If you have a problem, I will do the best that I can to help you but don't come crying on my shoulder. Don't expect me to be a big stroker because I'm not. And you do your job and tell me what you need to do it in the way of resources and I'll do my best to get them for you. So it was a kind of hard-nosed approach with an unwillingness to get involved with the emotional side."

This basic orientation was not tempered, as it is with some executives, by nonwork contacts to counterbalance the GM's work style—for example, "bending an elbow with the boys." The general manager explains: "I draw a very strict line between business activity and social activity. I have very, very little—almost no— social contact with the people with whom I work, even the assistant general managers. . . . So I guess that my nature, my personal nature, is to be a rather private person. But in the corporate or business setting, I do tend to reach out and touch and talk—that's pretty much my style."

These personal tastes and OD activities meshed only incompletely. Over the longer run, for example, perhaps most of the MARTA cadre came to accept the GM's biases as defining their working context. Nonetheless, those biases decreased the emotional component of the social support generated by OD activities, such as team building. Indeed, the conscious bias was on the other three components of social support—instrumental, informational, and appraisal—which not only have double-edged consequences but also seem less robust contributors to social support (House, 1981).

This deliberately truncated social support, in a critical case or two, set limits on the support necessary for key MARTA staff who had left familiar haunts, without such conventional support networks as families, and who for various reasons were not able to meet their nonwork needs in Atlanta. The conscious bias toward specific types of social support—instrumental, informational, and appraisal, as contrasted with emotional support—contributed to the low visibility of some tough personal predicaments. There was the case of the MARTA executive, sitting in the Atlanta airport, determining whether to attend an important meeting or to fly off to a seriously ill parent in a distant city. The meeting won out, and it was only later that the person's anguish became known, for the executive did not feel free to raise the issue with his colleagues.

In addition, the business/social separation did not suit the preferences of many in MARTA's cadre. Those numerous new employees with military backgrounds were the most likely to miss the "clubbiness" associated with their earlier careers, and many others with strong personal orientations also were uneasy with the business/social dysjunction. At the extreme, for example, several prominent members of the MARTA cadre complained of a basic imbalance. OD designs such as task-oriented team building "milked" participants; there was "too little cuddling after coitus"; and so on. "When the task-relevant things were done, *it was all done*," one observer reported. "For the GM, it was mostly take and little give. For us, almost all of the time, it was the other way around."

The general manager agrees with the characterization but believes that it has been modified by experience. "I think that my style is changing somewhat," he observes. "I am less of a taker and more of a giver, although I still think I'm more on the side of taking than giving." He explains: "I am demanding. I used to do very little stroking. I would spend a good bit of time with individuals, but usually to make it clear what I wanted them to accomplish. And I would spend time on my ideas as to how they might accomplish it, although I tried to give them a fair amount of freedom. But this is different from trying to provide emotional support. Now, I think, I approach my staff on a more personal level, trying to see whether the individual is weathering the storm well and whether there are any problems they need to discuss or need support for."

A second "balance" had to do with accommodating OD to political realities. All OD interventions constitute inherently political acts connected with who gets what, when, where, and how in organizations—for example, changing the character and quality of communication in an organization. So it comes as no surprise that some of the more delicate cost-benefit judgments in MARTA's experience involve the political sphere. Two points illustrate this pervasive theme, and they provide (in turn) broad and narrow perspectives.

Broadly, *the* issue at MARTA related to the dynamic interplay of determinedly integrative norms in an environment that was pervasively distributive in character, and sometimes unredemptively so. In politics "folks can be out to get you," especially when the stakes are high, as they were in the MARTA project. So common wisdom encourages "chesting your mitt" or revealing its contents only in quite selective ways. But OD processes/values prescribe broad sharing of information, with publics both internal to MARTA as well as external.

This tension was not resolved in MARTA in any definitive way. There was a substantial leaning toward "open communication," and particularly so at start-up. And the early risks with fostering openness proved at least benign and usually constructive, in substantial part because a blue-ribbon board of directors insulated MARTA from many normal political jostlings for nearly two years. The board gave the GM plenty of support and leeway, and this discouraged end runs by MARTA staff with information to local constituencies. When the original board was replaced by the several local city and county governing bodies that fund MARTA, the new board opened with attacks on the staff, which had the effect of furthering the cohesiveness of the MARTA management cadre, especially the senior staff. As the general manager recalls: "That experience pulled the staff together. We were constantly getting shot at, and we, you know, we circled the wagons. That was an ill wind that blew us some good. I think that experience helped to really pull the staff together. And my recollection is that we had a couple of OD experiences during that period which further reinforced that helpful shove by the new board."

The tension about information sharing nonetheless remained, to be resolved situationally at different times for various actors in several spheres.

Consultant: Do you recall any instances where you said to yourself: "Here, I am busting my gut to share information with people, and they take that information or even self-serving forms of it and make end runs. I could deal with them one on one, compartmentalize a lot of that information, and hence reduce my risks."

General Manager: Yes, that feeling was present. And, to some extent, that's the way I dealt with them.

So the commitment was not essentially to "OD values." Rather, quite specific judgments were made concerning costs and benefits. One decision rule applied. When things were going well, OD values concerning openness and confrontation got less attention. When matters deteriorated, these values would get ushered front and center, generally by both the general manager and the relevant portions of the managerial/professional cadre, but especially by low-power members of the senior staff.

More narrowly, the use of OD approaches also implied costs and benefits. Consider the bus property acquired by MARTA and its once owners/managers who were retained by the newly created Authority. The perceived benefits relate to a range of outcomes that can be considered political. The multiple levels of team building could have helped moderate awkward possible outcomes, for example. Witness this exchange:

Consultant: How about some aspects of that fear? Were you concerned that the [bus management] would become a clique in a political sense—making life difficult for you as the GM? Was team building one way to neutralize this possible clique?

General Manager: That was not a major theme after the first six months or so. I guess I was apprehensive initially, but as I got to know these people, I found that they were very committed to MARTA, not disloyal.

OD approaches also served a range of other purposes in connection with the bus managers and their work force. These included developing acquaintances between bus managers and the new MARTA cadres—which often involved linkages between older and younger people, locals and those from all over the country, those with OJT (on-the-job training) only and credentialed specialists, whites and blacks, those whose normal workdays were at several field locations and those with headquarters offices, and so on. Moreover, various OD activities helped unfreeze the thoughtways of some of the bus managers, so that they were more willing to accept new objectives and values.

These OD approaches also had their downside, from the GM's point of view. Consider contests over leadership. Often muted in organizations, they could be overt in MARTA—in large part because the OD activities provide forums for airing grievances, legitimate expressions of broad ranges of opinion, provide useful arenas for generating support, and (perhaps most significantly) limit the GM's potential for punishing or even discouraging challenges to leadership. Consider this discussion of the general acceptance of the sharp line the GM drew between private and business life, or—perhaps more precisely—between the emotional and technical aspects of work:

Consultant: X made personal or emotional demands on you that transcended business demands. He couldn't work with people who didn't really like him, he said to all of us.

General Manager: To some extent, that's true, and X also tried to take over the social leadership of the organization. Of course, X made no secret of the fact that he wanted my job, and I think that this was one way that he was trying to demonstrate that if he was the general manager there would be a different way of relating.

Consultant: The steely glint in your eyes suggests that you really remember that.

General Manager: Oh, yes, I do. That was an interesting test of wills and personalities that I had with X.

The strongest case for the benefits of OD approaches at MARTA involved the technical realm. Strangers had to quickly develop useful ways of working with one another; MARTA had to change from a bus property, to a basic concern with rail design, then to construction, and finally to rail operations integrated with buses in an urban transit system. The general case for dispatch has been sketched at several points. In specific if oversimple terms, each day of delay in the system would cost some $250,000 *in added interest charges alone.*

But even on technical issues, costs of the OD approach can be reckoned. Thus, sometimes issues would be "stored up" for off-site resolution, in opposition to placing greater reliance on OD values and processes in "everyday business." Relatedly, especially as the project was roaring toward and beyond early milestones, resorting to an "OD mode" could be perceived as dilatory and delaying by those with milestones fixed in their sights. "When we didn't have rail stations," one executive observed, "we had OD. Now we have stations."

Variable Visions of "Team." Metaphors can be powerful channelers of thought, feeling, and behavior, and that certainly was the intent of Kiepper's emphasis on "team." A massive project required multiple technical specialties, creative talents, and political skills and contracts. And these had to be variously blended, at often unpredictable times, for initially unclear or even contradictory purposes. "Team" often meant the *absence* of things: delays, surprises, embarrassments, and so on.

Clarity and consistency of ideas about what *presences* defined "team" varied. Two basic views could be distinguished. There was Team 1: a cohesive and permanent but quite permeable group of individuals aspiring to set and meet common goals while contributing to one another's growth and well-being via colleagueship, caring, and perhaps even friendship. And there was Team 2: a very broad metaphor that was eagerly if imprecisely attached to various *ad hoc* assemblages bringing together people who basically operate in individualized modes until things go poorly or somehow become stuck. Team 2 highlights people who "can take it," who are no "crybabies," who do what requires doing with little or no "stroking," and who (perhaps above all) "keep the flak down" in the process.

Despite major ebbs and flows, on balance, Team 2 it was. The general manager recalls: "I'm not sure I viewed 'team' in either of those lights—you know, I mean as a clear model, at that time." But practice tended toward a pattern: "Give people a tough job with demanding goals; let them stick out there on the point; fight it through; and if they didn't have the moxie to do it, they'd have to leave." A case adds useful detail: "So in a sense Y was on the point; he was our scout out there. You know—the point is a high-hazard job in the military, and in our organization that was an important area. I didn't want any bullshit coming from that area. We couldn't afford it. That had to be dealt with, and problems had to be nipped in the bud, and Y had to be willing to take some body blows in the process. And he did. Of course, it took its toll on him—on poor Y." The intensity of those "body blows" did not become clear to even knowledgeable observers until essentially after the fact, in part because of the general hegemony of Team 2 notions.

But Team 1 had its moments, and the GM sees movement toward it as one of the ways in which the MARTA experience modified some of his attitudes. He notes that he now "assumes more responsibility for being sensitive and responding to tension and stress" on his staff. He adds: "I look at myself and the way I operate now, and I spend a lot more time in talking with my principal subordinates that I observe under stress, rather than closing that side of them off as I used to do. I am much more tolerant now of the fact that people need support, and sometimes it can only come from above. That's the only place where it really means anything, sometimes." The roots of this expanding sense of "team" were intermittently clear to the general manager. "I don't have a strong feeling of guilt," he observes, "at least that I'm aware of." The GM concludes, "I guess a lot of my current attitudes toward people and the way I treat them have to do with mellowing, where I am in my life and career." The MARTA position came to him in his early forties. He left a position that was fulfilling all his early aspirations and for the first time had to build a large organization from scratch, and in the context of major doubts about the very future of mass urban transit. These concerns "were not something that pervaded my being, but they were there, and sometimes intensely so." Age fifty-five is a very different time. He explains: "I remember a line from *The Tea House of the August Moon,* where the captain says, 'I've made peace with myself, somewhere between my aspirations and my limitations.' And that's a pretty good feeling. You know, I'm not going to be the president of the United States, but, by the same token, I've achieved a level of respect in the field of public administration that brings me a lot of satisfaction. I used to run scared a lot of the time. I was very nervous about my job and the fact that it might be in jeopardy. I don't have that fear any more, although I'm sure that conditions are probably as hazardous now as they used to be." Being uptight, in short, can induce a kind of closing off of self from others. An executive, the GM concludes, "can't afford that luxury. I now think that he's got to be willing to have the capacity of kind of setting his own fears aside, not denying them but not letting them consume him to the point that he's oblivious to the feelings of others."

Consultant Seeks to Assess Value Complementarities and to Avoid Judas Goatship

This section deals with when a consultant can ethically provide technical assistance by focusing on "value complementarities." Being a "servant of power" never satisfies in this regard. So what degree of agreement with the general manager's values justified in one consultant's mind the risks to self and others inherent in seeking to help develop a high-involvement organization like MARTA? The technocrat need not ask such a question or seek an answer. He or she serves only as the Judas goat. Recall that Judas goats lead animals to slaughter while avoiding it themselves, if usually temporarily—without any responsibility for that "assistance" and perhaps even without consciousness of that fate.

This section provides no definite answer to the question. But it does suggest a procedure, and it illustrates a personal perspective. Specifically, some areas of strong value complementarity did exist in MARTA, and these areas initially encouraged technical participation even in the face of areas of lesser complementarity. The latter grew in the consultant's mind, however, and eventually led to his separation from the MARTA project, after a deliberate change in the consultant's orientation. The following narrative charts these several comings and goings—providing further context for the decision to provide technical assistance and also adding to the list of the several value incongruencies already introduced—the view of OD as damage repair rather than as preventive, and the focus on products of OD rather than on its underlying values and processes.

Several Strong Value Complementarities. In six senses joining the MARTA enterprise posed no problem for the consultant, because strong value complementarities existed between the consultant and the general manager, as well as between MARTA's demands and opportunities and the consultant's needs and aspirations. First, the MARTA project was a "good project," conceived from its earliest days in terms that included a range of sociopolitical objectives as well as economic considerations. For many people, including both the general manager and the consultant, MARTA was in effect another way of keeping busy in a city that earlier had symbolized its official attitude toward race relations in graphic terms: Atlanta—the city that's too busy to hate. For these individuals the enhanced mobility possible via an integrated bus and rail system had far more to do with avoiding class conflict than with moving people.

Second, MARTA was firmly committed to affirmative action. Overwhelming evidence indicates that the commitment was not just so much public puffery. From top to bottom, MARTA had strong minority representation. Indeed, "overrepresentation" more adequately described the reality: the average minority employment approximated 45 percent during the period covered by this analysis. Relatedly, the rapid expansion of the bus property created a substantial addition to Atlanta's black middle class. Prior to its purchase by MARTA, the Atlanta bus property had mostly white drivers. Subsequently, the much enlarged cadre of bus drivers was basically black, and with incomes that began in the $20,000 range and could escalate into the $40,000s.

Third, MARTA began under great pressure, and this challenge gave added meaning to the project, for all concerned. MARTA became bigger than life: MARTA's record might well determine the fate of federal support for mass transit in the United States. A local sales tax had been adopted to help support MARTA, but the project was impossible in the absence of very large federal contributions. If MARTA failed or succeeded lamely, that might well mean the last major infusion of federal funds for any American city's mass transit. These stakes attracted both the general manager and the consultant.

Fourth, the MARTA team posed a major technical challenge for all. Specifically, the 150 new managers had been recruited by national searches. Generally, they were youngish, with variable experience in mass transit and with little big-project experience. For the consultant this technical challenge had important value implications that encouraged his participation. Specifically, consultants had long argued for a basic strategy in organizational transitions—developing necessary skills and attitudes among the existing work force, which minimizes reliance on discarding people when change is necessary. MARTA posed an extreme test of this basic bias.

Fifth, local cynicism was high, and MARTA in this sense really involved a test of community and regional self-esteem and provided a severe test of developments in race relations for which Atlanta had become a model. Had Atlanta really gone "too far" in its efforts toward racial accommodation? Were too many people placed in key spots for political reasons only? The cynicism came in all colors. The white business community was clearly upset, and perhaps even hurt, by the rejection of the blue-ribbon board of directors that had guided MARTA through the prereferendum phases as well as through the referendum's immediate aftermath. Some even recommended that Atlanta authorities bring in the firm that had built the Disney World rail system, a recommendation motivated in equal measure by sardonic jest and by exasperation with the lack of apparent progress under the "new board." Among many blacks the MARTA project also took a cynical turn, as is reflected in a new meaning for the system's acronym: MARTA was translated by some as "Moving Afros Rapidly Through Atlanta." The reference was to the east-west rail line, which was to be built first. Some saw it as a way of getting black domestics—who often lived in the West End—to the affluent and white suburbs in the east and north.

Sixth, MARTA constituted a classic case study of fast-tracking a project, which required that multiple transitions needed to be made quickly and smoothly. The technical challenge attracted the consultant, who was convinced that fast-tracking was an appropriate mode for numerous nondefense public projects, which, however, might not be initiated in the absence of clear object lessons. Hence, success at MARTA might have broader significance than enhancing local civility, comfort, and mobility. The dimensions of the fast-tracking challenge can be suggested by a chance encounter with the head of a state Department of Transportation. "MARTA was doing nothing we could not do," the head announced, "but it would take us about thirty to forty years." The MARTA timetable called for less than a decade. The issue was not simply one of time. Any appreciable delay in the system's schedule might so raise the cost of the system as to scuttle it, especially given the fears that major federal support for rapid urban transit would wane, if not disappear.

These six value complementarities were reinforced by some positive earlier experiences between the general manager and the consultant. They had worked together some years earlier, when the general manager was a county manager in Georgia and widely recognized as a comer in the city management profession. One intense situation involving race relations in 1967 left the two with a strong conviction that their values in this matter were very similar. The consultant had developed a great admiration for Kiepper because of his willingness to risk public exposure on a still delicate matter, when even minimal native cunning indicated the multiple attractions of discrete silence for political appointees like Kiepper.

Several Variable or Low Value Complementarities. These six strong value complementarities had to be discounted substantially, however; for they were counterweighted by several variable-to-low complementarities, four of which get brief attention here.

First, the general manager—as noted earlier—had a far greater interest in the products of organization development than in its values. On occasion this commitment to OD might appear to be superficial or even narrowly manipulative. "Give me the team I want and need, and I'll promise you anything" provides an apt paraphrase of this now-and-again appearance. No doubt a more benign interpretation applied in most cases. Kiepper merely exhibited a short attention span, which is reasonably associated with his strong task orientation. When one problem was remedied, his focus shifted suddenly to other pressing issues, and the carryover between the situations might be moderate or even low. For example, a retreat might provide senior staffers with an opportunity to deal with a problem in a direct and participative way, and *that* problem might be solved. But the same mode might not be applied to a succeeding issue. In the senior staff members' view, Kiepper had an autocratic, one-on-one style as his preferred mode, with group participation as a backup when things went awry. To the consultant, in the main, Kiepper *was attracted* to OD values and processes, but he *was driven* by task exigencies or apparent exigencies that often overwhelmed or outflanked his real normative interests.

Second, the general manager's approach could be characterized fairly as low on socioemotional or maintenance behaviors, as well as high on task. So he would be a difficult target for the several interaction-centered designs relied on in the early team-building efforts, whose effects in part depend on meeting the affiliation needs of participants. In part, also, the general manager's profile explains the lack of attention to what is often called empathetic or emotional support.

Third, relatedly, the general manager had very definite and stable orientations toward his work. Some viewed this as "hard-headedness"; that is, they concluded it was very difficult to deflect or permanently influence the man in those areas that had become "set." Others proposed that he had a formidable array of personal defenses, even a uniquely impervious battery. However, the consultant preferred to view the general manager as a "cast-iron sponge," in two senses. Thus, everything "went through him"; that is, the general manager was an acute observer and interpreter of both ideas and feelings. At the same time, as befits a cast-iron sponge, very little "bent him out of shape" as a result of that observing and interpreting. Rather than the new data becoming the basis for possible choice or change in the person, to put the point oversimply, the data were seen more straightforwardly *as conditions to be overcome*. This feature implied good news, and some bad. The good news involved Kiepper's monitoring and goading of the project, where his staunchness was never in doubt. The bad news related to concerns about his influencability, which could have the effect of discouraging feedback to him even from otherwise resolute senior staffers.

Fourth, the general manager reflected over time a variable appreciation of OD values, and a respect for them in action. Roughly, appreciation and respect wavered at start-up, were strongest in the gearing-up phases, and diminished swiftly in the final rush toward the major milestones. In the last phase, basic reliance shifted from OD values as guides for behavior toward reliance on "pushes" or "crises" as motivators.

Consultant Resigns from the Project

The consultant's two resignations from MARTA conveniently anchor the three phases. Early on, the general manager agreed to a decision in a participative mode and then unilaterally changed his position. The consultant publicly resigned, on the grounds that decisions could be changed only in the arena in which they were made. MARTA employees could hardly assign much credibility to

OD efforts seen as "advisory only" in cases where they had been advertised as conclusive and binding. The general manager accepted this point of view, and the original decision was reinstated. Several years later, in the rush toward milestones, the consultant again suggested resignation, this time in private. The general manager did not dissent.

In the period between the two resignations, even though value complementarities tended to fall, several factors encouraged a continuing consulting relationship. Paramountly, the project was still a "good project." Moreover, the consultant's role broadened in several ways that encouraged continuing involvement. At the same time, however, the quality of the consulting relationship shifted in a significant way. Basically, while the project parameters were still being formed—and hence might yet be influenced—the reaction to falling value complementarities was not disguised but was directed toward finding viable accommodations between consultant and OD values, on the one hand, and MARTA's needs and especially the general manager's preferences, on the other. As the project parameters became more and more set, so did the consultant's strategy incline toward more preemptive positions concerning value incongruencies. The consultant's second resignation occurred as a result of one such preemptive position. "If we cannot make an accommodation on such a critical issue," the consultant noted, "I don't see how either one of us can have confidence in the other guy's values or views of how the world operates."

Looked at from another perspective, the consulting relationship involves judgments about "using" and "being used." The issues are devilish and the dynamics are subtle, but a brief description must suffice here. The consultant was concerned about "being used" as a Judas goat to encourage extraordinary effort by MARTA employees through episodic OD efforts, a concern heightened by the consultant's growing belief that sufficient and continuous attention was *not* given to OD values and emotional support. The consultant also was concerned about "using" MARTA for his own purposes, in the sense of seeking to maneuver it toward greater attention to emotional support and OD values, absent strong and continuous executive support. "Using" is bad consultant strategy, placing the emphasis on consultant needs rather than on reasonable progress toward greater responsible freedom for those in the system being served. At some point, *both* "being used" and "using" can constitute such dangers that dissolution of the consulting relationship becomes necessary.

Issues of "being used" and "using" often were highlighted in two core concerns, as conditioned and cushioned by the past and positive relationships between GM Kiepper and his major external OD resource. The core concerns were interacting: differences about the guiding metaphor for OD activities and the failure to employ internal OD resources. At MARTA, only external resources were used—for process consultation, surveys, one-to-one counseling, third-party conflict resolution, and so on.

The prime contenders for guiding metaphor have been introduced. The GM favored "damage-control experiences" and the external consultant emphasized "preventive maintenance." Those biases were least discordant around start-up, but the divergence accentuated as major milestones approached and then were achieved. For several years major OD interventions often were sanctioned by the GM as damage control but the consultant sought to transcend that focus by negotiating broader features for OD interventions. Systemic interventions basically ceased in the last year of MARTA's "high" period.

Relatedly, the consultant and the general manager differed about the key issue of institutionalizing OD activities by hiring internal resources. The consultant favored substantial internal staffing, but the GM was unenthusiastic. Again, the differences increased as milestones approached. MARTA's momentum then was such that OD values required a continuing and prominent presence, from the consultant's point of view. "Storing things" until retreats were held became an increasingly unrealistic and unsatisfactory strategy, notwithstanding the general usefulness of the strategy at earlier stages in the project. The general manager preferred as lean a staff as possible; he was concerned that internal consultants might have less independence and hence lose credibility; and he was satisfied with things as they were.

These core contentions were both conditioned and cushioned by reciprocally positive associations and past experiences. The high value of the MARTA project as both transportation and social intervention united both men. Moreover, the consultant had for a decade been convinced of the GM's skills and attracted to his social values—especially in connection with race—in some mutually experienced tough situations in Georgia in the mid-1960s. The GM in his turn generously concluded that the special character of their relationship provided great scope for the consultant: "I had developed a respect for your skill in being able to communicate with, shall I say, both sides of a controversy, or to take a variegated group and be able to establish some credibility and rapport with all of the various elements. And you were sort of a unifying force."

Three Perspectives on GM's Cost/Benefits

This overview can be detailed usefully in three senses, all of which bear on the costs/benefits perceived by the general manager. First, the role of the consultant, or intervenor, expanded in various ways over time, even as the gap between values in action increased. From the consultant's point of view, this permitted preventive initiatives at several levels, and especially so with the MARTA board of directors; and it inhibited the burgeoning of feelings of being used in a narrow cooling-out role. Typically, these initiatives would be seen as mutually appropriate by the general manager and consultant. On occasion, the latter would say to the GM: "Unless you strenuously object, I propose to . . ."

From the GM's point of view, the tradeoffs were mixed but generally positive. Particularly on issues involving the intervenor and the board, the GM entertained questions such as "Now, who does that guy work for?" The GM adds: "Yes, I worried about that— in thinking that those discussions might work to my disadvantage. I might be put in an awkward or difficult position. There is some risk involved. You have to be willing to pay that price." Some details suggest the possible "price," which in the extreme could (but did not) develop into tussles over influence between the GM and the intervenor. Did the GM have concern about such a possibility? He remembers: "On occasion, yes, I was edgy about the board. One of the things that you did with the board was to try to help them develop a sense of their own identity. I mean—what the hell is the board? What is it supposed to do? What kind of accountability standards should it have for the general manager? How should the GM's performance be judged? How should the board establish and articulate policy? How should it judge whether that policy is being carried out? Well, those were all appropriate things for you to be discussing and challenging them to deal with. But they still made me edgy for a while."

Why pay the price? The general manager emphasizes several points. The external consultant might help see the forest rather than the trees, and in that sense could provide the perspective of the person with no organizational axe to grind and not subject to daily pressures, with the narrowing of vision that often results from them. Beyond this point, the GM saw two basic benefits that also implied risks. The GM believed in going with experience, and successful experience in turn generated both greater scope for the consultant and risks for the GM. As he notes:

General Manager: One of the values in having someone come from outside the organization is that they can, more clearly, I think, in some respects, discern decisions that need to be made or areas that need attention. But someone coming in completely cold would be at a great disadvantage.

Intervenor: So you suffer the person because of that possible usefulness?

General Manager: Yes. My feeling is that a person like that is useful to the organization, even though they may at times raise questions and identify issues or heighten problems that I might have let lie fallow for a while.

Moreover, the GM was willing to help build credibility for the intervenor, even if that meant some risk for the GM or for MARTA as a system. Indeed, that credibility often will require such risking. As GM Kiepper explains: "The total impact of the intervenor, if you will, is positive to the degree that he has a bit of license to identify and raise issues, some of which may be sensitive. And that, I think, helps his credibility in the organization. Everybody who is dealing with him knows that this individual is free to raise and identify issues, even though they are issues that the general manager might not want to touch. And I think that helps credibility."

Second, the consultant on occasion served as "point man"—often by common agreement—as the consultant's relationships with the politically appointed board illustrate. Some stabilization of board norms and policies in the long run would simplify the general manager's life but in the short run required a prodding role by the consultant, which the GM might encourage but in which he could not join without exposing himself directly in ways that could jeopardize his role as project head. Here the consultant was given plenty of rope, with the mutual recognition that the consultant, in doing what seemed necessary, might well come to swing at the end of that "rope."

This approach departs from the stereotyped role of the consultant as facilitator only, but it constitutes no long-run substitute for the principals getting on with it. For openers, and for helping logjams get unstuck, the approach has its real benefits as well as political costs. The GM recalls: "Well, I would say that the intervenor was a prod often times, maybe a bit of a gadfly trying to push for certain decisions that he felt were a key to the organization. I didn't always respond to those prods. I guess that when it comes to decision making I have to reach a certain level of internal satisfaction with a decision."

Third, all major participants sought to define the consultant's role. The role specifications included potency but stressed "objectivity," which referred to knowledge and background and excluded narrow self-interest. The general manager circumscribes the choice of an intervenor in these terms: "The person that's chosen has to be someone who has high professional ethics, and he's not trying to take advantage of the situation in order to ingratiate himself with either the chief executive or the board of directors or a clique within the organization. If someone were inclined in that direction and thought that their nest might be feathered by currying favor with one group or another, that would be very destructive. But if a person is objective and has high professional ethics, then I think that the process can be very positive."

A dilemma inheres in this definition of the OD intervenor's role. MARTA failed to institutionalize OD by hiring internal resources, and that (in part) is a consequence of defining the required "objectivity" in terms of the consultant's external status as university employee and research professor. In the short run, then, the consultant's perceived "objectivity" aided and expanded OD initiatives. In the longer run, the externally rooted definition of "objectivity" set limits on OD approaches and values in MARTA.

Nothing Is Forever

So this retrospective view of MARTA ends: OD approaches/ values at once constrained and focused executive power, with attendant personal and organizational costs that may be reduced the next time around. At the same time, the consultant sought to make progress toward OD values while basic value complementarities first rose, then fell.

What does the narrative add? It certainly does not settle the issues of using and being used, or of Judas goatship. But the narrative should serve a consciousness-raising function, and it illustrates an orientation to monitoring the subtle relationship between those "on top" and those "on tap," between executive power and technical assistance. And the narrative adds perspective on the conditions surrounding the fateful provision of technical assistance to hierarchy in engaging human resources and psyches, given the major implications for freedom and privacy that must be balanced against that usually changing constellation of factors recommending or urging OD interventions (see Walter, 1984).

Paramountly, perhaps, the overview provides kaleidoscopic chapter and verse on two themes: nothing is forever; and better or worse can be made of situations. Both themes had been leitmotifs of the several OD interventions, one of which (for example) encouraged caution in a motto alluding to the Crusades: "More went than came back."

This review seeks to support these two propositions with a concrete experience in a large project, which, I hope, illustrates that the extremes of dropping out and selling out may be avoided by risking both of them.

Power in the Bottle:
Informal Interaction
and Formal Authority

John Van Maanen

Ethnographers have a penchant for examining the most ordinary and mundane matters of social life. Descriptive concreteness is an obsession within the clan. From the construction by islanders of an ocean-worthy outrigger canoe to the wary, self-protective tactics of the besieged urbanite living in an American slum, ethnographers seek to present the so-called native's point of view with detail and vividness. Abstractions such as society, structure, and the construct behind this volume, power, are typically viewed by fieldworkers

Note: The research reported in this chapter was accomplished while I was a senior Fulbright research scholar in England during the 1983–84 academic year. I am very grateful to the United States–United Kingdom Educational Exchange Commission for providing me the opportunity to do the research. I must thank also the many officers of the Metropolitan Police Department who made my research so enjoyable. This must surely be one of the more open police agencies, for they did everything they could to make the study possible and productive, including extending the invitation to do it in the first place. While in England I held a visiting faculty post at the University of Surrey in the department of sociology. Students, staff, and colleagues were very kind and helpful to me during all phases of the study. In particular, Nigel Fielding assisted me in uncountable ways. Various readers of an earlier version of this chapter deserve honorable mentions: Peter Manning, Mitchel McCorcle, Edgar Schein, Lotte Bailyn, Gideon Kunda, Deborah Kolb, Andrew Pettigrew, Stephen Feldman, and Thomas Blue all provided useful critiques. Of course, whatever errors of fact and judgment remain in this chapter are, alas, my responsibility.

with some suspicion—not because such abstractions are deemed entirely empty of content but because they are too often invisible, hard to pin down to specific settings, mean different things to different people, and force generalizations from a world of situated particulars.

Ethnography is essentially the science (and art) of social description. It is of great value when the routine practices of some identified social group are of pressing interest. If one wishes to penetrate façades, contrast public and private behavior, reveal cognitive categories, examine face-to-face interaction, or uncover the formal and informal norms associated with a relatively small social system, there exists no better method. If, however, one wishes to take up grand themes—such as the distribution of authority within a society, industry, or large organization; trends in public (or scholarly) opinion on the nature of leadership; or, for that matter, population trends in India—ethnography is obviously wanting.

This is simply to say that, as a self-proclaimed ethnographer recently returned from a lengthy stay in the field (exotic England), I find the general topic of this book, "executive power," a bit daunting. Certainly I have considered power in the abstract before and even written about it (obliquely) as displayed *ad terram* by police officers (Van Maanen, 1978, 1983a), fishermen (Van Maanen, Miller, and Johnson, 1982), and MBA students (Van Maanen, 1983b). But, as a theme in my research writings, only sparse and tentative references are made to the uses and abuses of power. More to the point, perhaps, much of my writing concerns the constraints and contingencies surrounding the use of power rather than treatments of its unbridled force. It is with some trepidation, then, that I embark on this chapter.

As representative of my approach over the years to the study of things organizational, I generally begin with an observed social practice that strikes me as possessing something more than passing interest (that is, as out of place given my own set of background expectancies) and try to work backward, as it were, to the set of circumstances and social knowledge that seems to produce and give meaning to the observed practice. I try to select practices that are, to my knowledge, important to the group studied and therefore likely to be shaped by the membership as something akin to a cultural invention that solves (or is thought to solve) particular recurrent problems facing that group (Arnold, 1970; Cohen, 1974; Becker, 1982). At times more general themes emerge from the description and interpretation of these practices, themes that reflect classic sociological concerns, such as social control, deviance, and socialization. This approach has worked reasonably well in the past—well enough anyway for me to try it at least one more time. It is, however, a modest tactic and one that very much complements my sense of the massive difficulties involved in making general, theoretical statements about the social world. It is also a tactic that runs somewhat against the grain of organizational theorists, who, in their usual rush to say something relevant, say too much.

Accepting the risk of saying too little, this chapter provides a description of a particular social practice, drinking at work; in particular, police officers drinking at work; and, even more limiting, CID officers (Criminal Investigations Division) drinking at work in a British police agency (London's Metropolitan Police Department). Behind the description are two analytical aims.

First, I wish to say something about how drinking is patterned in this police context and, at least by implication, suggest that drinking is likely to be patterned in all occupational and organizational contexts (patterned, for example, by age, gender, rank, specialization, shift, location, and so on). Drinking is, after all, one of the more popular pastimes in American and British life, and it would be surprising indeed if we were suddenly to learn that such a frequent and pleasurable activity is governed merely by personal whim or uncontrollable urge. In this regard the notion of an "organizational time-out" is introduced and used to order my data.

Second, I want to link the observed patterns of police drinking to the distribution and negotiation of power within the organization (and small occupational groups) of study. In part, I want to demonstrate that power considerations are ubiquitous in modern life and penetrate deeply into all our dealings in the social world (dealings that may be sacred or profane, work or leisure oriented, guarded or spontaneous). From this perspective the material reported here concerns the tacit, unseen, and typically taken-for-granted aspects of power. Some interesting ideas emerge concerning the use of power when one examines those sometimes frivolous and lightly regarded episodes in organizational life that are thought by participants to be occasions of good cheer, devoid of instrumental purpose, ceremonial or expressive, and (perhaps most misleading of all) unstructured. "Having a few with the boys (or girls) in the office" is a normal, ordinary activity, but it is one that reflects far more than individual fancies. As the late Erving Goffman (1967, p. 91) quipped: "The gestures we sometimes call empty are, perhaps, in fact, the fullest of them all."

Setting and Method

The Metropolitan Police Department in London employs roughly 25,000 sworn officers. Seventy-five percent of these officers are deployed across seventy-five divisions, with each division carrying (normally) between two and three hundred officers of assorted rank and function. A given division is headed by a chief superintendent. He and his immediate subordinates (usually, one superintendent, two chief inspectors, and one detective chief inspector) comprise the "senior officers" on a division. They are known to the officers ranking below them as the "guvnors." Each division operates within broad mandates, rules, and policy guidelines set by both law and higher police officials housed in district stations (twenty-four in number) or at New Scotland Yard (the "Yard"), headquarters for the Met. But in its handling of the trivia of day-to-day relations with the public, the day-to-day problems of maintaining and operating its technologies, and the day-to-day problems of seeing that its largely reflexive police tasks are carried out, each division is remarkably self-governed.[1]

The principal distinctions to be made within a division concern rank and function. Rank, running up the chain of command, goes from police constable (or PC), to sergeant, to inspector, to chief inspector, to superintendent, to chief superintendent. Function includes a wide variety of specialist assignments as well as the traditional "reliefs" responsible for routine foot and motor patrol of the division, responding to emergency calls for assistance from the public, communications at the police station, and running the front office of the station (affectionately known to all as "the nick"). In practice, officers posted to the nick sort themselves into one of two categories: Uniform or CID. The term "Uniform officer" can be misleading, however. Essentially, it means "not in the CID," even though the particular officer to whom it applies may not wear a uniform, work a relief, or be any longer designated a PC.

The Uniform and CID distinction is crucial. On paper, one way of depicting a CID officer is simply as a police specialist, on a par with other specialists like, say, dog handlers, traffic officers, or homebeats. And, like other specialists, an officer joins the CID as a detective constable (or DC) only after a period of service as an ordinary PC, after passing through a selection screen, and after completing a departmental training course. But to consider the CID equal to other functional groupings in this police agency would be a grave mistake. Historically and currently, important differences exist.

First, the CID is by far the largest special function performed by the Met. Its membership represents 14 percent of the total officers on the force; and, on the division, its numbers account for about 10 percent of the manpower (only about 3 percent of CID officers are women). Second, CID officers have greater opportunity to draw overtime pay and, on average, make more money than their rank equals in most other parts of the organization. Third, despite repeated attempts to "break up the CID," there remains a separate and parallel rank structure within the organization wherein the prefix "detective" is reserved for only those officers of the CID. Officially, the highest-ranking CID officer on a division (the detective chief inspector, or DCI) reports directly to the chief superintendent of that division. In practice, however, there is a good deal of ambiguity (and conflict) surrounding the CID chain of command and its supposed subordination to the Uniform side of the organization. For present purposes it is merely worth noting that an officer in the CID can carve out a rather splendid career by staying strictly within the specialty.

Fourth, and most important, most members of the CID press their distinctiveness by cultivating a separate and exclusive identity. These detectives of Scotland Yard not only have popular fiction, TV dramas, and numerous London legends to assist them in this process; they have a number of organizational conventions as well. CID officers do not wear uniforms.[2] At the divisional level, they typically work very closely together out of cramped quarters housed in the divisional nick. The tasks of a CID officer are highly discretionary, investigating "major crimes" in a fashion that an officer's own style, mood, interest, and skill dictate. Supervision is relaxed. It is, for example, quite difficult for a naive observer to visibly separate the officers from their charges. Ranking CID officers (DIs and DCIs) are distinguished primarily on the basis of the administrative tasks they perform (for example, reading diaries, approving overtime slips, or organizing occasional raids) and the more serious crimes they themselves investigate (for example, rape, murder, or spectacular arsons). Detective sergeants do not supervise but perform the same tasks as the DCs, who, in theory, report to them.

In sum, there is much truth to the CID officer's favorite description of the function, "a firm inside a firm." Separateness, exclusivity, status, and the relative freedom to pursue one's work without direct supervision characterize assignments in the CID. As one might imagine, it is a characterization that provokes more than a little hostility and envy from many Uniform officers.

My work with the Met took place between September 1983 and June 1984. During this eight-month period, I worked three to four days a week as a participant-observer in several divisions of the organization, performing the usual range of fieldwork tasks: formal and informal interviewing; touring with officers of the division; attending meetings; observing police work in various locales, such as the charge and interrogation rooms; collecting official and unofficial documents; going to court with officers; socializing with officers after (or during) a tour of duty; and so forth. Much of this work, except for the focus on detectives, differed very little from previous work of mine and is described in tedious detail elsewhere (Van Maanen, 1979, 1981, 1982).[3]

Organizational Time-Outs

Midway through the afternoon of my second day of fieldwork in the organization, a quiet Saturday, the senior officer with whom

I was chatting about the business of his division reached down to his bottom desk drawer, withdrew a bottle of aged malt whiskey, and asked if I'd care to join him in a bit of a nip. My past experience within American police agencies suggested that such a gesture of friendliness was uncommon, but it was not entirely outside my previous experience. We proceeded to go through a good part of the bottle before we parted, me to go home and he to make his dutiful tour of subdivisional stations and inspect the books. I have, of course, no way of knowing just how often he engaged in office drinking of this type. If subtle disclaimers are to be believed, it was relatively rare. "Nice to have someone visit us from across the lake," he said. "We don't get to exchange views very often, and God knows the sort of talk we've been having this afternoon is good for the soul if not the constitution."

Making my way unsteadily home, I spilled the day's observations and interpretations into my trusty tape recorder and labeled most of the research day a waste, partly because I couldn't remember very much of it and partly because I was convinced that my talk with the senior officer, while cordial, did not get very far. Our conversation, it seemed, rambled on in a boozy sort of way, touching here and there on matters of mutual (and serious) concern but more often than not generating stories which were now only half remembered. We both seemed to take more delight in the moment by providing personal anecdotes embedded in those mannerly ways that polished both our characters. Only later did I come to label this interlude as an "organizational time-out," and only later did I come to recognize just how much there is to learn about things organizational during such time-outs.

Donald Roy (1959–60) has written eloquently and sensibly about similar time-outs (although considerably shorter ones and geared into a far more tightly run, production-conscious work context). "Banana time," "coke time," and "shut-the-window time" were all routine and ritualized activities breaking up the workday for the otherwise highly scheduled human cogs attending to stamping machines on a small shop floor. But, as Roy rightly argued, such episodes allowed workers to attach certain meanings to the workplace and to the social relations that obtained there, provided occasions of mutual support and entertainment, and, generally, allowed for a more fulfilling experience at work than might otherwise have been the case.

Melville Dalton (1959), writing about middle managers in a large corporate environment, also suggested just how frequent time-outs were for those men he studied. He noted that many executive offices stood empty for goodly portions of the midday, while, toward the end of the workday, these offices often hummed to the tune of social interaction made rhythmic by alcohol. Moreover, Dalton, like Roy, pointed out some of the instrumental functions served by managerial time-outs, such as long lunches, business dinners, office parties, and the sharing from a bottle tucked away in the third drawer of the filing cabinet.

Both writers observed that what I am calling time-outs play very important roles in the business of business. In addition to whatever expressive functions time-outs serve for workers, it is apparent in these writings that time-outs are intimately connected to getting the work itself done. By helping to pattern and maintain social relations, by smoothing the harsh edges of often banal and boring activity, and by providing a dramatic stage on which one's major and minor attributes (and blemishes) can be enacted, time-outs are not only valuable but inevitable.

Sociologists continue to depict usefully situations wherein the expressive order, or the maintenance of social relations, seems to be the primary purpose of the gathering (see, for example, Goffman, 1967; Irwin, 1977; Bell, 1983). But—with a few exceptions, such as Berger (1964) and Riemer (1979)—there has been little attention in the organization literature(s) to the time-outs that both Dalton and Roy had in mind.[4] It is curious, too, that—given the recent spate of books, papers, and pronouncements on the symbolic nature of management and the presumed presence of those deep and spiritual corporate cultures created by those who produce computers, soap, and aspirin—little or no space is given to the downtime (or, more awkwardly, the nonwork work time) of organizational life. Aside from the pastoral company picnic where the beer flows freely, the members of the sterling corporate cultures so applauded by Ouchi (1981), Deal and Kennedy (1982) and Peters and Waterman (1982) seem always to be at work, excitedly mixing things up, slapping backs, being creative, and sloganeering. This may indeed be a faithful picture, but we are nonetheless left with a somewhat bland, if not empty, description of what the members of these happy corporate cultures do when they are not zealously attending to the missions symbolized by their respective company flags.

For my purposes an organizational time-out represents a gathering of organizational members during which some of the ordinary social relations and norms of the workplace are situationally redefined. Importantly, these periods are patterned and involve normative pressure on the participants to conduct themselves in particular ways (that is, they are rule governed). Broadly conceived, time-outs allow for discourse on nonwork topics, allow behavior patterns on the part of those present to deviate from those that obtain when they are working, and allow for the expression of sentiments typically unheard (or hushed) during the pursuit of organizational purposes. In most ways, time-outs denote autonomy for the participants (at least of a collective sort) and a general sense of freedom from organizational constraint. Time-outs are temporally positioned in a liminal, betwixt-and-between location relative to ongoing organizational activities and are familiar to all of us. In academic circles the professor in the beer bar surrounded by students is a standard example. The sales meeting that finds its way to the golf course or tennis court is another. And, of course, my pleasant afternoon with the senior officer is still another.[5]

Organizational time-outs are occasions launched by some sort of sign. Typically, there are strong symbols involved. Time of day and location are certainly obvious illustrations. The symbol of interest to me in this chapter is, however, the drinking of alcohol by two or more co-present persons who are members of the same work organization. As MacAndrew and Edgerton (1969) argue in their classic cross-cultural study on *Drunken Comportment*, alcohol has become an almost universal and powerful time-out symbol in a number of societies, the American and British among them. The raising of the first glass, bottle, aluminum can, or paper cup is, then, the sign that participants may take to mean a relaxation of ordinary work rules. Precisely what rules and norms are lost and, crucially, what different rules and norms come into play are, therefore, the basic empirical questions of interest.

Time-Out for a Drink

The materials in this section are presented in a manner that follows Lithman's (1979) splendid ethnographic study of a hard-drinking Canadian Indian community. As suggested by Lithman, I will argue that drinking sometimes allows people to communicate with one another in ways that would be impossible under other circumstances and to do so in a context where they may not be held responsible later for whatever was said and done. I will also rely on some past work describing what has been variously called the working, occupational, or street-level culture of police organizations (Van Maanen, 1974; Manning, 1977; Reuss-Ianni, 1983). Part of this street culture are the relatively well-defined working roles found on the Uniform side of the British police divisions (especially those separating "officers" and "men"). That such clarity rarely emerges within the CID is both a cause and a consequence of many alcoholic time-outs among the studied detectives.

Following Lithman, a distinction must first be made between those occasions where alcohol use is strictly incidental to the activities that surround the time-out and those where alcohol is the central, focal activity itself (and consumption will persist until the participants disband). The former category of events is certainly the most common among the police I observed and, for the most part, the least interesting analytically. The second category of occasions involves those where alcohol serves to bring forth a likely chain of events, certain topics of conversation, and claims of drunkenness on the part of participants. When alcohol is incidental, its presence is usually fleeting and seldom missed when it is gone. When it is central to the occasion, its presence is keenly felt and sorely missed when it runs out (thus calling for its frequent replenishment). I shall dispense with the first category quickly.

The specific occasion for incidental drinking might be a pub lunch attended by six or seven officers in the CID before undertaking a raid on a local villain. From my field notes:

We went to the Boy and the Donkey for refreshments. Most of the men ordered a pint along with the Ploughman's Special, and a few put down two or three pints before we piled in the cars to "hit" Peter Olsen's place. The DI drove the car I jumped in, and we talked over his plans for the raid as we drove toward the council flats.

Or the occasion might be a ceremonial dinner in the officers' canteen on a divisional station. Again, from field notes:

Several bottles of French wine were on the table. After dinner, brandies were served alongside the tarts and the silver service coffee setting. The chief superintendent made a short speech, the district commander another, and the traditional "to the Queen" toasts were uttered. Even the CID officers, despite jokes to the contrary, were well behaved and somewhat out of character. From cocktails before dinner—beer, sherry, or wine—to the gradual filing out from the elaborately decked-out canteen, the entire do lasted about three hours. Everything was well planned, polite, stiff, yet rather charming and pleasant. Unfortunately, some of the guests still had a tour of duty to perform before the workday would be over for them.

Or the incidental drinking occasion may be quite unintended, as is the case recorded below, when I accompanied a sergeant on his regular rounds of checking on those in his borough who applied for a gun license to enable them to keep a weapon in their homes.

Sergeant Weatherwax and I went next to the fairly posh house of an ex-chief superintendent. We were warmly welcomed even though Steve told me he had never met this man before. The elderly applicant asked his wife to bring us three brandies ("never did like port, always went up my nose") and we went to the sitting room. Steve and I gratefully sipped our drinks while the ex-guv told long, involved tales concerning a variety of police misadventures in the good old days ("not like that nowadays, eh lads?"). Eventually, Steve got around to examining the gun pedigrees associated with the various weapons, as well as looking over the suitability of the storage plans the applicant had for the guns. With station sergeant crispness, Steve proclaimed, "All correct, sir" and we took leave shortly thereafter.

As a final example, consider another incident structurally noteworthy for the almost perfect display of asymmetric power relations (fully in keeping with the disciplinary images maintained on the Uniform side of the organization) as well as for the uneasy response of the sergeant involved.

While I'm sitting in the chief inspector's office talking with him about the problems of staffing the special Christmas patrols, Sergeant Lindsey knocks on the door, apparently to ask a question. The chief inspector and I each have a glass of scotch in our hands, and, when Lindsey enters, he is asked to pour himself a glass and join us for a minute. Lindsey does but keeps glancing somewhat nervously toward the still-open door and soon says in half jest: "This will get around the office fast. Me sitting in this upstairs office having a drink. Very hotty-totty like. How can I tell me lads not to drink when I'm having one with the guv?" We all laugh and the chief inspector tells Lindsey he's sure he'll find a way. Much later in the day, I run into Lindsey again in the canteen over coffee, and he tells me he's never had a drink in the office with a senior officer before today unless one counts the hello-goodbye parties (exit parties wherein the officer leaving the nick—on transfer or retire-ment—"puts on a bottle" for his left-behind mates) or the annual Christmas bash (where senior officers serve drinks and food to their subordinates as a supposed token of their gratitude for loyal service).

These examples could be multiplied many times over. The specific event seems to be either a round of drinks in the midst of the flow of everyday activities, which are later picked up again, or a round of drinks offered as part of a formal, planned, and highly structured affair of some sort. No one gets drunk. No one loses control. No one seems affected in any way by the alcohol consumed—although, at times, this amount can be substantial. Any signs of drunkenness arising during these events are likely to be ignored, treated as a joke, or, as happened on a few occasions, attended to quickly (and discreetly) by someone taking the offending officer for a short walk and a long "cuppa" (usually coffee). Conventionally defined roles and duties are respected, demeanor is strictly "sober," and whatever responsibilities the participants carry into the incidental drinking occasion will be carried out by them as well (Lithman, 1979, pp. 123–124).

In these instances it is apparent that situational demands rule the manner in which the alcohol is used by organizational members. When the drinking is over and time-in more or less declared, no one complains or suggests that more alcohol be brought on. The amount consumed is usually rather modest and all signs of drunkenness are sternly discouraged. In the cases of illustration, no one wants a drunk along on a police raid, spoiling a formal dinner put on with some care and expense, acting rowdy in the sitting room of a solid citizen for whom an inspection is being performed, or lurching and leering at midday in the tidy office of a senior officer.

More to the point, these episodes are not the sort that have given the police in Britain and the United States a rather well-established (if perhaps overblown) reputation for heavy, raucous drinking. Nor do these sorts of episodic and casual drinking events correspond to the kinds of evaluations Holdaway (1983) makes about the centrality of "hedonism" and its constituent elements, "hard drinking, brawling, and speeding," as key elements of the British police culture. Nor do these incidental drinking occasions have much in common with the sort of behavior that Punch (1979) regards as part and parcel of the "cult of masculinity" embraced, in his opinion, by most policemen everywhere. In what situations, then, do police officers drink and get drunk?

Pubs, Parties, and Identity Displays

Three different types of drinking encounters can be identified where the use of alcohol seems highly related to the forms of social interaction observed.[6] Drunkenness is very likely to be displayed in all these occasions, which differ with respect to (1) the participants they typically attract, (2) the allegiance maintained by various participants toward each other and others not present, (3) the patterns of interaction and inclusion in the setting, and (4) the turn of events and conversations that develop over the course of the occasion. The men of the CID figure far more prominently in all three types than do the men of the Uniform branches, who, when they imbibe seriously, seem to do so in rather quiet, private, segmented, and less ritualized ways.[7] Women, when they are present at all (infrequently), play largely a background role in these settings and rarely exhibit as much drunken behavior as their male counterparts. There are, no doubt, some structural reasons here too, although they are not the sort that I have the space to develop.

While my description of each of these drinking encounters resembles a self-contained or closed model, situational peculiarities, such as a chance meeting with others not recruited for the original escapade, can change one type over into another. Moreover, some of the drinking situations that begin as purely incidental affairs can turn into any one of the three situations discussed below—such as when CID officers arrange a meeting with an informant (a "snout") in a local pub and the informant never appears; or when, as once was the case, the informant appears well after the transformation has occurred and a full-blown time-out is seriously being worked on, leaving the informant with stories only he could tell.

Pub Tours. Coming back to the CID office after a series of enquiries about the whereabouts of a suspected ("sus'd") villain, Thomas and Colin invite me to come along with them to a neighborhood rugby club for a couple of pints. I'm told the rest of the office will be there and it should turn out to be fun. When we arrive, other CID men are already on the scene, all DCs except for DS Rourke and a couple of odd characters who turn out to be no more than regular patrons of this semiprivate club frequented by the detectives. I'm told by Duncan that this is a CID pub: "just us and local villains." Most of the crowd seem a bit drunk when we arrive. Thomas and Colin soon fall in with the general demeanor at the long table where we sit. A good deal of the conversation focuses on the various, obviously uncountable, stupidities of the Uniform officers: "a bunch of scarecrows standing around in uniform hoping to frighten off some slag."

The frankness of the discussion is surprising as I learn just what last month's Skipper (the Uniform station sergeant) was "done for" (put on report). I learn, too, of the various theories held by the men as to why Probationary Constable Peter Nash never made it to PC Nash. Tales are told of verbals (words put into a suspect's mouth that didn't come out of it) gone sour, of successfully sus'd out leaks within the nick (a window washer in criminal records was said to have escaped attention for years), and prospectively, just who was going "to take the mickey" out of whom. Personal revelations are far less common than revelations about others; but, still, candor is notable as the men cover office politics from their own peculiar perspective. DC Owens, for instance, tells this story:

> "I was sitting in the office working on my fishing flies when that wooden-top Inspector Dorkley comes marching up the back stairs to tell me they've got some yob downstairs just nicked for breaking off car aerials over behind the Rose and Crown. 'Would I care to come down and interview him' he says. I didn't want to go down and chat him up, mind you; but here was the inspector waiting for an answer. It was down to me, so I jump outta the chair [demonstrating some swift moves in the pub], throw the ties on the desk, rub my hands together like this, and say, 'right, Guv, let's go push this little yobo around and maybe he'll shop us an axe murderer. I hope he's a

fucking nignog too, I hate them fucking coloureds.' I
left him standing in his own piss in the middle of the
office thinking he'd just released a nut case on some
poor, unfortunate young lad."

The participants in this little social drama of the pub all
became self-proclaimed drunk as the night wore on. There were the
typical loud voices, some falling down and staggering when going
to the toilet, and, as suggested, some rather blunt talk concerning
the CID's version of the wonderful world of police work. Yet, all
in all, the conversation was mostly able, sometimes witty, and
altogether coherent. Tales were told that had recognizable
beginnings, middles, and ends. By closing time, it was agreed that
a good time had been had by all.

Several days later I had a chance to ask DC Owens what had
happened to that "poor, unfortunate lad" in his story. After I
reminded him when, where, and what he had told me, he scratched
his head and muttered, "Did I tell that story again? I must be getting
on 'cause I can't remember telling you. Dorkley's been gone now for
some time, over at King's Gate, I think. Must 'ave been the booze
talking."

My field notes contain a number of structurally similar
episodes that could have been provided in place of the one above.
A few of them involve Uniform officers from the reliefs or
beatcrimes, and one involves a gathering of collators at a private
sports club. Most involve the CID. There are several points of
interest associated with pub tours that deserve summary mention.
First, the participants are virtually all of the same rank and
function. The only time I saw CID men of different ranks drinking
together outside the office on more than an incidental basis was
during the winding-down phase of what had begun as an office
party. Second, the topics of conversation, while not tightly defined,
center on establishing the distinctiveness of the little group gathered
together and serve perhaps to enhance and reestablish trust among
them. Moreover, sentiments of hostility are focused on traditional
out-groups. For some CID officers, the list is long. An illustrative
list might include (in no particular order) senior officers on the
division, except for the DCI; the Uniform branches; court officials;

women in the organization (often regarded as "plonks, PCs with cunts"); rotten villains (as opposed to "good villains," who "throw up their hands when you nick them fair and square"); and most of the personnel posted to headquarters. By directing "aggro" (aggravation) toward these groups, the men affirm, by contrast, their loyalty to one another.

Third, these events seem unplanned but nonetheless regular. Often they begin when two CID officers announce that they are going to such-and-such pub (on one occasion, to an officer's flat) and anyone in the office (loosely defined) who cares to join them will be welcome. By reputation, this happens two or three times a week on some divisions. These tours often include a series of pubs, and, in the process, the tour will pick up and lose participants. There appears to be a regular core of participants who always go, but everyone assigned to the office is expected to come along fairly regularly. Officers who have not been pub crawling for a few weeks are noticeable by their absence and often made sport of (as aloof, "Hooray Henry" types) to their face by regulars. I never met any nondrinkers in the CID and suspect that, if they exist, they have very thick skins (although I did meet some modest and "smart" drinkers).

Fourth, and perhaps most crucial, because drunkenness is the state participants claim to achieve, they are not held responsible for their talk and action in the same way they are otherwise held in check by office norms. Pub tour conversations take place within a domain of sanctuary and are defined as "drunk talk" and therefore treated (publicly at least) as "too unreliable" to feed directly back into workaday matters.

Office Parties. The party for Andrew's transfer to the Yard began fairly early in the afternoon, about three o'clock. It came about somewhat by chance, since no one knew for sure whether the DI or the DCI had other plans for the afternoon. Everyone agreed that no party could take place without their presence. Andrew had brought in a bottle of good whiskey and a couple of cheaper bottles several days before. Barry had stockpiled his normal supply of beer, and all knew that others would bring more. One ranking officer was well known for always bringing his own port and brandy to mix together, a habit he claims he picked up years ago while up on the

Flying Squad. Collections for replacements will be organized as required, for the office party "kitty" is currently empty—a result perhaps of the busy social calendar of the Christmas season, during which this party occurs. The affair gets going when the DI finally responds to a DC's gentle reminder that Andrew's last day in the office is supposed to be this Friday. "Right," says the DI, "let's go see what's in the closet." Everyone knows what's in the closet, of course, but the signal has now been given in the proper fashion to let the party begin.

Aside from the regulars in the office, other officers on the division are invited up for a drink. The party begins with only six or seven people present, but soon the office is crammed with perhaps twenty-five or thirty people, and others are spilling into the halls and offices surrounding the CID quarters. The CID office on this division is located upstairs, above the charging room, and is relatively distant from the small public areas of the station. But anyone past the front desk would have very little difficulty knowing that there was a party in progress and just where it was taking place. Noise does drift astray, and several times the skipper appears and pleads for a little restraint ("We've got some juveniles and their parents downstairs"). The station sergeant, on interrupting the flow of the party, is hooted at, plied with a drink, mollified to a degree (but never promised peace and quiet), and sent on his increasingly merry way back downstairs to keep the nick running.

There are many ranks represented at the party. Senior officers appear and proceed to pour their familiar and strange brews. One high-ranking Uniform officer briefly puts in an appearance (bringing with him an honorary bottle of wine for Andrew, bearing the label "Chateaux CID, 99% Rotten"). A senior CID officer from the Yard shows up and stays for several hours, as does another from the district. Eventually, most of the DCs and DSs on the division arrive to stay for the duration. Some of their friends from other divisions come, too, with glasses in hand. A friendly barrister drops in, as do several police solicitors (lawyers), who are apparently good friends with some of the men in the office.

As people arrive and mingle, others leave. Recruitment to this party seems fairly haphazard aside from the core group of divisional CID officers. A number of Uniform men are even present.

It is clear, however, that the party group is made up of friends. Persons unlikely to get along with the hosts of this affair do not appear, or, if they do, they are made to feel uncomfortable through the choice of conversational topics. Statements such as "Lemme tell you just how thick the Homebeats really are" (or Uniform officers, or chief inspectors, or SPG members) drive the unwanted from the room. On the whole, there is an open door to these parties, but a good number of guests arrive and depart with dispatch; to them the party is merely another incidental drinking occasion, perhaps a distasteful time-out for the quick caller to the party.

These parties are marked by an obvious emphasis on being drunk. The men swagger, swear, stumble, and put on an ostentatious but convincing display of drunkenness. People are obnoxious, aggressive, and physical and seem to have lost any pretension of courtesy. The few women present are sometimes fondled in meant-to-be-seen ways, but they are mostly ignored unless subjected to bawdy commentary or outright scorn. Moreover, the usual deference that CID officers provide one another during ordinary working hours (or even on pub tours) slips from view. Interaction among the officers is marked by uncharacteristic hostility. Between the ranks there is an interactive separateness in the room as the more senior officers cluster at one end of the room, abandoning the remainder of the party territory to their rank inferiors. Verbal swipes are taken at one another within each of these groups, but such swipes are most notable between the ranked groups. When they occur, attention is riveted on the exchange, slowing down the party and sometimes bringing forth lengthy collective arguments concerning a particular grievance(s). Consider the mutual "bollocking" (verbal critiques) that took place across the ranks:

> "You've got to stop fucking around with this nowhere Peters case, Guv. We've got to show some results sometime. I'm sick and tired of chasing down the numbers on all the videos that have been done in Greater London for the past month."

"Why are you winding me up, Sunshine? I'm doing my job and if you were just doing yours like it's supposed to be done, you wouldn't be coming on to me now."

"Come on David, don't be a cunt. You know everything we've got on Peters so far is dodgy. Its not going anywhere."

"You're the fucking cunt, Barry."

It seems that the question of how officers and men of the CID are to relate to one another during (and, presumably, after) the party is of much significance. It is also a complex matter in light of the overlapping duties, sometimes interdependent tasks, independence, and high visibility of their work (or lack thereof) relative to other police functions. CID officers form something of a clan wherein expressions of distrust or dissatisfaction with one another within and across the ranks are normally taboo. Yet there is, at least in this unit, a good deal of frustration with what are perceived to be low detection rates, uncaught villains, unsympathetic courts, inadequate dedication of the men to their jobs, tight constraints on overtime, odd obsessions of senior officers (or DCs and DSs), lack of skill and loyalty within the fold, the current apprenticeship program, and what is generally seen as the department's desire to "put the CID in its place."

In short, the conditions surrounding CID work make for relatively fragile relations between ranks and, sometimes, within a rank. Each expects more of the others than the others seem willing or able to provide. To talk about some of these matters openly during the course of the normal workday would be very difficult for the parties involved. Communication across the ranks is typically restricted to practical matters of immediate interest. A serious discussion about some of these believed personal and organizational shortcomings might trigger heated debate, arguments during which those involved might say things they would surely come to regret.

Given this microenvironment, the office party allows for some often blunt discourse across the CID ranks. With alcohol obvious and everyone drunk, an officer is not seen as responsible for what he says and does. Higher officers can criticize lower ones, and, more importantly, lower ones can "go on about their complaints" with higher ranks (occasionally with remarkably higher ranks). It is also possible, because of the public venue of the office party, to discuss what might otherwise be viewed as individual "personality conflicts" as if they were work or collective problems; in some instances these "discussions" seem to produce tension-relieving procedural changes (the officers working the Peters case, for example, were asked several days later to move on to some "more urgent" homicide enquiries). Sometimes much-desired transfers seem to result from the mixing and discussion that takes place inside the office party. In any case, participants will almost always claim that they were thoroughly "out of their minds" at the party; rarely will they admit to remembering much at all, other than what horrible hangovers they had the following day. The office party seems, then, to have the consequence of allowing officers with differing and often strong views on their work to talk to each other and, like the Indian participants in Lithman's (1979, p. 133) house parties, to do so in such a way that the results of the talk need not be directly faced.

My field notes contain a number of descriptions of structurally similar affairs. They are, in some divisions at least, rather frequent events, and few weeks are said to go by without at least one party's taking place. Exits and entrances to the unit provide typical reasons for "putting on the bottle," as do debriefings after raids, monthly "management meetings," certain holidays and local events of traditional significance, birthdays and births, and, if nothing else is available, a weekly "do" can be justified on the same principles used by American college students who invent pseudoholidays such as TGIFs (Thank God it's Friday). I never witnessed a party on the Uniform side of the organization (in or out of the nick) that came anywhere close to duplicating the atmosphere, content, and dynamics of the CID parties.

I did see one variation of this "intergroup conflict" theme occur when groups of CID officers (sometimes across ranks) drank with local villains or informants in certain so-called criminal pubs on the district. Here hostility was vented not so much toward one another in the division as toward one's counterparts on the other side of the law. Again, because the social relations between these two groups are delicate (to say the least), information and views are exchanged in "drunk talk" that could not be exchanged otherwise. I was privy to only one such occasion but frequently heard accounts of others, some of which were said to involve the CID on one side and SPG groups, relief officers, or other pockets of Uniform party types on the other side. Some of these variations on the theme are said to conclude by the breaking of chairs, bottles, and heads, a consideration that takes us directly into the next and last category of drinking when it counts.

Identity Displays. In late January I went on a pub tour with John, Thomas, Cliff, and Clive, all CID officers of undistinguished rank. We began by putting down pints in a familiar pub close to the nick. All the assembled are concerned with the way the new burglary screening program is working. The men are not happy with the current screening situation. They smell changes afoot that they do not like:

> "Those buggers [Uniform officers] will keep all the good crimes for themselves. Mind you, they've always given us shit in the past, and it's not going to change now. What winds me up the most is watching those silly blokes go out together on cases and spend hours on one trivial report. They've got a list of enquiries as long as my arm just sitting on Bill's desk downstairs that are turning yellow they're so old. The Boy Detective [a term CID officers often used to denote a particular senior officer on the Uniform side of the division] will be squirming if this keeps up. To top everything off, Bill's got the bottle [courage] to put that note in the Parade Book about the rape case Christain fucked up. God damn Herberts. It's all going downhill. Pretty soon there won't be any CID in the Met, and won't the villains be pleased? Thank God I'll be gone by then. It goes back to Mark, you know [a former commissioner infamous among the CID for his so-called anti-corruption campaign to "Clean up the Met"]. It'll never be the same."

The pints keep coming, and the talk turns increasingly bitter. As the evening wears on, the tired lament concerning the declining status of the CID officer is heard again and again. Eventually, the men, led by Clive, decide to move on to another pub. I bid everyone a drunken goodnight and drive home, thinking vaguely that I've just been on another pub tour. I found out later, however, that the men piled into Cliff's car feeling rather "stroppy" and proceeded to descend on the Three Virgins, a club thought to be frequented by Uniform officers. Apparently no one from Uniform was present, but the men ordered multiple rounds anyway and, according to John, stood around the bar talking loudly with each other about the silly people who frequent the Three Virgins. They claimed to have left no doubt in any of the customers' or employees' minds that they were from the CID. Not only were they CID but they were also not the sort of men who liked being insulted by people who exhibit oddly shaped heads (a pointed reference to the bobbie helmets Uniform officers sometimes wear). One of the patrons was said to have started toward the door during an allegedly moving monologue by Clive, and the others jammed him back on the bar stool with the remark, "You gotta stay put when DC Cooper is enlightening you."

The atmosphere, according to local lore, was electric; and, to a listener, whatever order remained in the club was clearly not the doing of the police, who claimed they were entitled to a brawl. Eventually things were said to cool down as the clock moved on toward closing time and it became apparent that no one else would be arriving for a quiet drink this evening. Final rounds were put down without further incident, and the men again piled into Cliff's car for the ride back to the station car park.

This incident differs in several important ways from pub tours. First, it is readily recalled the next day. This episode became known to some in the office as "Stalking the Downstairs Wally" (referring to a particularly disliked Uniform officer) and was told and retold with relish. It does not possess all the character of a truly legendary CID tale that circulates throughout the department, but, for the moment, to those in the local office, it will do. Second, recruitment to this event is far from random. Had I remained with the drinking party, I suspect that a normal pub tour would have been the result. Third, the four CID men who stayed the course were all rather good friends. Their talk throughout the evening apparently produced something akin to a tacit agreement that things were going badly for them and they should try to remedy the situation. Group dynamics is important here, for apparently a fever pitch was reached and these self-appointed avengers of CID honor decided they had a duty to perform. Nothing could really be done about the situation, of course, since it was the result of powerful forces located well beyond the divisional boundaries. But some protest was possible, and "Stalking the Downstairs Wally" was the form that it took. In essence, what occurred in the pub was what can best be called an "identity display," a demonstration that CID officers are CID officers and Uniform blokes are Uniform blokes. Whatever one is, the other surely is not.

No one in the CID would claim that these men did not know what they were up to when they went to the Three Virgins (although to outsiders they might disguise the meaning that the event held for them). Moreover, in many ways the group behaved in the most stereotyped and unflattering ways to outsiders—the image of a reeling and drunken CID man is well established in many police circles. They tried to start a fight (perhaps only halfheartedly) on the presumed turf of another divisional unit, a unit they were known to be squabbling with over the screening program. It seems that what these men were up to was merely to enliven the evening with an uncontested, familiar performance of the "drunk, tough, and nasty CID man" acting true to form and out for a little fun.

Other similar episodes in my field notes would fit this category. They are, however, in the form of stories told to me by some officers on the divisions I studied. These tales are no doubt inflated and pitched in ways that, at least for the detectives that tell them, cast honor, not shame, on the CID. Some concern the distant, glorious past (the "Golden Age") and some are current. All are told with obvious pride. Exemplars in this regard are the frequently told "Boxing Day" stories. These concern the annual department-wide bash for CID officers, which traditionally is said to get out of hand when officers are unleashed after the main event and go crawling to their most detested and villainous local pubs, there to bust up the place and anyone who gets in their way. Sometimes the "enemy" is inside the organization, sometimes outside. The results of identity displays are the stuff of which memorable experiences are made and conveyed. The features and functions of these displays are seen also in what Lithman (1979, p. 123) labels "ethnic brawls" pitting Indians against whites in an expression of "oppositional ideology."

Comment

What do these various drinking occasions teach us about power and its enactment in organizations? Most critically, I think they demonstrate how central a role power plays in the social relations that mark organizational life. Power is, of course, never limitless; but, even within the relatively loose context of organizational time-outs, the power of a person or category of persons over others is critical when one is trying to understand who does what in various situations and why. Because the exercise of power is, on balance, agreeable yet subtle, and its precise location is very difficult to pin down, there are virtually no questions organizational members can pose that are as vexing or divisive as those surrounding "Who does have power and what benign or vicious use do they make of it?"

I have suggested that power lies, in part, in the very situations in which it appears. It is, in this sense, definitional of the situation itself and, as such, penetrates all occasions of social interaction. Power, then, derives from organization and is exerted, alongside its more familiar forms of overt coercion and instrumental inducement, through the molding of belief and action. Episodes such as time-outs, as well as the taken-for-granted features of hierarchy, provide rough and ready guidelines for proper thought and behavior on the part of the organizational membership. Yet to see these guides as affecting members' lives, for better or worse, requires knowing just what the "true interests" of the membership are. Few of us today have even a remote idea of just how any such thing could be known. Moreover, it is quite hard to imagine how any perspective on "true interests" could be genuinely open to researchers.

What is clear, however, is that power has another face beyond the direct imposition of an actor's will upon another, and this face is usually masked by structure and ritual (Bachrach and Baratz, 1962). The basis of power and the social system that embodies it is sustained, as Lukes (1974, pp. 21–22) rightly points out, not only "by a series of individually chosen acts but also, most importantly, by the socially structured and culturally patterned behavior of groups, and the practices of institutions." In this regard, consider again some of my police observations.

In most respects, senior officers on the Uniform side have more power over their subordinates than their counterparts and rank equals within the CID.[8] Police constables, by and large, do their jobs well within the broad outlines set by the senior officers of the division. They may not like these officers, but they do their bidding. They virtually never talk back, and, despite grumblings for what are seen as the foibles of senior officers, they perform most of their required services in civil and competent ways (at least most of the time). CID officers are, however, another story. They are, perhaps by occupational socialization, a distrustful lot. They bicker among themselves and constantly thwart, with some success, the aims of their superiors. What might explain this pattern?

Bearing in mind that this discussion is a highly relative one, we can approach the pattern by noting first that managerial performance standards on the Uniform side are far less ambiguous than on the CID side. Uniform supervisors have access to many standards or conventional rules of thumb to judge the performance (or lack thereof) of their officers. While some observers may find these standards woefully inadequate, police supervisors do not. The arrest book, the PAS (person-at-station) book, the traffic book, the inquiry book are examples in this regard. By listening in on the radio communication of officers on a district, a reasonably aware sergeant or inspector will soon come to some judgments about who is working and who is not. Importantly, the men so judged will typically attest to the accuracy and (usually) the relevance of such judgments. There is little overlap or sharing across jobs (except in the generic sense of "patrol"), and visible uniforms and insignia support the mostly clear and orderly social relations that keep everyone in his place.

There is little of this sort of information or formality on the CID side. Access to information is personalized and often kept very private. Officers working particular cases are reluctant to discuss much about them, even with each other, during the ordinary workday—for fear of leaks; poaching; appearing to be unduly confident, incompetent, lazy, or lying; or being drawn away from the case at hand (see also Manning, 1980, pp. 218-252). CID officers are even more suspicious of written documents than are their Uniform brethren. Supervisors lose power accordingly, since structurally there is very little opportunity to see what their officers do all day and, informationally, there is little they can learn about what the officers do unless the officers choose to tell them. Commands in the CID, at least those at the local level, take the form of requests subject to amendment by those to whom they apply.

It is very tempting to conclude that drinking in the mannered ways described here is, for the CID, something of a functional but informal equivalent to some of the more predictable and formal channels of communication operating on the Uniform side.[9] Under some pressure to produce, CID officers work in a low information context, under strained interdependencies; and they face, for all practical purposes, detection goals that are usually impossible to meet. Executive power in the two areas of police work are, then, of a very different sort.

Looking at drinking occasions as ritual is also suggestive of just how power relations are maintained, if not strengthened, by organizational time-outs.[10] The incidental drinking episodes represent rather frozen but entertaining rituals wherein power is masked and largely ignored. Both high ranks and low ranks talk and behave on these occasions as if they were status equals in a common community. The rules suggest, however, that the ritual is strictly a reaffirming one insofar as category differences are concerned, for it is virtually always the higher rank who initiates and closes the time-out. Provided one does not upset the interlude by behaving as if the time-out were for serious drinking, the incidental drink honors the common pursuits and interests of distinctly unequal organizational members.

When drinking becomes central to a gathering, ritual becomes more specialized. Pub tours for little groups of CID officers provide occasions whereby they can distance themselves from and contrast themselves to others in the organization. Through gossip, tale telling, and the rigors of joint drinking, trust is at stake and typically confirmed while the values of rank camaraderie are celebrated. Office parties offer opportunities for rituals of resistance as official taboos are momentarily set aside. Evil talk is legitimized, and challenges to everyday divisional routines and power relations are allowed. The framework and temporal boundaries surrounding these challenges are more or less fixed and apparent to all participants; but the mere frequency with which these festivities appear on the ritual calendar of the office and the intensity of feeling generated on such occasions suggest that these parties provide welcome opportunities for persons and groups to dramatize their contrasting interests and problems. Finally, identity displays ritually symbolize in some very concrete ways the common aims and values of the membership. The power of the collective body is of concern here. Stories (Martin, 1982) and myths are created that provide the membership with memorable events; these stories and myths aid in demonstrating and therefore institutionalizing the character, strength, and style of the CID.

All this is to say that power has both structural and ritual forms. An instructive place to observe these forms of power and its enactment is in the time-outs created by organizational members. There is irony here, too, because time-outs are often thought by those who take part in them to be among the least rule-governed and power-dependent occasions associated with organizational life; but, as I have argued, they may be among the most.[11] Essentially, time-outs of the sort explored in this chapter provide support for the status quo of power relations among the membership. Moreover, time-outs stretch power and its uses into a more expressive domain than is commonly associated with workaday matters. Power may expand or contract during time-outs, but it is far from absent. Time-outs may even have much to teach us about who is powerful in the organization and why. Collectively, the Uniform branch of police service, in contrast to the CID, is instructive precisely because it lacks the elaborate and frequent peer group rendezvous, the high jinks of office parties, and the extensive library of heroic tales documenting the distinctiveness of the division.

As a way of closing this chapter, several general points are worth mentioning. First, much of the literature on power and its many forms and uses strikes me as exceedingly barren of those concrete nitty-gritty details about the everyday contexts within which power is put on display. This chapter is, in part, a reaction (some might say an overreaction) to the vacuous prescriptive literatures on power (for example, how to get it and use it) as well as the daringly abstract theoretical explanations for the functioning of power in organizations that rarely provide detailed examples to assess the value of the argument.[12] That the descriptive literature on power remains thin may suggest only that we prefer reading about what could be or should be done rather than what is done. One possible cause for such a condition is the historical fixation of the field on solving formal, managerially defined problems. Abstraction and prescription obviously prosper in these fix-it domains. A look into the cracks of organizations—at time-outs, for example— may be of some use in this regard.

Second, if these cracks are to be examined, ways must be found to harness elements of them that are describable. I have tried here to suggest that social relations and power are always relevant to contextual description. Pettigrew (1983 and in this volume, Chapter Six) argues much the same thing in his call for "contextualist research" in organization studies. The small group may also have to be rediscovered for this purpose, because that evidently is where a good deal of the meaning of power in organizations is constructed, displayed, debated, and affirmed (Schein, 1985). To understand what one can get away with inside (or outside) an organization requires a rather elaborate theory of power and its use (folk or academic). These theories, if they are any good, must be situated ones that involve a good deal of contextual sensitivity (for instance, as to timing, place, local history, application, and risk).

Finally, to draw again on the spirits informing this chapter, I must note that a good deal of the preceding analysis rests on the unexamined and questionable cultural assumption shared by

Americans and British alike that alcohol unhinges the tongue, allows for true exhibits of thought and feeling, eases the flow of social interaction, and promotes disclosure, trust, and warmth. I doubt seriously that any of these functions is performed by pouring liquor down our throats—at least in any direct or causal fashion. What alcohol does accomplish, however, is to bring these assumptions into play such that the meaning of behavior shifts when we are drinking from the mundane and instrumental to the seemingly fresh and expressive. Meanings are discovered in organizational time-outs that are simply not available during time-ins. This is, I think, a good lesson to hold steady when lofty matters of power are discussed. If we can take a statement such as "power is the ability of person A to get person B to do something he or she would not otherwise do" as a meaningful or operational definition of power, then, like the drunk who believes power is in the bottle, we will believe anything.

Notes

1. For various glimpses of how the police task is accomplished, Rubinstein (1973), Manning (1977), Punch (1979) and Holdaway (1983) are superb primers. The best available materials on the Met in particular are found in Smith and Gray (1983).

2. Though they do not wear uniforms, CID officers do wear distinctive clothing. The three-piece tailored suit with highly buffed shoes is popular at the moment. Trouser length, jacket style, tie choice are all matters of considerable discussion and debate among CID officers. They have no wish to be seen as similar to plainclothed Uniform colleagues, whom they regard as very sloppy dressers. Whether one regards the CID style as high fashion or not depends on where one stands in and toward the fashion world itself. The CID regards its styles as "sharp"; for example, no wide, flapping cuffs were to be seen in the office this season. Some observers regard the CID style as patterned after East London thugs; others see it as High Prole. Most CID men would be hurt by either characterization, since they regard the style as rather gentlemanly, a style thought to be firmly set by the amateur gentlemen detectives of Old (very old) Scotland Yard. It is clear, however, that a CID man

would much prefer to be taken as a right villain (a successful one) than as, gasp, a Uniform bloke. Some of these matters came into view during the early days of my fieldwork, when some CID men felt that I dressed like a "social worker." I tried to alter my attire somewhat, but about the best I could do was become a "better-dressed social worker."

3. Following ethnographic conventions, all names and places more specific than the organization itself and its functional divisions have been given pseudonyms. Furthermore, I must note that the consumption of alcohol among the police, especially to the point of apparent drunkenness, is considered something of a scandal, a violation of a sacred public trust, and is thought by many, including most of those high in the police hierarchy, to interfere seriously with the proper performance of duty. Since I report on some delicate and potentially embarrassing matters, all the incidents described here, and the people taking part in them, have been disguised and otherwise modified in general ways designed to protect my informants. For a thoughtful consideration of some of the ethical dilemmas involved in publishing ethnographic data, see Punch (1985).

4. Other exceptions would include Kanter's (1977) consideration of certain informal and exclusive socializing mechanisms in corporate worlds, Trice's (1984) inventory of rites and ceremonies in organizations, and much of the Chicago School occupational studies, of which the Becker, Greer, Hughes, and Strauss (1961) study is exemplary. Current concern for organizational culture may force analysts to reckon with time-outs; but, to date, much of the culture mongering seems narrow and aimed primarily at displaying how a particular cultural form promotes certain managerially approved outcomes, such as productivity, commitment, and harmony. Trice and Beyer (1984, p. 653) soundly critique organizational researchers for their tendency to focus on single, discrete elements of culture (such as symbols, myths, or stories) and note that such restrictiveness violates anthropological conceptions of culture.

5. There were few days during my research when alcohol did not figure into what I was doing. I tried as best I could to stay sober but not come off as some sort of moral entrepreneur. Most of

the time, I could beg off drinking involvements on the grounds that I had business elsewhere. Obviously, sometimes I could not so easily glide away (nor did I always want to). The majority of drinking was purely incidental, but the amount of it that went on struck me then and now as an amount above that to which I was accustomed in American agencies. In terms of drinking off duty, the two countries are probably on a par. It is true, too, that fieldworkers-at-forty are probably more likely to be offered drinks than fieldworkers-at-twenty-five-or-thirty (the ages during which much of my American work was accomplished). Why this is so is an intriguing question itself but one that probably bears heavily on the fact of my having easier access to those higher (and older) in the organization, who also possess the keys to the liquor cabinets and have fewer watchful eyes surrounding them. Police in Britain, as in America, are not to drink on duty. They do, everybody knows they do, and most of the time this causes no complaint. In both countries, however, there is considerable administrative concern over "sneak drinking" and its correlate, "alcoholism." My evidence on these matters is extensive only with respect to gossip and rumor.

6. When examining drunkenness in this section, I do not follow the medical model, which assumes a direct relation between alcohol consumption and certain "mental states." Nor do I think much of the "Dear Abby" effects thought to be triggered automatically by alcohol—effects such as "loose talk," "feelings of potency," or "uninhibited behavior." A number of sociological studies challenge the medical and folk views, especially those views assuming a correlation between drunkenness and normlessness, however defined (Cavan, 1966; Spradley, 1970; LeMasters, 1975). Psychologists, too, have provided suggestive materials surrounding the cultural context of drunkenness (Peele, 1984). Of particular interest here are the McClelland studies (McClelland, Davis, Kalin, and Wanner, 1972), which examined, under highly controlled conditions, alcohol consumption and "power displays." The position I take follows Lithman (1979) and flatly denies any direct relation between consumption and comportment. As MacAndrew and Edgerton (1969) have shown, people have a very discriminatory sense of how to behave when drunk. Thus, whatever inhibitions are

shed during such periods are no more accidental or irrational than they are directed by neuron firings.

7. This is as good a time as any to note that whatever indication I provide about the frequency of drinking in particular domains is, at best, a nervous guess. There is no control on my groups or observations, and I have only my field notes on which to base my rough counts. I trust my data far more than I would a questionnaire, but I recognize their limits as well. In the textual comment that prompts this disclaimer, I am simply reporting that drinking in the office was a very uncommon activity in the Uniform areas of the stations I observed. It took place in my presence on a few occasions, and I heard stories of more. But, compared to the CID, where alcohol was often present, there is little doubt in my mind that drinking in Uniform is not a public or highly organized activity as it is in the CID. For similar views on this matter, see Smith and Gray (1983).

8. This statement should not be taken very far. I am making a relative comparison here, not an absolute one. Even on the Uniform side, one would be hard pressed to demonstrate that the guvnors very often exercise their powers. By and large, much of the police control inside the organization is ceremonial, staged, and highly ritualized (the parades before each relief; the streams of memos and orders that appear in various locales of the nick from senior officers; the traditional visits to the substations, where occasionally an inspector will put his hand on the engine bonnets of Panda and R/T cars to see whether they've been driven lately; a nocturnal tour of the canteen to see who is playing cards or pool or reading). Such ritual is not entirely empty, however, because the work of the division does get done and usually rather well (here the comparison is with the United States patrol divisions). This is an entirely different kettle of fish, which deserves—and will get— separate analysis. The appearance of power is treated well by Goffman (1959, pp. 83–108), and matters concerning command and control in police agencies are well covered in Punch (1983).

9. I yield now to more temptation. Simply linking drinking patterns to social relations may not be going far enough. Several other general features seem to be involved in the calculus of consumption rates. Obviously, the norms of the group must reflect

an appreciation, not a condemnation, of alcohol. This, for the United States and the United Kingdom, is hardly much of a restriction. But, within such contexts, alcohol might be popular when trust is vital to the functioning of the group yet is itself a problematic, variable quality that must be continually worked on and reaffirmed. Liquor may flow more freely in those groups where strong loyalties and identities are being threatened; and, where the belief systems support such causal reasoning, identity displays are made more likely by courage in the bottle. Ironically, the CID is under siege currently, in part because its officers are seen to drink too much, but the siege itself simply amplifies the pattern.

10. To decide on a working definition of ritual from the disputes of social anthropologists is no easy matter. Leach (1968, p. 526) writes: "Even among [ritual specialists] there is the widest possible disagreement as to how the word 'ritual' should be used." I bypass this debate and adopt Lukes' (1975, p. 290) definition of ritual: "rule-governed activity of a symbolic character which draws the attention of its participants to objects of thought and feeling which they hold to be of special significance." This is useful for my purposes, since organizational time-outs gracefully slide in under its cover. Moreover, as Lukes suggests, this definition allows ritual to be seen as a mode of exercising power, because it compels the analyst to specify just what is of "special significance." By drawing attention to certain objects, relations, or activities, it deflects attention from others, and power is exercised in tacit and unseen ways. (See Chapter Six of this volume for a more elaborate discussion of Lukes on power.)

11. There are, of course, acute interpretation problems involved in the study of ritual (Turner, 1969, 1974; Lukes, 1975). The most vexing among them concerns just how to establish the validity of one interpretation over others. The analyst cannot merely accept the members' interpretation (if, indeed, there is one), for this too must be interpreted (Van Maanen, 1979). The interpretation of the ritual time-outs I provide in this chapter are obviously theory dependent (that is, the central role that power and social relations play in organizational life). But these interpretations are not entirely uncontrolled either, since the substantive and procedural details of the rituals are empirically established within

a given context. Fundamentally, however, my interpretation stands (or falls) on the basis of logic and plausibility, compared to whatever alternatives the reader and future research may suggest.

12. There are several noteworthy exceptions in this regard. Pfeffer (1981b) is one, and Pettigrew (1973) is the other. There are, of course, many superb treatments of power in the more general social science literatures, but these are far too numerous to begin mentioning here.

TEN

Power and Participation:
The Coming Shake-Up in Organizational Power Structures

William A. Pasmore

The rafters supporting the power structures of traditional forms of American organizations are shaking. They are reverberating from a quake that began with its epicenters in the Hawthorne works of the Western Electric Company, the coal mines of England, and the factories of Japan. Its tremors were felt during the human relations movement and the later involvement of many leading corporations in organization development activities. More recently its aftershock has culminated in a multidisciplinary, multinational, multipartite movement toward more participative organizational structures, wherein our current concepts of executive power are as much in need of revision as Newtonian physics in the face of Einstein's theories of relativity. Some advocates of greater employee involvement in decision making claim that executives will have no place in the flatter, power-equalized organizations of the future (Kralj, 1976; Rothchild-Whitt, 1979). Organizational theorists such as Bennis (1970) and Perrow (1972), on the other hand, maintain that, while notions of egalitarian organizations are enticing, hierarchies offer the only effective solutions to the many complex problems of human organizing. Is either correct? Should executives fear the onset of employee-involvement activities, or should they embrace them? Who will make business decisions in the future and how will they be made? Will the dynamics of executive power undergo a transformation? The answers to these questions are open to influence; and the actions of executives today will to a large extent determine both what the answers will be and what degree of upheaval will surround the emergence. The tectonics of organizations dictate that a larger quake in power systems will occur; will executives be prepared to withstand it?

This chapter will explore the use of power in organizations by examining the forces that are reshaping interactions between those who lead and those who are led. This system of forces needs to be understood if we are to comprehend both the limits that are being placed on the traditional use of executive power and the shortcomings of participative management as an antidote to experiences of executive powerlessness. Drawing on the literature pertaining to employee involvement and my own experiences as a consultant, I will offer suggestions to those executives who both fear and welcome the changes at hand and to all those who would seek to make organizations more effective and more human at the same time.

Arguments for Greater Participation

To sharpen the contrast between the views of those who support new, highly participative forms of organizing versus those who continue to advocate traditional hierarchical structures, we shall consider the arguments for the most extreme variant of participative design: workplace democracy. Then we shall present some actual cases, which reflect the difficulties that may be encountered as executives attempt to bring about transitions intended to enhance participation.

A quick perusal of the literature on participation is enough to reveal that there is substantial disagreement concerning what is meant by the term "participation." Clearly, the thrust of all definitions is toward the greater involvement of members at all levels of organizations in decisions that affect them. The form and nature of such involvement appear to vary across a wide spectrum. Mason (1982) notes that participation is in reality a multidimensional construct; any particular attempt at increasing participation in an organization must, according to Mason, be assessed in terms of five parameters: (1) scope, the range of issues available for discussion; (2) extensity, the proportion of the community that participates in decision making; (3) intensity, the degree of psychological commitment with which members participate; (4) mode, the actual form that participation assumes; and (5) quality, the authenticity of participation. Mintzberg (1983) adds to this view perspectives relating to who participates and how. He distinguishes between representative democracies, in which individuals are elected to boards of directors to represent interest groups, and participative democracies, in which members of interest groups participate directly in making decisions affecting them. Mintzberg also distinguishes between democracies that involve employees and those that involve external interest groups, which also have a stake in the governance of today's large, complex organizations. Trist (1981) sets out four types of democracy: (1) interest-group democracy, by which he means collective bargaining; (2) representative democracy, which includes the election of workers to boards and to works councils, as is common in West Germany; (3) owner democracy, which includes employee-owned firms, employee stock ownership programs (ESOP), communes, and cooperatives; and (4) work-linked democracy, wherein workers decide how work shall be done at their level.

Because of the variety of definitions and models attached to the workplace democracy concept, it is difficult to be clear about who is talking about what and which results are comparable and which are not (Neumann, 1983). Nevertheless, despite the din of voices chanting different definitions and advocating different modes of participation, the chorus is clear about the values and objectives underlying the movement toward more democratic organizations. The arguments are these.

1. It is now widely recognized that employees bring more than their hands with them to work. As mature adults, employees make complex decisions concerning nonwork aspects of their lives, including participation in our democratic political system. Organizations with traditional power systems fail to tap the decision-making capacity of their human resources, thereby limiting their productive potential. Proponents of workplace

democracy argue that participation in democratic processes within the firm is the surest way to guarantee that human resources will be fully committed to the creative resolution of organizational problems (Elden, 1985).

2. Democratic participation fits with the higher educational levels of today's employees and their desire for greater involvement in decision making. Thus, the democratic organization benefits directly in two ways: (1) by taking full advantage of the creative resources at its disposal and (2) through the enhanced motivation of employees, who gain self-respect as they are recognized for their ability to contribute to the success of the organization.

3. Participation increases the commitment of members to the enterprise (Kralj, 1976). In a sense, participation changes the fundamental nature of the psychological contract between the employee and the organization. In the view of employees of traditional organizations, the responsibility for seeing that problems are solved is clearly that of management. In employee-owned organizations, this responsibility is shared by all. Even with representative forms of participation, the message sent by management that it is sincere about employee involvement is important (Mintzberg, 1983).

4. Although participative decision making is time consuming, the commitment it produces compensates for the time taken, because decisions are implemented more fully and quickly. One manager at Zilog, a manufacturer of computer chips, contends that the institution of participation has cut the average time it takes to make and implement a decision by two-thirds. He explains that under the old, nonparticipative system, decisions were made quickly but could take up to three times as long to implement. Participation eliminates the time-consuming steps of explaining to employees why the decision was made and helping them to understand what they should do differently.

5. Democracy is a means of dealing more constructively with the issues of interest groups that are demanding greater influence over corporate decisions and that view traditional power arrangements as socially unacceptable (Mason, 1982). Workplace democracy can provide open channels of communication between executives and previously disenfranchised groups, defusing harmful

conflicts and allowing productive compromises to be worked out. Likewise, outside interest groups can be brought together to discuss their competing needs and hammer out resolutions they can live with. In this way, workplace democracy can help to ensure that issues are put on the table rather than being pushed under it and ignored. An important potential consequence of interest group involvement is that participative organizations may become more self-regulating, reducing the need for governmental intervention into their internal affairs.

More broadly, it can be argued that no nation can call itself a true democracy if its major institutions are nondemocratic (Bergmann, 1975). By introducing greater participation in the workplace, we ensure that employees are protected from unfair autocratic decisions, just as our democratic political system protects citizens against unjust political leaders.

Thus, executives who support participation may do so for practical or patriotic reasons. Some social scientists, however, support participation for more ideological reasons. Beginning with early experiments by religious groups in communal living, and later drawing on the writings of Marx, participation has taken its strength from visions of utopian societies, in which the individual becomes fully developed in the course of helping the community to develop (Nord, 1977). The utopian community includes equal opportunity for individuals to lead and to follow; full and open self-expression; individual autonomy with the underlying support of communal interdependence; the pursuit of happiness in addition to the satisfaction of basic needs; collaborative decision making; continual evolution toward a more perfect society; opportunities for learning and self-actualization; the absence of coercive control or punishment; free and informed choice; the absence of dogma but the presence of shared beliefs and values; the sharing of resources; care for the weak and aged; the harmonious blending of work and life; the valuing of differences with the simultaneous recognition of fundamental similarities; the absence of class distinctions; and, most important, shared governance.

To some the utopian ideals of participation are synonymous with the American dream; for others the norms and values of the utopian society conflict with many tenets of the free enterprise system, such as rugged individualism, competition, making it to the top, and survival of the fittest. Staunch capitalists accuse those who favor greater participation of spreading Marxism, while advocates of workplace democracy explain that worker-controlled organizations have always been a part of our economy and operate in competition with other firms; few would accuse small, family-owned businesses of undermining capitalism, for example. Workplace democracy simply extends the entrepreneurial spirit to larger firms, such as Wierton Steel with its 7,000 employees. The resistance of some executives to participative structures is perhaps better explained by their discomfort with the fact that there is little room for executive power in utopian societies, unless sanctioned by the collectivity. Underlying the movement toward participation is an implied statement that our current modes of doing business, running our government, and managing our society need to change in order to allow the full expression of individual abilities and the total realization of our collective potential. This message can be frightening to those who fear that such changes will usurp the control they have struggled to attain.

However, as noted by Webster, the definition of utopia is "an impractical scheme for social improvement" and the definition of utopian socialization is "socialism based on a belief that social ownership of the means of production can be achieved by voluntary and peaceful surrender of their holdings by propertied groups." As long as participation is viewed as utopian socialism, it will continue to be dismissed by many as impractical.

Difficulties with Participation

Most of my own work has involved the introduction of participative processes in new and established organizations. I am, therefore, an advocate of increasing participation as a means of improving organizational effectiveness. Nevertheless, the difficulties I have witnessed in several attempts to increase organizational participation lead me to the conclusion that we have much to learn about creating effective participative systems.

The three short cases that follow are representative of what I believe to be commonplace efforts to enhance organizational participation. In discussions with managers and colleagues, I have found that some of the same issues raised in these cases have affected the outcomes of their efforts as well. Thus, it may be possible to draw some preliminary conclusions from these cases regarding difficulties that may be experienced in moving toward more participative systems.

The first case, in a food-processing facility, was instigated by corporate pressure placed on the plant manager to experiment with innovative work design. As noted by Kanter (1983) such a beginning is not unusual; many OD projects begin as something that the top orders the middle to do for the bottom. Despite his initial resistance and that of the union, the plant manager did eventually succeed in redesigning work in the plant. Employees were granted more autonomy and were involved in many decisions previously reserved for management. Employees expressed satisfaction with the changes that took place and labor-management relations grew more cooperative. Productivity soared. Nevertheless, some time later, the corporation reversed its posture and withdrew support for the innovations that had been introduced. The lack of uniformity across its manufacturing locations was creating problems in corporate planning and control systems. The plant manager was directed to return the operation to its traditional design. Despite employee protests, the plant gradually resumed "normal" operations.

In a second case, the manager of a data-processing facility wanted to experiment with more participative management techniques. He anticipated resistance from his middle managers who had little experience or training in participative management; he failed to anticipate that employees would prove as resistant to the changes as his managers. The computer programmers who worked in the organization viewed themselves as autonomous professionals and preferred to work alone. The thought of meeting in groups to discuss the work they were doing was not attractive to them; at best they felt it would be a waste of time—at worst, an invasion of privacy.

The manager would not retreat. He maintained pressure on his immediate subordinates to introduce participative processes and took every opportunity to explain his views to disgruntled employees. Gradually, over a period of nearly three years, the organization began to change. The performance of the organization improved. More important, in an industry that is plagued by turnover, some employees who had made plans to leave the organization asked if they could stay on.

Eventually, the manager retired. His replacement, being unfamiliar with participative approaches to management, felt uncomfortable with the arrangements he encountered in the organization. He took steps to tighten control systems and reassert the authority of middle managers. Some employees left, but most simply acquiesced to the new manager's style, just as they had adapted to the participative changes introduced by their former boss.

In a third case, this time in a hospital setting, a group of employees, administrators, and physicians was assembled to study ways of improving the cost effectiveness of laboratory services. The group noted that the introduction of new technology that automated testing procedures had left many technicians overqualified and underutilized for the work they now performed. The group suggested several ways that the excess talents of these individuals could be used to enhance the service provided by the laboratory.

The director of the laboratory reviewed the group's suggestions. He noted that the goal of the participative exercise was to reduce costs, not to improve the jobs of technicians. If technicians were overqualified and underutilized, the more sensible solution would be to replace as many of these individuals as possible with less-skilled, lower-paid employees. Although he did not actually carry out his plan, the group felt betrayed. The participative process had not changed anything; in fact, it had made things worse.

Several points of commonality exist among the cases. First, none of the interventions described dealt adequately with the issue of power. The power holders in each case decided the fate of the interventions from month to month and year to year. In the first case, the corporation decided to begin the process of change and then decided to stop it; in the second case, one director introduced the change, and the next eliminated it; in the third case, changes were never introduced at all because the data pointed to a less threatening solution for the client who had commissioned the study in the first place. In all three cases, employees in the organization were adaptive to the changes rather than proactive in initiating them. In each organization a few employees were strongly supportive, but just as many resisted the changes. In all three cases, most of the employees were neither excited by nor set against the changes; they were willing to bend with the prevailing wind. As Hackman and Oldham (1980) point out, human beings are remarkably adaptive creatures who are able to function normally after experiencing wars, deaths of loved ones, relocations, natural disasters, and other calamities; changes in the workplace are much less traumatic in comparison. Many employees simply are not that interested in change, even if it is intended to benefit them. If changes occur, the majority will adapt to them; and if there are no changes, life will go on. Executives like the director of the data-processing organization are often puzzled by the lack of enthusiastic participation in the change process by those whom the process is intended to benefit.

Beyond just these three cases, I have observed a number of other stumbling blocks in attempts to enhance organizational participation. Some who control capital resources are concerned more with producing short-term results, cutting costs, and getting the job done than with taking time to address social and organizational issues that emerge during the change process. Even when time is taken to allow employees to participate, the process too often produces frustration. Representative groups get bogged down in their own internal affairs; those not directly involved feel little ownership in the work of such groups; and the excitement generated during group discussions is seldom duplicated when ideas are implemented sometime later. Moreover, employees take more interest in the issues that affect them directly and less in global issues of organizational governance. Employees who attempt to participate in decisions on global issues are seldom prepared to do so; they lack the same information, training, and experience possessed by managers. Consequently, they frequently allow managers to dominate joint discussions. Thus, without additional training for employees, some participative organizations may in actuality be making decisions in a nonparticipative fashion. Even if these issues are addressed, there are a number of reasons why introducing more participative processes is problematic.

1. It is impossible for everyone to be involved in every decision without paralyzing an organization. Moreover, when specialized expertise exists, it should be brought to bear on problems. There will always be a conflict between the utopian ideal of total participation and the need for decisions to be made quickly and correctly.

2. Participation can also serve as a disincentive to those who prefer to work alone or who have their sights set on their own advancement. Participation, and the equality it implies, may be distasteful to those accustomed to individual competition in traditional hierarchical settings.

3. As a greater number of decisions are made democratically, organizations can become more rather than less bureaucratic (Garson, 1977). Once the right to make a decision is shared, the right to change the decision also becomes shared. In this way, an increasing number of decisions must be made through cumbersome participative processes that are themselves difficult to change.

4. Participation is not an antidote for every organizational ill. In some cases, external conditions may make success difficult or impossible under any circumstances. Rath Packing and South Bend Lathe employees discovered this; after they bought their companies from the former owners, their self-appointed leaders could do little to save the companies from the extreme competition they faced.

5. Participation does not guarantee that everyone will view the decisions made to be fair. Whenever there are different positions, decisions will benefit some and harm others. Participation in difficult decisions, such as who should work overtime, who should be laid off, or how profits should be distributed can lead to frustration with the participative process and tension among parties to the decisions.

6. Participation is not always rewarded. Superiors often evaluate subordinates more on the results they achieve than on their styles of management. Even when participation does produce

superior results, managers may find that their superiors are uncomfortable with participative approaches and therefore fail to recognize the results achieved.

7. The traditional use of power by executives also fits better with the highly engineered, fractionated, and specialized systems used by many organizations to turn inputs into outputs. Long-linked technologies—in which simple tasks are performed repetitively and coordination is achieved through standardization, regulation, and bureaucratization—leave little room for anyone, including executives, to make changes in how things are done (Mintzberg, 1983). The organizations that executives manage today reflect the influence of extreme specialization in work design, attempts to reap benefits from economies of scale, and long histories of adversarial relations between labor and management. Many executives who would like to experiment with innovative uses of their power find doing so difficult under these circumstances (Kanter, 1977, 1983). Given investments in capital and careers, Hackman (1978) states that it may be several decades before a fundamental shift in the use of power occurs.

8. In the meantime, there is reason to believe that many traditionally oriented executives, with power and resources at their disposal, will use a variety of methods to reinforce their authority. Even organization development, which is based on values of power equalization and the mature treatment of organizational members at all levels, can be viewed as strengthening the power of traditional managers by providing them with greater control over their subordinates, while still allowing important decisions to be made unilaterally (Elden, 1985). Many OD interventions are aimed at lower organizational levels, leaving power structures untouched. Few consultants in this country practice participatory research (Brown and Tandon, 1983), in which the powerless are mobilized to confront the powerful in order to bring about systemic change. Most consultants prefer to work through power structures (ostensibly because they have been taught to "start at the top" but also because elites can afford to pay) rather than against them. Thus, traditional leaders find support from many quarters, including behavioral scientists who on the one hand urge them to

give up traditional practices but, on the other, work with them to help maintain the status quo.

9. The war against traditional management is not particularly evident at lower levels of organizations either, where one would expect to find battle lines clearly drawn between the haves and have-nots. While American values strongly support equality, they also support individual initiative. In the land of opportunity, Horatio Alger still sets the example, and anyone can become president. Have-nots are taught that it is not the system that is at fault for their lack of success but, rather, their own lack of initiative; what one gets is what one deserves. This pertains to work as well; to admit dissatisfaction with one's job is to admit dissatisfaction with oneself for not taking steps to change the situation. The end result is that most people report being satisfied with their jobs and see little value in changing the status quo (Hackman and Oldham, 1980).

10. Finally, the case for maintaining traditional patterns of power distribution in organizations has been strengthened by several authors who view executives as symbols or carriers of organizational culture. Bennis (1983) speaks of the transformative power of the executive, which he defines as the ability of a leader to translate intention into reality and sustain it. Top executives with transformative powers create compelling visions, which inspire others to act; communicate these visions clearly and convincingly; maintain a laser-like focus on the objectives they have set out to accomplish; empower others to use their abilities to achieve the desired outcomes; and constantly review what is happening in order to make adjustments in plans as necessary. Similarly, Peters and Waterman (1982) maintain that excellent companies are run by executives who use a "hands-on, value-driven" approach that is action oriented, supports entrepreneurism, maintains close contact with customers, emphasizes the achievement of productivity through people, and allows for plenty of time for "MBWA"—management by walking around. Clearly, if an organization is fortunate enough to have a leader who can accomplish all these things, it would be foolish to replace that person with an inexperienced, indecisive, internally conflicted committee of representatives elected by 51 percent of the work force.

Managing the Transition to More Participative Structures

Clearly, there are compelling arguments both for and against increasing participation in organizations. Ultimately, the decision to move toward more participative structures must itself be a participative one, involving those who will either resist the change or help it to happen. If the decision is made to move toward a more participative organization, the transition will not be automatic. The transition involves at least four predictable stages, which are depicted in Figure 1.

**Figure 1. Movement from Traditional to Participative
Forms of Organizing.**

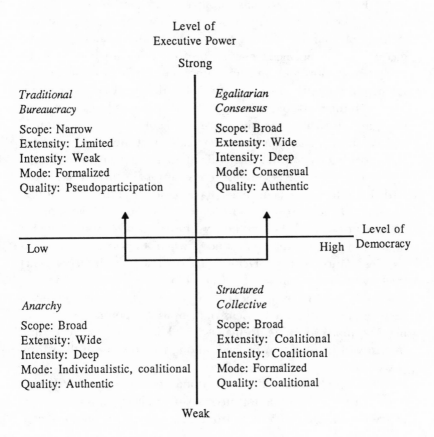

Level of
Executive Power

Strong

Traditional Bureaucracy	*Egalitarian Consensus*
Scope: Narrow	Scope: Broad
Extensity: Limited	Extensity: Wide
Intensity: Weak	Intensity: Deep
Mode: Formalized	Mode: Consensual
Quality: Pseudoparticipation	Quality: Authentic

Low   High   Level of Democracy

	Structured Collective
Anarchy	
Scope: Broad	Scope: Broad
Extensity: Wide	Extensity: Coalitional
Intensity: Deep	Intensity: Coalitional
Mode: Individualistic, coalitional	Mode: Formalized
Quality: Authentic	Quality: Coalitional

Weak

Using the dimensions of workplace democracy provided by Mason (1982), we can characterize traditional, bureaucratic forms of organization as featuring a narrow scope of joint decision making, limited extensity of involvement, no intensity of commitment to democratic processes, formalized decision making, and pseudoparticipation. In this case executive power is strong but democratization is low. At the other extreme, a smooth-functioning workplace democracy would feature a broad scope of decisions open to joint influence, a wide extensity of commitment to democratic processes, a consensual mode of reaching agreements, and authentic participation. In this case democratization is high and so is executive power, since the use of such power is endorsed by the collectivity.

Between these extremes are two transition phases. The first features low democratization and weak executive power; strong feelings of equality follow the ousting of traditional leaders or methods of management, making it difficult for anyone to assume unilateral authority. At the same time, democratic processes are not yet in place to support new forms of collective decision making. Although the scope of issues open to discussion is broad, extensity wide, and intensity deep, the mode is one of anarchy. Individuals and coalitions assert their interests as constitutions are pounded out, resulting in conflicts that can interfere with attempts by any group to lead. In the next phase, constitutional conflicts have been settled, but the agreements made have yet to stand the test of tough decisions. Leaders assume authority under the provisions of the agreement but find their authority limited. It takes some time for organizational members to know when their involvement is required. Once their involvement has been decided, leaders can act freely within the sphere of influence accorded to them by their followers. By this time the organization will be able to make decisions by egalitarian consensus; prior to this point, the decision-making mode is more formalized and both the extensity and intensity of involvement depend on one's support from the ruling coalition.

Living through the transitional phases can be difficult. There are no set formulas for success, since each situation is unique. A few organizations benefit from the help of consultants who provide guidance during these transitions in handling process issues, managing conflicts, making effective decisions, or undertaking work redesign. Given the difficulties associated with achieving successful participation, it is remarkable that so many organizations continue, despite the obstacles.

To make the transition to effective participation easier, we need to conduct further research into a number of organizational issues.

Environmental Adaptation. More attention needs to be paid to the effects of the external environment, reward systems, and control systems on the internal dynamics of participative organizations. To date, too much attention has been paid to bringing ideological values to life and too little to the larger forces that shape the behavior of members of all organizations, democratic or traditional. Participation alone will not overcome the effects of international competition, outdated technology, or being in the wrong market. Reward systems that continue to reinforce individualistic actions will not promote cooperation. Control systems that stress discipline for failure to follow policies will not enhance innovation.

Education. If workers are to become able participants in participative systems, they must be educated to make good decisions. Expressions of preference in the absence of logic or reason are little better than random choices. Workers need to understand the organization enough to participate not only in deciding which color to paint the cafeteria but also which business strategies to support. Participation is not genuine if the most important decisions continue to be made by a few.

Motivation. The biggest stumbling block to the spread of participation is probably not the lack of desire on the part of executive or leaders but, instead, a lack of motivation on the part of some workers. Organizations will not move toward democracy unless their members want them to; but employees, for the most part, have been content to follow. Executives who wish to tap the energy bank contained in their human resources need to find ways to promote more excitement about participation among workers.

Examination. More research needs to be conducted about what works and what does not—both across organizations using different methods of participation and within organizations once a particular form of workplace participation has been selected. Democracies that fail to examine themselves quickly fall out of step with the times and with the sentiments of their members—and become just as stifling as more traditional organizations.

Equalization. Participative organizations need to find ways to empower both their members *and* their leaders by increasing the scope, intensity, extensity, and quality of the democratic processes. No leader can direct an anarchy; and structured collectives that legislate all decisions leave no room for leaders to lead. The achievement of egalitarian consensus may be just shy of utopia and just as difficult to reach, but all substitutes are inadequate.

Reading the Tea Leaves

As I think about predicting the future, I am aware that many unforeseen changes have affected our lives in the past decade alone. Still, there do appear to be some visible trends in the examination of participation and executive power, and these trends may provide clues to where we are headed.

First, it is clear that both the traditional exercise of executive power and the participation movement are experiencing difficulties. Under the stress of these pressures, neither will exist in the future as it exists today. Executive power will become more shared and consensual in nature, drawing more heavily on the consent of followers. Given the changes we are experiencing in society, it is likely that the more executives resist this transformation in their role, the faster it will come about. On the other hand, executives who are genuinely interested in programs aimed at broader participation or even workplace democracy will be confused and dismayed by the jumble of ideas surrounding these concepts and the apathy of employees toward them. Participation needs to become more than an ideology; it needs to include a workable process for making sound decisions and translating them into action. For these reasons, neither executive power nor participation democracy can survive in the future, at least not in their present forms.

Eventually, executive power and participation will turn out to be mutually supportive rather than mutually exclusive. As Kanter (1983, p. 249) has noted, "Leadership—the existence of people with power to mobilize others and to set constraints—is an important ingredient in making participation work." Workplace democracies, even more so than bureaucracies, need the kinds of visionary leaders described by Bennis (1983): executives who can set a course, inspire others to join with them, and not let go until their objectives are achieved. Where will these leaders come from?

For a time visionary democratic leaders probably will be found in small organizations rather than in large ones. It is easier to manage democratic processes when fewer people are involved, and smaller organizations or subunits usually allow more freedom for innovation. At the same time, larger firms have begun to see the wisdom of building smaller plants and creating smaller businesses within larger ones; therefore, the democratization of larger firms may occur from the outside to the center and the bottom to the top. In the end, though, leaders at all levels will experience changes. Over time, as our current leaders are replaced, their successors will come from a wider variety of backgrounds and experiences than ever before. Organizations will find it to their advantage to prepare many more people to assume leadership positions, since leadership will be distributed more widely.

All this implies change for the organizational sciences and organizational consultants as well. To date, the empirical foundations of the field of organizational behavior rest on research conducted in the hierarchical, nondemocratic organizations that have dominated the American scene during most of the twentieth century. We have spent almost all our time studying the stultifying effects of bureaucratic constraints on human motivation and almost no time in studying what happens when such constraints are removed. We have been advocating that employees should be granted human rights for so long that we fail to recognize that many employees are just as happy to be left alone and do not know quite what to do when opportunities for participation are granted to them. As employees are being pushed headlong into quality circles, employee-involvement groups, and other processes to secure their commitment to organizational goals, the resistance of some is clearly evident. When employees have to ask, "What's in it for me?" it is obvious that we have not touched deep chords of self-empowerment or self-actualization through these vehicles. Fundamental transformations of relationships between individuals and organizations will take more than one hour a week. In the future, some exciting work will involve helping coalitions to articulate their positions, reach shared agreement, and translate their plans into innovative organizational processes that accomplish objectives while reflecting underlying ideals. In addition to providing more people with managerial training, we will also spend more time on follower development, as it becomes apparent that leaders are only as effective as their subordinates allow them to be.

Our research will need to reflect the complexity of the systems transformations we will be dealing with; two-variable studies will continue to be illustrative of basic dynamics, but studies using less traditional rigor and more innovative methods will allow us to capture and report more of what is really happening. Much more research on behavior in egalitarian systems will be needed as competition between peers, a hallmark of hierarchical organizations, gradually gives way to collaboration. We will also need to gain a better understanding of the emotional component of change, since tapping emotional energy will be important in ensuring ongoing participation.

The world is changing; and organizations, which are fundamentally social inventions, will change along with it. Executives who fear these changes will resist them, only to find that the harder they resist, the faster the changes will come about. On the other hand, executives who view the same changes as providing exciting new opportunities will encounter difficulties in turning ideological dreams into effective organizations. Further experimentation with new forms of organizing will require the blending of traditional conceptions of the role of the executive with more democratic ones. How soon this happens, and with what degree of trauma for executives, will, for the most part, be up to them.

ELEVEN

Making Room
for Individual Autonomy

Eric J. Miller

This chapter explores current shifts in Britain in the relatedness of individual to organization and their implications for the distribution of power and exercise of authority. It draws on my experience in consulting, research, and educational roles, working with a wide variety of groups and organizations, ranging from community groups to multinational corporations. The Tavistock Institute's Group Relations Training Programme, which I have worked with for twenty-five years and directed for the last fifteen, has enacted, in the temporary institutions formed in its conferences, contemporary versions of power and authority prevailing in the society outside. And specifically over the last four to five years I have been involved with a group of people in OPUS (an Organisation for Promoting Understanding in Society). We have been talking about our own and other people's changing feelings, preoccupations, concerns, anxieties, and ways of coping with their lives, and trying to tease out underlying patterns or trends, conscious and unconscious, in society as a whole (see OPUS *Bulletin*, vols. 1–15, 1980–1984). The primary objective of OPUS is educational: to provide citizens, as individuals, with a set of observations, questions, and occasionally hypotheses that make up our understanding of what is going on in society and to encourage them

Note: In light of subsequent discussions, I have made some revisions to my earlier (June 1984) version of this chapter. For detailed scrutiny and comments, I am particularly grateful to Jeanne Neumann; also to Mitchell McCorcle and Harry S. Jonas III.

to think about and examine their own involvement in their various roles and accordingly to exercise their own authority within them. Insofar as OPUS also has a research objective, its methodology is a crude form of interactive research. Correspondingly, this chapter also builds on my own experiences in the role of citizen. Beyond this, of course, I have drawn on ideas and concepts of many other people. Where I can, I acknowledge names and give references, but there are many influences of which I am not aware, and I doubt whether anything I have to say could be called original.

My main proposition runs along these lines: Between the end of World War II and the late 1970s, British society generally and its employment institutions in particular were dominated by a dependency culture, in which the individual's relatedness to the state and the organization was dynamically similar to that of infant to mother. This was associated at the organizational level with a consistent and persistent pattern of power and authority and at the individual level with certain common coping and defense mechanisms. These underlying patterns were remarkably resistant to the importation by behavioral scientists and others of newer "liberal," "democratic" values and associated forms of work organizations. Since 1979, which saw the installation of the Thatcher government and mounting unemployment, especially in the manufacturing sector, various symptoms of "failed dependency" have appeared in the United Kingdom. The welfare state and employing organizations have in reality become less reliable in meeting dependency needs, and the exercise of power and domination has become more overt. The unemployed—who, in losing their jobs, have lost crucial props to their identity—are merely the more obvious and dramatic cases of a far more widespread societal phenomenon, symptomized by psychological withdrawal from organizations, retreat into the past and fantasy, expressions of impotence in face of nuclear annihilation, displacement of aggression onto social subgroups, and a paranoid search for an enemy.

Paradoxically, the unemployed also are pointing the way to a positive alternative to the dependency culture. While widespread demoralization has prevented the unemployed from forming a critical mass politically, and the economic gap between employed and unemployed, the haves and the have-nots, is perceptibly widening, the presence of a significant minority surviving outside employment begins to undermine the Protestant work ethic. So there are signs that the employee is renegotiating the basis of his identity and shifting the nature of his relationship to the organization. (As noted later, although women are not immune to the crises described in this chapter, it is the male role and self-image that are the more threatened.) As instrumental values and more conscious compliance take over as the mode of relating to the organization, authority becomes personal authority to be exercised more outside employment than within it. Hence, a challenge for employing organizations—to which only a few are beginning to respond—is to find ways of reconnecting personal authority to the task of the enterprise.

The Dependency Culture

Postwar social policy in Britain was shaped by the widely acclaimed publication in 1942 of the Beveridge report, which essentially held out the promise of the welfare state as a reward for enduring the rigors of the war and winning it. Warriors could return to be suckled by the bountiful national breast. And the bounties were many: free education for all; free health care; child allowances; pensions for the old and disabled; subsidized housing; dole for the unemployed; supplementary benefits to ensure that no one fell through holes in the safety net; and a host of other provisions, from maternity benefits to funeral grants. Along with this, Britain embarked on a thirty-year period of economic stability and rising prosperity, based on Keynesian growth and high employment, and also of political stability, with government alternating between the two major parties, whose policies—after a short flurry of nationalization, denationalization, and renationalization—became more marked in their similarities than their differences. By the mid-1970s, many people came to feel that—apart from minor recessions—this state of affairs could be regarded as normal and would continue indefinitely.

A further important characteristic of these thirty years was a growing reliance on large organizations. This was a product partly of the welfare state (for example, the National Health Service, besides catering to our medical needs, became a vast employer) and partly of nationalization; but, in addition, a series of mergers and takeovers in industry meant that large companies accounted for a higher proportion of total employment than in any other European country. Medium-sized and small firms were relatively fewer. Correspondingly, a small number of powerful unions claimed the membership of most of the work force.

Nationalization, it must be remembered, particularly of industries such as coal and steel, was introduced as a safeguard against any recurrence of the exploitation and bitterness of the interwar years. Almost by definition, the nationalized enterprises provided security of employment comparable to the civil service and local government service, and this came to be expected of other major employers also; and by and large the rate of economic growth enabled it to be provided. Legislation furnished progressively greater protection of employees, and the unions were strong enough to keep the employers in line: if mother showed signs of being less than generous with the breast, father could be relied upon to step in to keep the milk flowing.

In many respects—economically, sociopolitically, and even to some extent psychologically—this was a satisfactory set of arrangements for all concerned. Economically, although return on investment was held down by relatively low productivity, overall growth generally kept profits at a level sufficient to satisfy shareholders while, despite inflation, wages steadily rose in real terms. When goods began to return to the shops after postwar shortages, there was money to buy them: "You've never had it so good," Mr. Macmillan was to tell us. Consumerism rapidly established itself. Also, wages actually grew faster than salaries over the period as a whole, and this, coupled with heavy taxation on higher incomes, brought about some reductions in inequalities of wealth. In monetary terms at least, the historical blue-collar/white-collar, working-class/middle-class distinctions were significantly blurred.

As Bott (1957) noted thirty years ago, two models of class system operate in British society: the prestige model, which postulates three or more classes and scope for upward mobility into all but the highest; and the two-class power model, which fosters solidarity of the working class through the shared belief that the route to greater individual prosperity is through the collective power of workers to gain a larger return for their labor—a bigger share of the "national cake." Sociologists in the 1960s were preoccupied with the phenomenon of embourgeoisement, which is essentially a shift from the two-class model and its associated values toward the prestige model; but if it was occurring at all, which some contested (see Goldthorpe and others, 1967), it was a process that made most headway in southeast England and much less in the main centers of heavy industry in northern England, South Wales, and southern Scotland. Unions after all could justify their claim that they were securing a higher standard of living for their members, and reminders of the 1930s could serve to encourage waverers to hold on to their working-class identity.

Persistence of strong unions, enacting the power model, was also convenient for the other, "management," side of the boundary. I put that term in quotation marks because top managers in the employing organizations were faced with the problem of securing the motivation and commitment of a wide range and growing proportion of supervisors, specialists, and other staff who did not necessarily have the title of "manager" and whose earnings were becoming relatively and even absolutely lower than higher-paid "workers." The solution to this problem lay in perpetuating a myth that they had been made members of an exclusive club called "management" and that through diligence and loyalty they could progressively gain access to the club's inner sanctums and to the power that went with it. (To put it another way, the organizational breast was on offer, but regulated by top management—in this case "father"—which demanded deferred gratification.) This promise of access to the club's inner sanctums implies the need for competitiveness and rivalry for promotion. Perpetuation of a perceived conflict with the unions could therefore mobilize what Bion (1961) called "basic assumption fight/flight" as a means of cohering an otherwise internally disparate and rivalrous "management" and differentiating it from "workers."

Therefore, the collusive fight between the supposedly exploitative management and the supposedly greedy and idle workers helped the unions maintain working-class solidarity and diminished the threat of embourgeoisement. Not until the late 1960s and early 1970s did significant numbers of the junior corps of "management" begin to defect and join unions themselves. Overtly, these employees were resentful at being excluded from significant management-union negotiations (often hearing about the outcomes from their subordinates rather than from their superiors); perhaps less consciously, they recognized—especially when expansion and therefore promotion opportunities slowed down—that the notion of club membership was indeed a myth designed to preserve the overriding power of top management. They were, however, subject to strong pressures to remain "loyal to the company," with the result that they neither left "management" nor fully joined the union, and their officials in particular were subjected to a good deal of role conflict and stress.

Psychologically, too, this set of arrangements was satisfactory, at least superficially. The employing organization, with its hierarchical structure, provided security and met dependency needs. The job, however unsatisfying the content, gave the individual a role in a production system and a social grouping. At the same time, resentment at dependency—the other side of the ambivalence—and the need to find outlets for expressing aggression and experiencing potency was also accommodated. For those on the "management" side of the boundary, peer rivalry in the struggle for promotion fulfilled this function. (Their interorganizational mobility, incidentally, was far lower than in the United States.) The others had their union to act it out on their behalf. Here, however, there was an added complexity. The level at which the union fought its battles with management was often so remote that the individual member's dependent relationship within the union hierarchy seemed to him not very different from his dependency within the work structure. For these reasons greater power became vested in shop stewards, who, being somewhat closer to the individual, were more satisfactory carriers of his needs to feel potent. Particularly in those companies where the price to be paid for dependency was exceptionally mindless work content or an authoritarian mode of management and supervision, union members tended to elect shop stewards whose relatively extreme left-wing views, advocating the overthrow of capitalism, more adequately reflected the rage experienced by members in their employee roles. In fact, the left-wing extremists implicitly played a significant role in the collusive maintenance of the equilibrium. Union officials and employers' negotiators were united by their paranoia about the disruptive influence of extremists on the labor force, and this led, during the 1960s and early 1970s, to many agreements on wages and manning that employers, at least, have since had cause to regret.

Before concluding, however, that those thirty years of the dependency culture was an only slightly tarnished golden age, we need to look a little more closely at what was happening at the level of the individual. Alienation remains as valid a description of the work experience of many employees as it was one hundred years ago; if anything, it is magnified by the greater size of employing organizations. The individual feels forced to do something that gives him no satisfaction by someone else who has coercive powers and steals most of the fruits of his labor. Talking to groups of manual workers and junior clerical staff in 1979 at a factory that was part of a large industrial group, I was struck by the coexistence of rationality and fantasy. At the rational level, these employees could give a clear and accurate account of the way in which their company worked: the market for their products; the relations between costs, prices, profits, and investment. Yet not far below the surface was a fantasy that all the profit went to the factory general manager, who took home a bag of gold at the end of the week. Articulating such a fantasy, they could laugh at its absurdity yet acknowledge that it was there. The coercive hold that the organization has over the individual, whether "manager" or "worker," is that it satisfies his dependent needs and his infantile greed, though it does so indirectly by offering him the pseudoautonomy of the consumer role. As a consumer, to be sure, he has choices; but it is pseudoautonomy in that the orchestrated pressure to spend and consume is itself a secondary coercion that reinforces dependence on an employing organization, which is to be placated through passivity and compliance. (Correspondingly, I postulate that, at least in Britain, embourgeoisement has been associated with only pseudoinstrumentality; that is, consumption patterns and class identification may shift, but the underlying organizational relatedness of dependency and coercion remains.)

The individual's rage and his wishes—not always unconscious—to destroy the organization have to be split off and suppressed or repressed. Psychoanalytic theories of splitting and projection illuminate this process. In the language of Klein (1952, 1959), there is re-evoked in the individual the primitive "paranoid-schizoid position," which is the phase when the young infant cannot yet distinguish between his impulses and their effects. His fantasy is that the objects he wishes to attack and destroy—notably the "bad," uncaring breast of the mother—are actually damaged and will take revenge on him with equal destructiveness. Hence, the dominant anxiety in that phase is paranoid, and the dominant defense to cope with that anxiety is schizoid: unconsciously splitting the "good object" (gratifying breast, mother) from the "bad object" (depriving breast, mother), even when there is conscious recognition that they are one and the same. In the adult this can lead to formation of a compliant "pseudo self" (Fromm, [1942] 1960) or "false self" (Winnicott, 1960, 1980), which, as Fromm put it, "is only an agent who actually represents the role a person is supposed to play but who does so under the name of self" (Fromm, [1941] 1960, p. 177). Split off from this and repressed is a private self, which may be what Winnicott calls the real self, the creative potential; but it is held incommunicado, locked in an unconscious world of infantile omnipotent fantasy. By means of this splitting, any questioning of the institutional roles that the false self enacts, almost ritually, is inhibited. Winnicott was discussing this defense as a form of individual psychopathology, but forty years ago Fromm was already perceiving it as a phenomenon of a society that increasingly "automatizes" the individual ([1941] 1960, p. 178); and work that I and others did in British industrial organizations during the 1970s suggested that employees had increasingly taken up a position of schizoid withdrawal (Lawrence, 1982; Lawrence and Miller, 1982), which affected all their social relations, not only those of the workplace.

And, indeed, Winnicott's description of the individual operating with a high degree of "false self-defense" is all too apposite to the observed life experience of a large sector of our population:

> In the healthy individual who has a compliant aspect of the self . . . and who is a creative and spontaneous being, there is at the same time a capacity for the use of symbols. In other words, health here is closely bound up with the capacity of the individual to live in an area that is intermediate between the dream and the reality, that which is called the cultural life. . . . By contrast, where there is a high degree of split between the true self and the false self which hides the true self, there is found a poor capacity for using symbols, and a poverty of social living. *Instead of cultural pursuits, one observes in such persons extreme restlessness, an inability to concentrate, and a need to collect impingements from external reality so that the living time of the individual can be filled by reactions to these impingements* [Winnicott, 1960, p. 150; emphasis added].

Television and videorecorders have provided a rich source of such impingements.

It may be added that this set of structural arrangements and individual defenses serves to maintain a particular conception of authority as concerned with superordination and subordination. Insofar as conflict is split off into union-management relations, the work organization is maintained as a hierarchy of dependency and compliance. The alternative conception of authority—exercise of capacity to contribute to performance of the task—cannot flourish in such a culture. Authority based on competence is always a threat to an organization that defines authority as based on position (if it is exercised by a subordinate, it is treated by the superior as insubordination), and so the imperative to maintain the dependency structure takes precedence over effective task performance. Hence, there is a collusive myth that the hierarchies of status and competence coincide. (Suggestion schemes are an ingenious but seldom very successful device for preserving that myth, in that (1) they imply that the subordinate's capacity to contribute to improved performance is an exception, almost an aberration; and (2) they reconfirm that the authority to implement improvements has to come from above. In addition, of course, they are an almost explicit acknowledgment that if the suggestion were made directly within the hierarchy, the immediate superior would experience this as a threat to his or her position and either suppress the idea or steal it for him- or herself.)

These structures and defenses proved remarkably tenacious and resistant to change. I have discussed elsewhere the processes whereby employment institutions "give a few selected individuals a monopoly on creativity and offer work—without creativity—to the majority, the so-called 'working class'" (Miller, 1983, p. 10); and I am far from the only person to be concerned not just with the waste of people's talents in organizations but, more generally, with the damaging effects of alienation on the individual and on society. There has been widespread awareness of the growing dissonance between the constraints on the individual in his role as employee and his relative autonomy in the role of consumer, between the authoritarian values of the workplace and the democratic values of the wider society. In the Tavistock Institute, for example, this has been the focus of much of our work ever since the late 1940s. Formulation of the concept of the sociotechnical system in the early 1950s opened up a whole new approach to work organization and stimulated many experimental innovations in places as far apart as Scandinavia, India, and North America. And one can list a long series of approaches/concepts/philosophies of intervention by behavioral scientists and others to try to do something about that dissonance: OD, democratization of the workplace, job enrichment, job enlargement, participation, industrial democracy, quality of working life—to mention but a few. The Case Western study, *Job Satisfaction and Productivity,* carried out in 1973–1975, analyzed some 600 cases and showed conclusively that autonomy, as an "important aspect of the work itself, the nature of superior-subordinate relations, and the organizational climate of work," is a "significant organizational factor related to both satisfaction and productivity" and hence a potentially effective action lever for improving productivity and the quality of working life (Srivastva and others, 1975, p. xvi). As I myself wrote subsequently, in relation to one particular experiment: "So we have here a conception that seems to have everything on its side. There is the immediate pragmatic argument: organizations that make better use of their human resources tend to carry out their tasks more effectively. There is the wider social justification: organizational misuse of people and consequent alienation incur a high social cost. And more generally this is in tune with social values: people matter; human dignity and rights must be respected; older notions of boss-worker relations are exploitative. On this basis one might expect sweeping changes to be taking place in a whole range of organizations. Reality, however, . . . does not support that expectation. First, successful experiments are rare. Second, the changes achieved, notwithstanding their evident benefits, often remain precarious. Third, there seems to be immense difficulty in disseminating innovations" (Miller, 1979a, p. 173). Why should this be?

One explanation is that such innovations are, almost by definition, a threat to existing power holders in the organization. So we see self-styled democratic and participative managers seeking to bestow autonomy without surrendering one iota of control; or the top management that can afford to profess advanced, even radical, views because middle management and supervisors can be relied upon to take the obstructive roles. Then there is the manifestly successful experiment that somehow fails to be replicated; or the innovation is transferred in such a way that success is improbable, since the requisite boundary conditions are not sustained. For example, Rice's original experiments in the work organization of weaving (Rice, 1958) remained effective over a long time period (one being still almost unchanged fifteen years later), and the method was introduced in other loom sheds. What was not transferred, however, was the crucial shift in the role of the supervisor (supervisors had no training in how to work with semiautonomous work groups, as distinct from individual workers); as a result, the potential benefits of the changes were vitiated (Miller, 1975). So there is much evidence to suggest the "Speakers' Corner" syndrome: power holders accommodate radical or dissenting views by providing a limited, legitimate outlet for their expression—thereby encapsulating the threat to their power and, as a bonus, demonstrating their liberality.

Unions as established power holders may also obstruct such innovations. Here the position is more complex. They can argue persuasively that management's motivation in introducing innovations in the work organization is not entirely altruistic, that management simply wants to screw more effort out of the workers. Moreover, it is more difficult for unions to command the loyalty of workers with high job satisfaction. Whether or not diminution of union power is an overt intention of management in endorsing these developments, it is often a consequence. It is a common belief on both sides of the boundary that less power for the unions means more power for management. The notion that it is the workers actually involved in a program of, say, job enlargement who gain in power may be given lip service but is not always borne out behaviorally. Our own experience of interventions has been that unions' anxieties about losing power are often voiced in the negotiation of a project, and they sometimes succeed in blocking it by limiting their members' participation.

However, the resistance has not been located only in the union. Managers contemplating an experimental change that might involve greater exercise of authority and discretion by subordinates are seldom unambivalent. Given the available management-union split, differences of views within management tend to get suppressed, and unvoiced doubts and objections can be and are projected onto the unions—the "common enemy" syndrome.

Our experience further suggests that, as an intervention goes forward and shows signs of "success" in the sense that employees are operating with greater authority, it is management rather than the union that is anxious about a threat to its power. In one instance, colleagues and I worked over a period of five years with a subsidiary company of a larger group. (The earlier phases of this project are described in Miller, 1977. See also Miller 1983; Khaleelee and Miller, 1985.) It had about 1,000 employees, and initially we worked with some 120 managers, supervisors, and technical staff. Within eighteen months outcomes were impressive: internal coordination improved; chronic problems got solved; there was a general increase in self-confidence and purposefulness, especially in transactions across the boundary of the organization with group headquarters; and, more concretely, there was a surge in manufacturing output and profits. Meanwhile, we were extending our involvement to the subsidiary company as a whole and provided consultancy and training for a range of internal groups, including the executive management team and a joint trade union committee. With some success we provided a "space" in which people in the organization, regardless of level, could take up what we called a "third role"—not as members of a work group or as union members but as "citizens" of the organization as a community, from which they could reconsider their actions and attitudes in their other two roles. This "space" approximated what Winnicott (1960, p. 150), in the passage quoted earlier, described as "an area that is intermediate between the dream and the reality"—an area of play, of the use of symbols, of emergent creativity. (With the schizoid defense, no such space is available between external conformity to normative reality and internal flight into infantile fantasy.) Progressively more employees became involved in the program, and it was evident that we helped many people recognize that they could use their authority to influence the operation of the organization and their own roles in it in creative ways. Financial results continued to be impressive; and, in relation to the larger group, having started out at the bottom of the league in terms of profits, our client was now at or near the top. What my colleagues and I had not sufficiently taken into account was that this achievement was a threat, both to other subsidiaries in the group, whose managers were being pressed for higher performance, and, more importantly, to group management. Our client organization was guilty of cultural deviance. Elsewhere in the group, the dependency culture of compliance and conformity prevailed; here it was one of exercising authority and taking initiatives. Headquarters perceived this as insubordination, since the assertion of competence undermined the hierarchy of status. The fact that effective decisions were being made was less important than who was making them. Group management applied various forms of pressure on the management of the subsidiary to toe the line and close down the program, including withholding promotions, and eventually installed a new general manager. So the consultancy came to end.

It is therefore extremely tempting to interpret this outcome and others like it solely in terms of the threat to executive power and to postulate that if we, as consultants, had been politically more astute we would have acted to co-opt group management in supporting the program: "Organizational development cannot be effective without also being a political activity, involving changes in the distribution of power" (Miller, 1979b, p. 231). My proposition here, however, is that this threat, though a major part of the story, is not the whole of it. Members of our client organization were just not innocent victims of a coercive top management. Even the staunchest supporters of the program were not without ambivalence, and when headquarters closed it down, their response of shock and dismay carried undertones of relief.

Elsewhere, Lawrence (1979) has reported on another project in which he and I were involved—in this case the design of a new factory based on semiautonomous work groups. Again, it had all the appearance of a success story. The new work groups fully demonstrated the influence of autonomy on productivity and satisfaction, and they were progressively enlarging their range of activities. In this case management terminated the project, saying explicitly that it had "gone far enough." Indeed, at various times some managers had voiced anxieties that the project might put them out of a job. Again, therefore, it seemed that the threat to managerial power was the stumbling block. But in this case, too, our interpretation was that there was something more. As Lawrence (1979, p. 246) put it: "The other reason probably lies with the workers. On what journey was this project to take them? While they could and did express a high degree of satisfaction with conditions in the new factory, it may be that the demands were too high. . . . My hypothesis is . . . that the project and its new work experiences put into disarray the taken-for-granted assumptions made by most workers about the relatedness between themselves and management [—management in its meanings] both as a status and political aggregate and as a process."

These two cases are not atypical. At one level management, as what Lawrence calls a "political aggregate," was undoubtedly concerned to protect its power and status. But at another level, there was also collusion to maintain management at the apex of a dependent hierarchy. As I have written elsewhere about the former case, "Opportunities [for employees] to reflect, to question, and to innovate are exciting; but they are also a threat to primitive needs for security and dependency. Those needs lie in all of us and are met by stable institutional structures and cultures. Upsetting those structures raises anxiety [in employees] that their schizoid defenses will break down and their destructive impulses will erupt into violence and chaos. Reassertion of control by headquarters served to patch up the defenses" (Miller, 1983, p. 17).

One further point needs to be made. It can be argued, perhaps, that workers' resistance to innovations of the kinds discussed here results not from the schizoid defense but from the operation of much more straightforward instrumental values. That is to say, workers seek to minimize their involvement in the workplace because their interests, satisfactions, and indeed their identity are invested in their lives outside. This would be the embourgeoisement thesis. I can certainly think of examples, but my impression is that they are a minority. Supportive evidence for the wide prevalence of the schizoid defense comes from studies of what happens to people when they lose their jobs. If instrumental values predominated, the main problem posed by unemployment would be reduction of income. But a study in which I recently took part in West Yorkshire (Khaleelee and Miller, 1984) confirmed the findings of other research that money is, though a problem, not the major one. Over and over again, people equated employment with respect (self-respect and respect of others) and unemployment with worthlessness. Depression, diminished mental functioning, impotence, mental illness, marital breakdown—these well-documented consequences of unemployment are not consistent with the instrumental theory, which posits an identity securely placed outside the world of employment. The other significant concern demonstrated in the West Yorkshire study, as in others, is that employment is equated with order, while unemployment is equated with anarchy. Couple this evidence with the frequent observation on the behavior of unemployed men—that they shut their front doors, watch television, and never come out except to collect their dole—and it appears that the hypothesis of the schizoid defense is only too well confirmed.

My argument in this section, therefore, is that between the late 1940s and the late 1970s Britain in general and employing organizations in particular were characterized by a pervasive and collusive dependency culture. (And it may well be that the shifting values in society, especially during the 1960s, which generated uncertainty and left the individual less secure about his or her own identity, actually increased the implicit demand that work organizations should meet needs for dependency and security.) The dependency culture was sustained in two ways: structurally, through the almost ritualized split between unions and management, which provided a safe outlet for destructive impulses that might otherwise have imperiled the hierarchical structure; and intrapersonally, through the schizoid defense, which also protected the structure by passive, compliant conformity—to the employing organization or to the union, as the immediate circumstances demanded. In total, there was an integrated defensive system in the classical sense (Jaques, 1955; Menzies, 1960), and it is hardly surprising that interventions based on "autonomy" values should be difficult to sustain.

Failed Dependency

High employment was a major element in the culture of dependency. Until the early 1970s, the rate of unemployment was typically below 3 percent, which meant that, even though the size of the labor force was increasing by nearly .5 percent per annum (and for women at a much faster rate), virtually everyone seeking a job could get one; and the numbers of long-term unemployed, those out of work for over a year, were considerably below 1 percent of the labor force. (Given such a low rate of unemployment, the low level of job mobility at all levels is telling evidence of a dependency culture.) Between 1974 and 1976, unemployment doubled (from 2.6 to 5.4 percent) and it remained at just over 5 percent until 1979. This was felt to be immorally high. Moreover, the rate of inflation was escalating; the country's competitiveness overseas was declining; the manufacturing industry was in particular difficulty; and there was widespread recognition that Britain's economy was in a mess.

In electing the first Thatcher government in 1979, after the Labour party had been in power for eleven of the previous fifteen years, the voters were almost explicitly asking to be punished for their infantile greed. Margaret Thatcher had warned that productivity was too low and wages too high and that she was going to make the country live within its means. There was much talk of having to take nasty medicine. Few people foresaw, however, how nasty the deepening recession would make it. In 1979 registered unemployment stood at just under 1.3 million; by the beginning of 1983, it passed 3.2 million (13.5 percent) though most economists put the true figure nearer 4 million—about one sixth of the work force. Employment in manufacturing had fallen dramatically. Within three years it had shed one fifth of its remaining labor— nearly 1.5 million people. Long-term unemployment had risen to over 1 million, more than one third of the jobless total; and, despite the big expenditure on youth training and other schemes for young people, more than a quarter of this number were under twenty-five.

The nasty medicine had other side effects. Cuts in education expenditure, ending of free school meals for children from low-income families, greatly increased prescription charges in the Health Service, and a host of other measures combined to suggest that the welfare state was being eroded. (For a recent discussion, see Stern, 1982.) Nor did it pass unnoticed that such measures impinged most heavily on those with the lowest incomes, while changes in the structure of taxation made people in the higher income brackets not only relatively but also in real terms far better off.

Since 1980 OPUS has been attempting to identify underlying preoccupations, concerns, and processes in society, using a fairly crude methodology. Associate staff, who are based in different parts of the country, meet every three months to pool their observations and experiences; their shared perceptions and emerging hypotheses are reviewed by a forum consisting of a cross section of people from very different walks of life; data are amplified through meetings of other linked groups; and the results are published in a quarterly *Bulletin*, which is intended to offer readers a reference point—

OPUS's understanding of what is happening—against which they can begin to think about their own part in processes of which they may not be fully aware. Here I will describe briefly a few, mostly recurrent, themes that appear to be responses to failed dependency. (I am drawing heavily on Khaleelee and Miller, 1983.)

One continuing theme has been withdrawal and retreat—hiding from reality. This is manifested in all sorts of ways. The world of entertainment has always played into nostalgia for a fantasied Golden Age, but this appears to have been accentuated since 1980. Television, for example, has produced a crop of plays and other programs set in the eighteenth and nineteenth centuries. Cinema has offered escape to a supernatural or idealized future (*Star Wars, The Empire Strikes Back, The Alien, Close Encounters, E.T.*) or to a mythical and magical past (*The Sword and the Sorcerer, Excalibur, The Dark Crystal*)—films that present in an extravagant way the archetypal struggle between good and evil. Best-selling books have had a similar quality. Architecture, interior decoration (for example, of bars), and even gardens have gone back to the 1930s or to Victorian fashions. In organizations, too, the phenomenon of withdrawal has been pronounced. I shall come back to this point later.

A second dominant theme has been fear of the nuclear holocaust and people's impotence in face of it. For a minority the peace movement and the Campaign for Nuclear Disarmament (CND) have provided the reassurance of togetherness and the release of action to mitigate the anxiety; and the sisterhood of the Greenham Common women, sustaining continuous protest at the United States Cruise missile base, has supplied a model of potency that cannot be ignored. But for most the Bomb remains a diffuse threat, sometimes acknowledged, often repressed—a sword of Damocles under which they somehow have to go on living. This allows the individual to feel, or to behave as if, there is no point in doing anything himself as a citizen because it is all futile: a dreadful uncontrollable force may wipe him out. Voicing of the fear and support for the CND seem to be closely correlated with the increase in unemployment and the linked fear of the employed that they will be made redundant. So there are grounds for postulating that the individual's sense of impotence in relation to British society and indeed to the rest of the world is being projected onto the nuclear threat. The real threat is also a vivid symbol.

Third, society's anger and fear have been split off to be carried selectively by the young and the blacks. Aggression and nihilism in the wider society have been expressed through punk culture, skinheads, or the National Front. The 1981 riots in parts of Liverpool and London (with "copycat" disturbances elsewhere) were more concentrated expressions of anger and rage. There was a mounting fear that violence could sweep out of the inner-city ghettoes into the middle-class dormitories. The convenient familiar myth is that the young and the blacks are intrinsically unstable and violent. The fact that society has so arranged its affairs as to impose the brunt of increased unemployment onto these groups, and therefore deserves retribution, obviously generates fears of spreading violence but is seldom explicitly acknowledged. (See note at end of chapter.) By a similar process of splitting, Northern Ireland continues to serve the rest of Britain as a repository of violence, and this is not perceived as having any connection with a level of urban unemployment that has long been the highest in the United Kingdom.

A fourth theme has been the identification of a "real" enemy against whom the population could enact its anger. The crisis over the Falklands was a convenient vehicle. Because of the war, for example, dock workers decided to refrain from striking; but once the fighting with the Argentinians was over, the industrial disputes at home resumed. So the apparent collusion with Argentina to fight over the Falklands provided the governments of both countries with short-term palliatives for domestic dissatisfaction and disintegration. Momentarily, the British knew who they were again. When the excitement died down, the old feelings and problems returned: impotence, worthlessness, apathy.

The phenomena just outlined—withdrawal and retreat, impotence in the face of nuclear annihilation, displacement of aggression into social subgroups, and creation of an external enemy—can be interpreted as societal defense mechanisms developed to cope with the anxiety, fear, and anger generated by the experience of failed dependency. The state, the institution of employment, and the trade unions have all three displayed themselves as unreliable in meeting needs for dependency and security. Church and family—the other institutions with the traditional function of catering for dependency—are, respectively, discredited and beleaguered. And the fundamentalist religious movements, which have been burgeoning in many parts of the world and which serve to sweep away uncertainty and to confer on the individual a clear-cut set of meanings, have so far gained little ground in Britain.

Returning now to look specifically at the phenomenon of withdrawal and retreat in relation to employment institutions, we can see that there was, of course, an immense amount of involuntary withdrawal. Whole departments and even whole factories were closed down, with massive redundancies, or layoffs. "Reducing head count," "shedding labor," and—a particularly telling *double entendre*—"demanning" were the terminology of the times. In some large organizations, including some nationalized enterprises and also universities, an attempt was made to manage the process with kid gloves. A major chemical company, for example, spent large sums to find highly paid jobs in the Middle East for surplus employees. Also, such organizations set up generous and costly schemes for early retirement and voluntary resignations. What surprised many personnel managers, particularly at the beginning of the recession, was the eagerness with which these offers were taken up: there was a rush for the door. Doubtless many volunteers were bemused and seduced by the size of the offers (if take-home pay, after tax and other deductions, is £100 a week or less, £20,000 tax free seems like a fortune), but this was the first indication that at least some people regarded employment as less of a privilege or even necessity than employers may have imagined. In other organizations, large and small, dismissals were much more arbitrary and the terms much less generous. Instead of the caring family model in employment, we were back to the military model with a vengeance: casualties are inevitable; people have to be thrown out of the boat so that it can continue to float. Some managements quite openly enjoyed the opportunity to reassert their power vis-à-vis the unions. (Excessive power of the unions had, of course, been one of the planks on which the Conservative government had been elected in 1979, thereby undermining the Bullock report, which two years previously had proposed a significant shift toward industrial democracy in British industry; see *Report of the Committee of Inquiry on Industrial Democracy,* 1977.) However, even among overtly more circumspect and generous employers, the high price they were prepared to pay to shed labor suggested that they were at least as much concerned with assertion of power as with restoring economic viability.

Apart from the involuntary and voluntary leavers, withdrawal was also manifested by those who remained in employment. "Don't stick your neck out"; "keep your head down"; "keep your nose clean"; "cover your arse": those were the prescriptions for survival, expressed in stark physical terms, as if one's own body were at risk. This also became manifest in the Tavistock Institute's group relations conferences: preoccupation with learning the "rules," the "right" ways of behaving, so as to "get by"; distrust of groups and a search for safety in secret pairs and trios; privatization of learnings generated at the conference and a strong resistance to the idea of applying it to roles at work. Correspondingly, in these outside roles, a consistent theme has been a withdrawal of identification with the outer boundary of the organization and a falling back onto smaller groupings to support the individual's identity and need for meaning. The notion of loyalty to the firm gets eroded when a person fears that he himself may be the next for the axe; yet he also has to deny his vulnerability. One widely observed phenomenon has been the severance of contact with the victims of redundancy—a tendency among those remaining to obliterate the fact of their existence. The groups left behind close their boundaries even more tightly. "Enclave" became a word of the times. Such "survivor" groups may also cross the boundaries of the organization. Survival, however, is not the only connecting link. It is sometimes reported that such groups, almost conspiratorially, experience a regeneration of creativity, which had been blocked in the larger structure. Members of such groups gain a new confirmation of their individual identity. More commonly, however, survivors seek to derive their identity negatively from their position of "nonunemployment"; besides seeking increased material rewards, which will further differentiate them economically from those (including ex-colleagues) who are on the dole, they are inclined to adopt that set of values which defines "the unemployed" collectively as inadequate, lazy, and shiftless: "They could get a job if they tried." The fact that they themselves have jobs can then be attributed to their own merit and virtue.

Postdependency and Employment Institutions

Failed dependency may be thought of in terms of the predicament of an infant being abandoned or even assaulted by hitherto dependable parents, yet also aware that this is a fate he has brought upon himself by his own greed and destructiveness. He is outraged and terrified, angry and depressed, and in a state of shock does not know what to do with his conflicting feelings. How to survive? The aspect I am particularly concerned with here is the loss of well-established meanings and ways of coping. Failed dependency may be seen as a transitional phase, in which that loss is being dealt with and acceptable new meanings and coping mechanisms begin to emerge. I postulate that a postdependency culture is just beginning to take shape in British society. The most recent (1985) evidence, mainly from the soundings of OPUS, indicates that, although the crisis is far from over, new models may be coming forward; and these new models have profound implications for the relatedness of the individual to the employing organization. Executive power and authority, as they have been conventionally conceived and exercised, are called into question.

A first observation is that the nostalgic element of withdrawal and retreat is moving into living memory, instead of lying in a prenatal past. Britain's most popular TV serial, *The Jewel in the Crown*, was set in the 1940s. So also were the extraordinary celebrations of the fortieth anniversary of the invasion of Normandy: whatever the political motivations of the national leaders, the immense media coverage beforehand indicated that a popular chord was being touched. Undoubtedly, there was a big element of harking back to the days when Britain could boast an empire and win a war. But *The Jewel* also portrayed the less creditable aspects of the British in India—racial discrimination, oppression, and torture; and the Normandy celebrations underlined Britain's dependence on its Western allies in defeating Germany. A possible hypothesis, therefore, is that, alongside an escapist flight to largely imaginary past glories, there is emerging a need to incorporate the past into the present. The 1983 Beatles revival, followed by a growing preoccupation with the meaning of the 1960s, supports that hypothesis.

The major strike of the National Union of Mineworkers against the National Coal Board in 1984 seemed to suggest that splitting, polarization, and fight were alive and well. It was an up-to-date conflict with archetypal overtones, a struggle between good and evil; unlike the *Star Wars* films, however, the strike enabled onlookers to choose for themselves which was good and which was evil. Was the hero Arthur Scargill, the mine workers' leader, who was defending a major industry and the workers in it from a government determined to destroy the mines and miners and using police brutality as an instrument of repression? Or was the hero/heroine Ian MacGregor/Margaret Thatcher (mainly the latter), who was introducing economic rationality at last and reasserting law and order against the use of violence by the miners' pickets? The fight continued so long because it offered the public such splendid opportunities for the vicarious experience of potency: either Scargill or Thatcher could be used as the bad object, to be blamed for all sorts of felt grievances that had nothing to do with coal. And perhaps also it was a last plea for a continuing dependency culture. If my parents are divorcing, I have to pin my hopes on one of them: was it to be mother (Thatcher) or father (Scargill)?

On the other hand, in parallel with this pattern of splitting, action, and confrontation, which is seen as the "male" mode, there is evidence of an upsurge in the "female" mode, which is orientated more toward process; toleration of uncertainty; integration and synthesis; and also a longer-term perspective, a preparedness to wait, to make do. There is a high correlation between the two modes and the two genders. (Thatcher is a frequently cited exception—variously admired, hated, and envied because she out-males the men.) Certainly there are signs that women are becoming contemptuous of men's posturing, of the seriousness with which they take their little games. Greenham Common is a continuous reminder that women can manage without men. Employment institutions have told a great many men that they are not needed; now they are beginning to get the same message from women.

All this, I suggest, has a bearing on the basis of individual identity, particularly male identity, and on the relatedness of the individual to the organization. The schizoid defense was part of the collusive preservation of a belief in the dependability of the employing organization, or at least of the institution of employment, as a satisfier, or satisficer, of multiple needs: for structure and order, for affirmation, and for money. The work role embedded in a hierarchy met dependency needs; the role of union member offered the experience of solidarity, power, and a vehicle for expressing fight. But the costs were high—alienation from the work itself; the experience of coercion—and the defense was a necessary coping mechanism to sustain the system. Widespread experience of unemployment has shown all too vividly the centrality of employment in conferring on the individual from outside a sense of identity, self-worth, and potency. (During the West Yorkshire study, one refrain of many women was "A man's not a real man unless he's got a job.") Correspondingly, it confirmed the operation of the schizoid defense by showing how many individuals evidently lacked an identity built around inner resources. A great many unemployed men (and here I am explicitly discussing men, not women) want only to get back into a job and can envisage no other way of being.

Massive unemployment, however, has also exploded the myth of the dependability of work organizations. Those men who do get back into a job are conscious of its precariousness and tend to adopt the "heads-down" strategy of survival described earlier. In addition, there is evidence that a growing number of people can and do survive without employment. Alternative role models are multiplying. Here I identify five.

Least salubrious of these models is that of passing the time, of existing without purpose. Being without doing can be a difficult and challenging process of self-examination and self-development; but the pattern I am identifying here is one of drifting from day to day. The followers of this way of life include many long-term unemployed men, especially in towns that industries have deserted, and a large set of young people. They are the casualties of failed dependency, not valued by society, not valuing themselves, surviving on state benefits and, often, petty crime. Among the younger of these lost generations, the hedonistic search for pleasure and excitement increasingly leads to drugs.

However, the remaining four role models all reflect real and positive alternatives to the conventional concept of employment.

Self-employment—selling one's skills directly—is the obvious alternative. For some accustomed to the dependency of employment, the shift to independence and self-management is too big to make, but those who achieve it tend to report that they work harder while experiencing much greater satisfaction. The spouse is often at least partly involved; and Asian and other immigrants have displayed the success of family businesses in the full sense of the term.

The third model is not tied to a specific profession or trade but to making a livelihood through a mix of activities, part planned, part opportunistic. Often, though not always, this mixture of activities falls within the "black economy"; state benefits provide the basic income.

Whereas these latter two are both economic models in that the primary concern is to make money, in the fourth model it is what one does that is primary. Its proponents are devoted to an activity, a cause, a set of values: making music, getting further education, doing voluntary work, campaigning for clean air. If such activities do not generate income, these individuals get by on the dole or through part-time or occasional earnings.

Finally, the fifth is the mixed model—that is, adopting different models at different phases of one's life: a period in full-time employment, a spell pursuing a chosen activity, another phase in a part-time job, and so on. If this model sounds familiar, that is because it has been a common model among women (the intervening "activity," of course, being child rearing); and its availability has partly cushioned them from the demoralizing effects of unemployment. Only now is it beginning to be perceived as a viable option for men, too.

All this may well imply, as many people said during the West Yorkshire study, that the Protestant work ethic is breaking down, that we are in the throes of the much-heralded paradigm shift. (For an important discussion of this, see Emery, 1982.) However, I am more immediately concerned with the growing evidence that it is the employment ethic—the notion that the normal and proper thing for a man to do is to devote his life to full-time paid employment—that is breaking down. The separability of "work" and "employment" is beginning to be recognized. For example, the West Yorkshire study (Khaleelee and Miller, 1984) exposed "a feeling that much of what is done in 'employment' . . . isn't 'work' in the sense of doing something that you can feel is creative, or even useful" (p. 28), along with acknowledgment that "a great deal of work which is useful or indeed essential to society is done outside employment" (p. 29)—child rearing being an obvious example.

For the individual, this paradigm shift means reconstructing his or her identity on different bases—forming a new integration of past and present, inside and outside, and even "male" and "female." Undoubtedly, the collapse of the dependency culture, by undermining the schizoid defense, has produced many casualties. These are people who had invested their "false selves" in enactment of organizational roles; and when these roles are removed, their other selves are trapped in an autistic inner world. There are nevertheless signs that many others are moving toward a fresh and constructive integration.

Essentially, high unemployment is producing a much more penetrating questioning of taken-for-granted assumptions about the institution of employment, not just by academics but by employees themselves, at various levels, struggling to cope with their day-to-day experience. I postulate that one significant outcome of their experience of the last five years is the demolition of the myth of authority. My argument runs as follows: Social order in the work organization has been sustained through legitimation of a hierarchy of managerial authority, with a consonant structure of status and rewards. Supervisors and junior managers in the lower reaches of the hierarchy, where there were some discrepancies between remuneration and authority, have been co-opted, as we have seen, through admission to the management "club" and the implied promise of promotion within it. Continued economic growth until the early 1970s and beyond produced enough actual evidence of promotion to make this implied promise credible. It could be believed that competence would be recognized and rewarded and that by and large there was a correlation between level of competence and level of authority. Evident cases of noncorrelation could be accepted as exceptions and aberrations from the norm; basically, cream would rise to the top. With the shift to zero growth and then retrenchment, first there was a reduction in upward mobility and then many managers discovered that club membership made them no less vulnerable than workers to the exigencies of redundancy. Not merely individuals but whole levels of management were eliminated; and many others at the lower levels justifiably felt insecure. Moreover, the processes through which some managed to secure their positions while others were extruded have displayed that competence is often a less important factor than influence and patronage. Surviving junior and middle managers, with diminished scope for promotion themselves, therefore become much more conscious of the discrepancies between competence and authority; and, as the underlying relationships of power and domination become more obvious, the myth of legitimated authority is eroded. The underlying master-servant model is uncovered—and they, too, are servants.

Disillusionment, therefore, may be almost as prevalent among those who remain in organizations as among those who have been made redundant. Whereas the relatedness of the worker to the organization (and "worker" here includes many technical and administrative staff) had tended to be one of passive compliance along with schizoid withdrawal, the self-perception of the line manager more typically resided in his exercise of authority and his place in a structure of authority and status, which it was his duty and in his interest to defend. Now there is as much pressure on him as there has been on the rest to be compliant in order to survive, except that he also has to go beyond that and display energy, enthusiasm, and commitment that he does not necessarily feel.

Among employees at all levels, there is a continuing attempt to hold on to accustomed defenses and myths, but in the face of the palpable shifts both outside and inside the organization, these are becoming more difficult to sustain. To survive as a person (as distinct from simply avoiding losing one's job), there is a need to create a new set of meanings around which to reconstruct one's identity. These meanings, to be viable, cannot afford to rest at all heavily on the organizational role; they have to be built on a new integration of internal resources and external affiliations. The consequent relatedness to the organization is much more consciously and genuinely instrumental. And it is sustained by an internal conviction that the individual could survive and make a sufficient livelihood outside that organization and possibly outside any organization.

To the extent that the individual is able to dispense with organizational position as a prop to his identity, he is in a position of strength, from which real choices can be made. He is able in a fuller sense to exercise his personal authority. (I conceptualize "personal authority" as a function of managing oneself in relation to role and task performance, while "power" is concerned with maintenance and enhancement of status and with control over other people.) In doing so, because his personal functioning is less keyed into defensive use of the structure and culture provided by the social system, he is less constrained by unconscious anxieties and dependent needs. On the one hand, he can choose calculated compliance: to support the objectives and norms of the organization only insofar as is necessary to serve his own, externally oriented, objectives. On the other hand, he can choose to exercise his authority in the service of the task of the organization and derive ego satisfaction from pursuing competence and excellence in role performance. This is the more risky option, since commitment to task does not necessarily mean, and indeed is unlikely to mean, commitment to the prevailing power structure or to the established ways of doing things. Although he does not set out to tilt against the system (my ideal type corresponds rather to Winnicott's description, quoted earlier, of "the healthy individual who has a compliant aspect of the self . . . and who is a creative and spontaneous being"), he will often be taking a critical stance and his behavior may well be perceived as insubordinate.

Commitment to task is sorely needed by the managements of today's organizations. Given the complexity of the problems to be tackled and the adaptive capability that is required, they cannot afford to go on giving a monopoly of creativity only to a few selected individuals (see Miller, 1983). In the past, when British managements have talked of the need for commitment to task, they have tended to behave as if the qualities they were really looking for were loyalty and obedience to themselves. Particularly in the newer technologies, with the knowledge base increasingly dispersed, the myth of omniscience at the top of the hierarchy is untenable; hence, obedience is the kiss of organizational death.

The idea (or ideal) of the individual exercising authority to manage himself in his role is far from new. For example, it has been the mainspring of the Tavistock Institute's Group Relations Training Programme since the 1960s and has guided much of the institute's organizational consultancy (see Miller and Rice, 1967; Lawrence and Miller, 1976; Miller, 1977; Lawrence, 1979). It is also consistent with Maslow's (1970) conception of self-actualization. This orientation lay behind the innovative forms of work organization, such as semiautonomous work groups, which have proved so difficult to sustain. The question is whether now, in what appears to be a rather different social and economic environment, there will be greater acceptance of a culture in which authority derived from task performance carries more weight than superordination/subordination.

Schwartz (1983), in a recent review of Maslow's theories, takes a pessimistic stance: "One might even hypothesize that those organizations that most require persons at the self-actualized level are least likely to tolerate them, since organizations whose myths are in danger of collapsing, who most need clear perception and creativity, are likely to feel most threatened by it" (p. 952). Dickson (1983) draws attention to one of the central myths: "*Managers believe they are the cause of subordinates' behavior* at the same time [as] they believe in equality and democracy as a principle of life in society" (p. 927; emphasis added). A great superstructure of "motivation theory" has been erected on this rather shaky premise. "Participation," on the face of it, recognizes and values the potential contribution of all employees to ways of improving performance of the task; but in practice it is often operated as a "velvet-glove" strategy to obtain employees' acceptance of managerial decisions that have already been made. The persistance of the managerial behavior that reflects these myths and assumptions, despite the efforts of many change agents and management educators, would therefore seem to justify Schwartz's pessimism.

Moreover, as we have also seen, many British managements seized the economic recession as an opportunity to reduce union power and exercise tighter control over the work force. Far from encouraging employees to use their own authority, they were demanding greater compliance.

However, there is another, slightly more optimistic, perspective. Managerial behavior is not a product simply of the kinds of people who occupy managerial roles, or of past processes of education, training, and socialization to which they have been subjected; it occurs in the context of a social system. The structure and culture of that system must be consonant with the behavior and even reinforce it; otherwise, it could not be sustained. I argued earlier that, although "resistance to change" can often be attributed to managements' defense of power and status, the perceived "beneficiaries" of changes—subordinates gaining more authority and discretion—are often ambivalent. In other words, there is a collusion, largely unconscious, to maintain the status quo, with its hierarchy of power and privilege. This is central to the dependency culture: there has to be the parental figure to receive the projections of love/hate, responsibility, and blame. If I am correct in postulating that British industry and society generally are moving out of that dependency culture, through a phase of failed dependency and toward "postdependency," and that an increasing number of employees are shifting into a more genuinely instrumental, "take-it-or-leave-it" relatedness to the employing organization, then that collusion is beginning to be undermined. Exercise of personal authority should become less ambivalent and more legitimate.

Although gross economic and sociopolitical changes have occurred in Britain in the last five years, changes in culture and attitudes move much more slowly. I certainly do not predict a sweeping, rapid change. As Schwartz indicates, many managements are likely to cling fatally long to patterns of the dependency culture. Many employees, too, will be reluctant to surrender their dependency. But, as the pressures of the collusion diminish, a growing number of managers will be freer to recognize that the people working with them are not quite the same animals as ten years ago, that the belief that they are "the cause of subordinates' behavior" is not quite so tenable, and that conventional theories of motivation and indeed of organization seem less and less appropriate. The new technologies do not of themselves make hierarchies dispensable, but they certainly flatten them, by calling into question the function of middle-management layers.

This process will be at times a turbulent one. Genuine empowerment is not something that can be given by management in controlled doses; it is taken by individuals who use their own authority to speak out, without necessarily waiting for permission. The leadership required of management is to define the task and to equip groups and individuals with the requisite resources so that they can manage themselves to perform it. If in that way the task itself becomes the leader, hallowed concepts such as subordination, obedience, and personal loyalty become outmoded and are replaced by negotiation between adults responsible for managing the boundaries of their respective systems and subsystems. This is not the familiar labor relations negotiation about pay and conditions; it is negotiation among people in their work roles about performance of the task. It is the task, and their competence in relation to it, that confers their authority on them.

It may well be, therefore, that a steadily increasing proportion of those now in employment, at all levels, will be perceiving themselves and expecting to be treated as, in effect, professionals. There is already a growing use of self-employed individuals and groups to undertake on a contractual basis work previously done by employees; and that trend may call into question existing assumptions about ways in which employees are managed. More conventional types of industrial and commercial organizations might usefully look for alternative models in those organizations that use large numbers of professionals—for example, universities and medical institutions, in which executive power tends to be more problematic.

Although the obvious need to experiment with new forms of work organization and management will understandably raise the anxiety of many managers, it may be comforting to realize that they are not moving into entirely unexplored territory. The kinds of

innovations that, despite their apparent success, met resistance in
the 1960s and 1970s are no less relevant today, and they should fare
much better with the decline of the dependency culture. And I
believe that the payoffs from reconnecting personal authority to the
task of the enterprise can be very substantial.

Note

In the West Yorkshire study referred to earlier, the
governmental Manpower Services Commission (MSC), which runs
the major youth programs, proved to be a universal scapegoat: "The
MSC is blamed if it provides realistic work experience and blamed
if it doesn't; it's blamed if it offers training and blamed if it doesn't."
We concluded: "Evidently the parental generation has ambivalent
feelings towards the school-leaving generation: it wants the kids to
have a decent future but sees them as a threat to adult jobs. That's
hard to acknowledge: it's easier to put the blame on MSC"
(Khaleelee and Miller, 1984, p. 16). In this context, it is hardly
surprising that a comparative study of British and American
students, carried out in 1982–83, showed the British as more cynical
and as having significantly less belief in the responsiveness of the
political system to the individual as an active participant. "Above
all, [the British students] appear to regard present political
institutions and their incumbents as lacking in legitimacy"
(Ranade and Norris, 1984, p. 56). The British sample was shown to
be distributed around the borderline between "protest participant"
(those who believed that they could affect their situation) and
"disgruntled apathetic" (those who believed that they could not).

TWELVE

Power Outside Organizational Paradigms

L. David Brown

As the world grows more interdependent and organizations are more subject to rapid external change, executives increasingly must work *outside* organizational boundaries. In recent years I have worked with many organizational executives concerned about problems in the larger society. This chapter examines the "functioning of executive power" outside organizational boundaries from the vantage points of conceptual perspectives on power and my own research and consulting experience.

The argument takes the following form. Theorists of power relations outside of organizations attend to dimensions of power that remain largely unrecognized by organization theorists. Organizational power issues are often resolved through "influence paradigms" that regulate the exercise of internal power. Community partnerships, which bring together representatives of diverse organizations to solve common problems, do not share such paradigms. As a result, executives are often ill equipped by organizational experience to work effectively in such partnerships. This chapter describes patterns of community partnership development, examines power relations within them, and suggests four factors that are central to "the functioning of executive powers" in such settings.

Power in Communities and Organizations

Power is an endlessly debated and defined concept (see, for example, March, 1966; Pfeffer, 1981b; Astley and Sachdeva, 1984).

I have been greatly influenced by the conceptual work of Lukes (1974) and its empirical application and refinement by Gaventa (1980). They propose a three-dimensional view of power that predicts different behavior when different dimensions are employed. The first dimension of power is observed when relatively equal parties openly contest a decision, each using available resources to influence the outcome. In such pluralistic power relations, *control over resources* is the basis of power, and the party with more resources mobilized has more influence. A second dimension of power operates when one party has less access to the decision-making forum. Barriers to participation or bias against one party can produce "nondecisions," in which conflicts of interest remain unexpressed. In this dimension *control over access and agendas* for decision making is key, and the interests of less powerful parties are not even discussed. The third dimension is observed when less powerful parties accept myths promulgated by more powerful parties and so support decisions that contradict their interests. In this pattern *control over awareness* results in cooperation and quiescence, in spite of conflicts of interest visible to outsiders. Table 1 summarizes the three dimensions.

Table 1. A Three-Dimensional Analysis of Power.

	One-Dimensional Power	Two-Dimensional Power	Three-Dimensional Power
Interaction Pattern:	Overt Conflict	Covert Conflict	Overt Cooperation
Decision by:	Pluralistic Negotiation	Nonparticipation	Quiescence
Sources of power:	Control over Resources votes money influence	Control over Access and Agendas barriers to participation built-in bias	Control over Awareness myths ideologies legitimate roles

This view of power is not pretty. There is potential for abuse, oppression, and manipulation inherent in power differences—a potential richly developed by the powerful groups, such as mine owners and union leaders, in Gaventa's (1980) historical study of power relations in Appalachia. The perspective on power emerging in the current organization and management literature has a different flavor. Power is seen as necessary for getting things done (Kanter, 1979), essential for adapting to external pressures (Pfeffer, 1981b), and desirable for handling interdependence (Kotter, 1978). Much of the literature on power in organizations examines "leadership," a concept with very positive connotations. Organizational researchers are much less suspicious and pessimistic about power and its use than community researchers are.

More important, organizational researchers have focused largely on the first dimension of power—influence in explicit conflicts through use of political resources. Some investigators have focused on *personal* influence, such as social attributes that confer power (French and Raven, 1959) or strategies and tactics for interpersonal influence (Kotter and Schlesinger, 1979; Kipnis, Schmidt, and Wilkinson, 1980). Others have emphasized the power conferred by organizational *position*, such as location for solving critical problems (Hickson and others, 1971; Pfeffer, 1981b); access to resources, support, and alliances (Kanter, 1979); or structural position in organizational hierarchies, resource pools, or central activities (Astley and Sachdeva, 1984).

Less attention has been paid to the second dimension of power—control by limiting access to or controlling agendas of decision making, and so preventing overt expression of differences. Political scientists have examined agenda control in communities (Bachrach and Baratz, 1962; Crenson, 1971), and occasional organizational analysts have examined how access to decision processes can be used to influence events (Pettigrew, 1975) or to empower individuals low in formal power (Mechanic, 1962). But there has been comparatively little analysis of how organizational subunits gain access to decision making, how organizational decision agendas are controlled, or what subtle biases shape the definition of "nondecisions" in organizational life.

Still less attention has been paid to the third dimension of power in organizational life—influence through control of participants' awareness to justify decisions that are not in their interest. Political scientists have recognized the importance of symbols and myths in the control of participant awareness (Edelman, 1964; Gaventa, 1980), and some organizational theorists have noted the importance of symbolic activities in organizational settings (Pfeffer, 1981b). But only very recently has the use of such "unobtrusive power" been systematically studied in organizational settings (Hardy and Pettigrew, 1985; Pettigrew, 1985a).

Why this lack of attention? One explanation is political: Organizational researchers need managerial support, so the political economy of organizational research discourages investigations of phenomena that managers prefer not to discuss. This argument has some force, particularly when managers participate directly in defining and supporting research activity (see Brown and Tandon, 1983). A second explanation is methodological: Unobtrusive power is inherently subtle and covert, and its successful use *prevents* overt conflict over decisions. Consequently, the occasions on which it has been used (Lukes, 1974) are difficult to identify. Furthermore, users of unobtrusive power are understandably reluctant to discuss their activities, since the future utility of their tactics often depends on their low visibility. Unobtrusive power relations are largely invisible to methods that do not permit richly textured analysis of complex situations; the investigations that focus on unobtrusive power in organizations often depend on participant observation and case studies, which remain relatively unfashionable methodologies in organizational research. A third explanation is organizational: Organizations are more tightly organized than most communities or societies, and that degree of organization can obscure the operation of subtle dimensions of power. Organizations typically formulate missions and goals that are accepted as legitimate by their members, and they coordinate member activity with leadership, formal structures, technological arrangements, and cultural expectations that define appropriate behavior (Brown, 1980). Over time and interaction, these factors converge to produce an *influence paradigm*, which defines who has organizational power, how it should be exercised, and what its limits are. This paradigm provides a shared context within which organization members initiate and receive influence attempts.

Influence paradigms define decision-making access and agendas—the second dimension of power. They indicate who should and who should not set agendas and participate in decisions. Janitors do not usually have a voice in marketing strategy, but they may influence wages-and-benefits decisions through collective bargaining. Individuals with little formal power but much control over access to decision makers, such as secretaries of senior managers, may wield considerable influence over what becomes defined as an issue and so placed on the decision-making agenda and what remains a "nondecision" (Mechanic, 1962).

Influence paradigms also shape subgroup awareness—the third dimension—by providing values, myths, and ideologies that legitimate decision processes that are apparently against their interests. For example, large bonuses to chief executives are explained as the result of impersonal formulas devised at a time when lower profits were expected and not easily changed after the fact. The utility of problem-solving mechanisms, such as an ombudsman or a grievance procedure, depends on how much legitimacy the mechanism has in the eyes of those it affects.

By establishing control over access and awareness, organizational influence paradigms reinforce and legitimate power distributions in organizations. But for paradigms to remain in force, all the parties must abide by their provisions. Bitter power struggles result from events that undermine paradigm legitimacy. No-holds-barred union-management struggles or dog-eat-dog acquisition fights result from lack of agreement on procedures to regulate conflict between the parties.

What do influence paradigms mean for "the functioning of executive power"? The Latin roots of the term "executive" (ex, sequi) mean "follow out," and influence paradigms provide maps for executives to influence organizational decision making. Paradigms define access routes and agendas for decision making, and they establish legitimate distributions of power and procedures for using it. Within these limits executives can focus on how to deploy their resources to affect decision making—or first-dimension power. Work outside organizational paradigms, in contrast, requires attention to access, agendas, and awareness in power relations.

Development of Community Partnerships

Community partnerships bring together representatives of different sectors—public, private, education, union, neighborhood organizations—to solve problems they cannot handle alone. Common interests vary across partnerships: the Jamestown Labor-Management Committee united to combat the economic decline of the community (Trist, 1979), while the National Coal Policy Project brought together warring producers, consumers, and environmentalists to find alternatives to constant legal struggles (Gricar and Hay, 1984). The use of such partnerships is rising. A recent survey found more than a hundred public-private partnerships operating in the state of Massachusetts alone (Governor's Task Force, 1982), and a national study group hailed community partnerships as important resources for solving major urban problems (Committee for Economic Development 1982).

Many complex social problems cannot be solved without the resources provided by coalitions of diverse organizations (Emery and Trist, 1965; Trist, 1977; 1983). Community decisions are greatly influenced by formal and informal interorganizational networks (Laumann, Galaskiewicz, and Marsden, 1978; Perucci and Pilisuk, 1970), but such networks have seldom been *consciously* designed to solve community problems. They more commonly arise from the hurly-burly of community politics and therefore often leave out important participants or include partners irrelevant to the problem at hand. But the creation of interorganizational partnerships does not have to be left to chance. The partners relevant to major social problems are often easy to identify, and social technologies now exist for handling conflicts of interest constructively. Conscious design and management of interorganizational, intercommunity, and even international partnerships can pay major social dividends in coordinating effort, reducing duplication of effort, preventing unnecessary conflict, and encouraging innovative solutions to complex problems. The following examples illustrate the evolution of several such community partnerships:

1. The Executive-Activist Dialogues were launched by a national foundation to promote cooperation between activists from disadvantaged urban communities and chief executives of major corporations in the same city. The dialogues brought participants together for a weekend retreat designed and facilitated by third-party consultants to promote communications and to find joint projects that would benefit the city. The first dialogue produced intense conflict and no successful project; the second produced much discussion, several projects, and continuing relationships among participants. The dialogues brought together representatives of the richest and most powerful elements of the city with representatives of the poorest and least powerful—a chasm seldom bridged by other efforts (see Brown, 1977).

2. The Committee on Residential Lending was initiated by a suburban city manager to deal with controversies over financial disinvestment by lenders' steering of buyers and realtors to racially segregated neighborhoods. Participants included citizen activists, realtors, lenders, and city government officials. After initial stormy meetings, the committee articulated shared goals, developed analyses of housing problems, proposed solutions, and worked with other agencies to promote reinvestment in the city. The committee evolved over several years from a collection of antagonistic subgroups who blamed each other for community problems to a cohesive organization working together to promote financial reinvestment in the community (Gricar and Brown, 1981).

3. The National Coal Policy Project brought together representatives of coal producers, coal users, and environmentalist organizations to discuss national policies for coal mining and use. Many representatives had long histories of conflict, and previous disagreements had typically resulted in acrimonious and expensive court battles. At the initiative of a coal company executive and an environmentalist agency leader, the project sought to formulate mutually acceptable national policies. Project participants met in task forces, used third-party consultants, and adopted special procedures to resolve disagreements. Eventually the project produced 200 shared recommendations for coal policies, some of which have now been incorporated in national legislation. The project produced agreements among participants accustomed to

bitter legal battles, and it demonstrated the potential of nationwide cooperative agreements (Gricar and Hay, 1984).

As these examples indicate, community partnerships are initially unorganized systems (see Brown, 1980), and they must cope with several issues as they organize themselves to act in concert. The most important of these issues are (1) identifying problems and participants, (2) negotiating shared visions and goals, (3) diagnosing problems and planning action, and (4) implementing decisions.

Identifying Problems and Participants. Community partnerships typically do not form unless potential participants recognize a compelling common problem and formulate that problem in terms that encourage cooperation. Frequently some participants define others as the problem and so come prepared to blame instead of cooperate. The Committee on Residential Lending, for example, brought together citizen activists (who perceived the problem to be irresponsible lenders and racist realtors) with lenders and realtors (who thought that radical troublemakers were the problem). The city manager formulated the problem as improving understanding and promoting community reinvestment—a redefinition of the issues that enabled participants to continue discussions.

Problem definitions shape participant selections, and the source of an invitation may determine its acceptance. The city manager successfully invited realtors, lenders, and activists to the Committee on Residential Lending, though lenders no longer talked to activists outside the committee. Many chief executives attended Executive-Activist Dialogues because of the sponsoring foundation, not because they expected productive meetings. When participants do not recognize a problem or accept the legitimacy of an invitation, partnership development is badly handicapped. Some environmentalist groups did not join the National Coal Policy Project, for example, because they did not see a problem ("We are already winning in the courts") or because they did not accept its convenors as legitimate.

To form community partnerships, in short, organizers must formulate problems that compel cooperation, identify relevant participants, and arrange credible sponsorship. Launching such partnerships is a very delicate business, especially when the needed partners have histories of conflict.

Negotiating Shared Visions and Goals. Getting representatives to appear is often just the beginning of the battle. Participants with histories of conflict are often strongly tempted to replay past engagements. Community partnerships must convince skeptical representatives that constructive outcomes are possible, for representatives will not stay long if the main fare is old battles. Therefore, initial discussions must generate a shared vision of joint work for common goals. Visions must simultaneously recognize diverse interests and articulate common concerns to hold the partnership together. Representatives to the Committee on Residential Lending brought initial goals so diverse that early meetings produced much conflict, but that conflict clarified differences *and* previously unrecognized common interests in revitalizing city housing stock.

Early negotiations set expectations, precedents, and norms for future meetings. Representatives decide future participation on initial experiences of influence or impotence, inclusion or exclusion. In the first Executive-Activist Dialogue, activists felt "railroaded" in early discussions by executive arguments and cohesive presentations. Halfway through the dialogue, the activists withdrew to "get our shit together" and returned to impose their own solution on the guilt-stricken executives. The activists won the battle, but at a high cost to future cooperation. In contrast, at the Committee on Residential Lending, the city manager encouraged analysis of problems and discouraged escalating conflict, and gradually consensus on committee goals emerged.

To summarize, initial discussions ideally clarify differences and common concerns on which shared visions can be based. Representatives tacitly assess each other in initial meetings, identify resources, and negotiate ground rules for future meetings. Events in initial meetings form the basis for future analysis and decision making—or for their absence.

Diagnosing Problems and Planning Action. Community partnerships in their ideal form provide the resources needed to solve complex social problems, the interrelated systems of problems that Ackoff (1974) calls "messes." Such messes require analysis and planning that integrate the varied resources of diverse organizations to achieve solutions impossible to any of them alone. But such

solutions depend on the partnership's capacity to use its differences
constructively.

Shared goals can provide the basis for constructive
management of differences. Community partnerships often
reorganize themselves after they agree on basic goals. They develop
structures that allow efficient use of their resources. The Committee
on Residential Lending, for example, broke into subcommittees to
analyze issues in depth and to formulate action plans. Those
subgroups brought back recommendations for approval by the
whole committee.

Sometimes difference management in community partnerships requires special procedures to facilitate decision making. The
National Coal Policy Project, for example, adopted the "rule of
reason" (Wessel, 1976) as a procedure for handling conflicts among
representatives, and so dealt constructively with some highly
controversial issues. The Executive-Activist Dialogues used third-
party consultants to facilitate initial discussions and to help the
participants work together. These consultants helped manage
conflicts at critical points.

Differences among participants are potentially the source of
innovative problem solving or the seeds of avoidance or conflict
escalation. The first Executive-Activist Dialogue produced a seesaw
of conflict. Executives dominated early discussions; activists later
rebelled and claimed "victory"; by the end of the retreat, both
parties were antagonistic and alienated. The second dialogue
produced exploration and long-term cooperation, in part because
differences among participants did not coalesce on the executive-
activist dimension. Participants articulated perspectives that united
individuals from both groups; they listened to each other; they
generated alternatives that responded to many interests.

Implementing Decisions. In the process of implementing
decisions, issues that were only temporarily resolved can again be
raised—especially if the cooperation of others outside the
partnership is required. When implementation of decisions largely
involves participants, previous agreements have considerable force.
Partnerships that survive to plan and implement action strategies
typically have developed their own influence paradigm to organize
problem solving on any issues that remain unresolved. In the

second Executive-Activist Dialogue, for example, several mixed subgroups of executives and activists planned projects and later carried out those plans. Problems were handled on the basis of patterns developed during the dialogue; so executives and activists shared assumptions about how differences should be handled and decisions made.

As noted, implementation plans sometimes require the cooperation of parties outside the partnership. The Committee on Residential Lending, for example, wanted actions from the city council, the Veterans Administration, the Federal Housing Authority, and local citizens. In a striking metamorphosis, the committee evolved from an arena for squabbling interest groups to a cohesive interest group exerting pressure on other organizations. Relations with outside groups can replicate or reignite problems experienced at the outset of the partnership. Tensions initially avoided may return to haunt participants. Contentious potential participants left out of the partnership to facilitate the management of differences at the outset may return to hinder later implementation efforts. The National Coal Policy Project sponsors kept the project to a manageable size and stridency by ignoring some parties and by not pursuing others who were skeptical. After the project had produced its policy recommendations, however, the lack of support from excluded parties undercut wider consideration of its recommendations.

Partnership decisions can be implemented by participants or by links to outside agencies and forces. Even when only participants are involved, implementation can revive old tensions. When outsiders must join forces to implement partnership decisions, problems of conflict and cooperation similar to initial negotiations may have to be managed.

Executive Power in Community Partnerships

Community partnerships present several special problems to executives. First, they are underorganized. Executives accustomed to the blueprints provided by organizational paradigms may find this lack of organization quite disconcerting. Second, community partnerships are often forced to share power in order to encourage participation by many relevant stakeholders (Trist, 1983). Such partnerships make decisions by mutual influence; so participants must deal with comparatively ill-defined hierarchies of responsibility and authority. Third, problems of loosely defined organizations and distributions of authority are compounded by questions about access to decisions or the legitimacy of decision processes; such questions are not so common in organizations with well-developed influence paradigms. Power in community partnerships requires skills for which the organizational experience of many executives is poor preparation.

I focus here on four aspects of power in community partnerships for which organizational executives are likely to be ill prepared. I will treat them roughly in the order in which they arise as community partnerships develop.

Negotiating Credibility. In most organizations position contributes at least as much to executive power as personal characteristics. Personal attributes seldom compensate for the absence of a structural base (Kanter, 1979; Pfeffer, 1981b). Not so in community partnerships. When representatives of organizations with histories of conflict come together, they may well suspect one another *because* of their organizational positions. Activists suspected chief executives in the Executive-Activist Dialogues; lenders were leery of citizen representatives in the Committee on Residential Lending; coal executives and environmentalists were old antagonists in the National Coal Policy Project. Suspicion is not universal, and participants often respect each other's position and experience. But respect for position is *not* automatic in community partnerships, as it often is within an organization.

A community partnership cannot succeed without some minimum of mutual credibility among its members. But that credibility evolves out of interaction. That interaction is shaped by personal characteristics of participants and by choices among issues and procedures for group discussion. The experience of two Executive-Activist Dialogues is illustrative. The most influential executive in the first dialogue was impatient with "inefficient" foundation staff and "unproductive" discussion, and he was shocked at "obscene" language used by activists, particularly a young woman from an activist Hispanic gang. He pressed successfully for a quick choice of a joint project. At dinner that night, the Hispanic participant horrified him by advocating the Chinese Communist economic system over capitalism. Later that evening she took the activists out on strike against his project. Initial skirmishes about impatience and language escalated into stereotyping ("ignorant young radical," "capitalist pig") and personal antagonism. The dialogue's focus on personal differences and the styles of two informal leaders produced escalating conflict and declining credibility for both.

In contrast, the informal leaders of the second dialogue—the chief executive of a multinational manufacturing firm and the leader of an unwed mothers' project in the black ghetto—interviewed and favorably impressed each other on the first evening. They sparred amiably with each other about leadership early in the workshop and later engaged each other more seriously over differences in their experience. But these interactions produced recognition and acknowledgment of their different resources: the black activist acknowledged the expertise of the CEO on economic matters, and he acknowledged her expertise on the realities of life in the ghetto. They argued over possible projects, chose to work together on a common venture, and continued to collaborate for several years after the dialogue. Their work together built mutual credibility and enabled personal contact that was rewarding to each.

What factors promoted the negotiation of credibility in these situations? Participants were impressed by evidence of competence and were quick to discount "bullshit." They also valued direct discussion of interests and agendas; they expected each other to pursue personal or group interests, but they were alert to and resented covert influence attempts. Frank discussion of interests enabled participants to recognize diverse interests as legitimate without feeling manipulated. Low-status participants were particularly impressed by high-status participants who genuinely wanted to learn about the experiences or problems of others. Participants generally were more able to listen when they felt heard and appreciated for their knowledge and resources. The development of credibility often coincided with the emergence of personal connections among very different participants—connections that developed on many different bases but included implicit recognition of some commonalities, however different the parties might be on other dimensions. These characteristics can be summarized as follows:

> Negotiating credibility depends on combina-
> tions of participants' personal characteristics, discus-
> sion topics, and group processes that promote (1)
> demonstration of participant competencies relevant to
> shared problems, (2) explicit discussion and recogni-
> tion of other interests as legitimate, (3) mutual
> learning about other participants and their situations,
> and (4) personal connection among representatives
> with different interests.

Negotiating credibility is critical at the beginning of a community partnership, for influence with other representatives cannot be assumed on the basis of position.

Formulating Inclusive Visions. Organizational visions integrate core values and ideologies to provide shared explanations for the members' experiences. The intricacies of visions, values, and ideologies in organizations are only now being examined in any detail, though their importance has long been recognized by some authors (Selznick, 1957; Child, 1972; Beyer, 1981). Organizational visions define reasons for existence, legitimate relationships with other institutions, and provide underlying rationales for the organization of human, financial, informational, and material resources (see Harrison, 1972). Organization leaders express core values of the organization (Mintzberg, 1979), though not always consciously. Members may not explicitly recognize organizational values, but they are often quick to recognize violations (see Brown and Brown, 1983). Visions provide a common ground of assumptions and awareness against which members act.

Community partnerships do not automatically begin with visions that include the interests of all participants. Their members bring a variety of inconsistent expectations, though they often hold some societal values and ideologies in common (see Lodge, 1975; Hofstede, 1980). When participants do not have vision, disagree-ments are easily polarized in value and ideological terms, and such disagreements are notoriously difficult to resolve (Brown and Brown, 1983). Without a shared vision, participants do not easily subordinate their immediate interests to those of the partnership. Few organizational executives have opportunities to practice formulating visions that include diverse interests and values, because organizational paradigms typically provide ready-made syntheses of values and ideology for their members.

Successful community partnerships create *inclusive* visions. Participants in the Committee on Residential Lending, for example, came with very different agendas: activists wanted to monitor lenders; lenders wanted to follow "sound banking practices"; realtors wanted to discuss problems created by federal loan programs. So initial discussions produced considerable conflict. Further discussion, facilitated by the city manager, clarified both differenes and similarities in interests, and gradually a common commitment emerged to "promoting reinvestment in the community"—a vision that included interests of all the parties. The discussion also reduced personal animosities as participants learned to appreciate the pressures operating on each other.

Formulating inclusive visions requires the exploration of differences in participant interests, values, and ideologies. Such explorations risk escalating conflict, and they require explicit discussions of diverse perspectives and goals. Participants often marshal different facts to support contradictory explanations for problems; and individual skills and group processes that enable individuals to share their views, listen to those of others, and develop shared diagnoses of the situation are essential. Ultimately, participants must synthesize their interests, values, and ideologies into a common perspective that integrates incompatible interests and articulates compelling mutual goals. Individual skills can contribute to this evolution (Eiseman, 1978; Fisher and Ury, 1981), as can group processes that focus on articulating superordinate goals to guide future activity (Sherif, 1958). To summarize:

> Formulating inclusive visions for community partnerships depends on (1) exploring similarities and differences in interests, values, and ideologies; (2) formulating analyses that build common understand-

ing of problems and possible solutions; and (3) articulating visions that integrate incompatible interests and provide shared goals and plans.

Inclusive visions are needed for specific planning, for decision making, or for implementing solutions. But they are seldom easily formulated at the outset. The details of common core values and ideologies often have to be identified or created in interaction. Understandings developed in early discussions provide a basis for subsequent influence. In creating a shared vision, participants begin to establish procedures and precedents that will shape decisions of the future—a partnership influence paradigm.

Organizing Decision Processes. Decision making in most organizations is organized by combinations of leadership activity, structural arrangements, technological imperatives, and cultural factors (Brown, 1980). The organization of decision making varies considerably across institutions. Leaders play a central role in some (Harrison, 1972); structural arrangements are critical in others (Kerr and Jermier, 1978); technological imperatives are important for still others (Woodward, 1965); cultural patterns are most important in others (Brown and Brown, 1983). In most organizations combinations of these factors regulate decision making in the form of generally accepted influence paradigms.

Community partnerships, in contrast, are initially *unorganized*—or at best loosely organized—and so make different demands on their participants. Without well-defined paradigms, such questions as who should be included (or excluded), what issues should be discussed, what alternatives can be considered, or how alternatives can be chosen remain ambiguous. Decisions are difficult without agreement on procedures and standards. Partnerships that continue over long periods evolve their own paradigms to organize decision making.

In the shorter term, alternative decision patterns may be needed. For example, community partnerships can rely to some extent on societal expectations to guide discussion and decision making. In the Committee on Residential Lending, potential escalations were retarded to some extent by the fact that participants lived in the same small city and could expect to meet each other again in other settings. They also shared common commitments to middle-class norms for civilized discussion and beliefs in basing decisions as much as possible on established facts. These agreements encouraged analysis of data and relatively polite disagreements in committee activity.

A second alternative to a well-developed decision-making pattern is agreement on a formal procedure or an impersonal arrangement. The National Coal Policy Project adopted the "rule of reason" (Wessel, 1976) as a formal procedure for resolving controversial issues. The second Executive-Activist Dialogue and the Committee on Residential Lending both used subgroups to analyze alternatives and plan for action, and so created small units that could informally resolve conflicts that would have paralyzed the partnership as a whole.

A third option is to authorize a third party to manage the decision process. The Executive-Activist Dialogues were largely managed by third parties, in the persons of foundation staff and consultants, who selected participants and designed initial workshop activities. In the second dialogue, participants gradually took over management of the discussion and decisions. The city manager played a pivotal role in the Committee on Residential Lending, bringing participants together and regulating their discussion as they struggled to define a common vision. He became less central after the subcommittees began work on specific issues and the committee became more able to regulate itself.

> Early decision making in community partner-
> ships may require (1) using societal expectations to
> guide discussion, (2) adopting impersonal procedures
> to regulate conflict, and (3) authorizing third parties
> to manage decision processes.

Different alternatives may be appropriate at different stages. Third parties, for example, can convene participants who would not attend at the invitation of interested parties. Formal procedures and impersonal arrangements may enable productive discussion of controversial issues, particularly when they are administered by a credible third party. Societal values and expectations can guide early interactions in the absence of agreement on procedures for handling differences. Successful partnerships will develop their own decision-making patterns in the long run, but pre-paradigm alternatives can facilitate initial decision making.

Empowering Diverse Participants. Organizational influence paradigms distribute power among levels and departments. Ideally, organizational power is concentrated where it is most needed for organizational effectiveness (Mintzberg, 1979). Resources are allocated to individuals to facilitate their contributions to organizational performance. Influence paradigms provide access to decision making for some and justify favoring some interests over others. Individuals seek to maximize their own power, or at least to minimize its loss, and they use information, support, and resources to do so (Kanter, 1979).

Community partnerships initially have no shared paradigms to define who has access to and control over decision making, or to justify unequal distributions of power and resources. They depend on awareness of common problems and shared access to decision making to recruit and hold participants. Patterns of activity in the partnership must *empower all the participants* if the partnership is to utilize their resources. Participants do not have to be equally powerful, but they do have to be mutually influential if the partnership is to survive. When partners feel disenfranchised or perceive no common interests, they are likely to withdraw. Empowering participants in a community partnership involves many dimensions of power relations: participants' awareness of their own and others' interests; shared access to agenda setting and decision making; mutually recognized resources for influencing actual choices (Gaventa, 1980). Executives who are trained to handle power primarily in terms of resource control and influencing explicit decisions may be at a serious disadvantage.

Partner *awareness* is critical to partnership effectiveness. Partnerships depend on participants' recognition of their own interests, the interests of others, and the intersections among them. The National Coal Policy Project convenors failed to demonstrate meaningful common interests to some potential participants, and so lost important allies. Citizens' recognition of their interest in community reinvestment was prerequisite to the formation of the

Committee on Residential Lending: lender interest in the committee was mobilized by the city manager's support and by citizens' threats to "go public" about disinvestment. Educational activities that clarify participant interests can empower previously unaware partners.

Empowerment activities can alter barriers to participation or built-in biases and so change *access* to decision making. In the first Executive-Activist Dialogue, the executive "united front" intimidated activists, informally excluded them from initial decisions, and set the stage for their withdrawal and counterattack. In the second dialogue, preparations prior to the meeting and selection of more diverse executives reduced subtle barriers to activist participation and biases in favor of executive control. Neither group dominated access to subsequent decision processes. Community partnerships in themselves can change participant access to decision making. Representatives of citizen groups on the Committee on Residential Lending felt empowered by the invitation to participate, and other participants felt more able to influence community-wide decision making because of their role in the committee.

Empowering parties by recognizing their *resources* may be important to improved problem solving. The city manager granted activists access to the Committee on Residential Lending, but he also stopped them from browbeating other participants and dominating discussions by sheer numbers. The definition of resources critical to decisions may not be highly visible. In the first dialogue, analytical expertise and general information were tacitly chosen as critical resources—a choice that automatically encouraged executive dominance of decision making. In the second dialogue, high value was also placed on personal experience with urban problems; therefore, activists were empowered to influence decisions.

> Community partnerships can empower participants needed for effective joint action by (1) encouraging awareness of all interests affected by joint decisions, (2) removing barriers to participation or biases that restrict participant access to decision

making, and (3) recognizing participant resources relevant to specific decisions.

Empowering activities continue to be relevant at many stages. The organizational experience of many participants may encourage them to centralize power in one party or another, but partnerships that seek to respond to many interests cannot allow centralization or fragmentation in place of mutual influence.

Discussion

I have argued that "the functioning of executive power" in most organizations follows blueprints laid down by organizational influence paradigms. These paradigms legitimate distributions of organizational authority, organize patterns and processes of influence, and define participants and procedures in decision making. The study of less organized systems—such as community partnerships, where power is neither facilitated nor fettered by shared paradigms—can illuminate the nature of influence inside and outside of organizations.

Community partnerships focus attention on issues of awareness and problems of access to decision making, since the paradigms that legitimate and organize organization decision making are not available. Partnerships evolve their own paradigms over time, but influence initially depends on processes that are less familiar to executives who operate within well-defined paradigms: negotiating credibility, formulating inclusive visions, creating alternative decision processes, and empowering many diverse participants.

So what? How many executives work in community partnerships? Partnerships are important, but only a small minority of executives will ever be involved in their creation. Why should executives worry about influence processes in such uncommon situations?

Community partnerships may be rare, but situations in which organizational influence paradigms no longer control decision making are increasingly common. At least four classes of situation call for the exercise of "power outside the paradigm" by executives. For example, extraparadigm power may be required by the *declining legitimacy of old paradigms* in the face of changes in the work force, new technologies, or market pressures. General Motors' increased emphasis on marketing in the mid-1980s requires changes in influence paradigms based on the primacy of engineering, production, and long organizational tenure. The decline of old paradigms requires the use of extraparadigm influence strategies as a new paradigm is being created.

Organizational influence paradigms are typically not shared with other organizations, and *interorganizational cooperation* requires the development of shared assumptions about the exercise of power. Joint ventures, mergers, and other forms of cooperation across organizational boundaries require influence processes that initially are outside the paradigms of the parties. As organizations become increasingly dependent on establishing and maintaining effective interorganizational linkages with consumers, suppliers, regulators, competitors, and other external constituencies (Pfeffer and Salancik, 1978), influence independent of shared paradigms will become increasingly critical.

A third example is the requirements of *initiating and implementing strategic change*. Major changes in organizational strategy may require altering influence paradigms by which decisions are made and carried out, and inability to develop and exercise power outside previous blueprints can hamstring needed changes. Pettigrew's (1985a) study of strategic changes at Imperial Chemical Industries demonstrates the importance of extraparadigm influence in both implementing and blocking major change. In short, the capacity to operate outside old paradigms and to create new ones suited to new circumstances is important to executives in many situations beyond community partnerships.

How can executives develop the personal skills and organizational mechanisms that enable effective influence outside shared paradigms? Conceptual recognition of the needed capacities can help, but there is no substitute for real experience. Most formal management education provides skills and knowledge appropriate to influence based on technical expertise rather than capacities for operating effectively in unorganized situations. The analysis presented in this chapter suggests that work with diverse groups to define and accomplish common objectives is an important ingredient in learning to develop and use power independent of paradigms.

Some organizational roles encourage relevant learning. Project managers and other individuals in integrator positions are forced to coordinate the work of diverse departments without relying on hierarchical authority (Galbraith, 1973). Kanter's (1983) research on middle-level innovators indicates that successful initiation and implementation of changes requires developing a network of lateral contacts and formulating visions that include many different interests and parties. Roles that require executives to cooperate with peers and develop common projects encourage them to learn how to work outside departmental paradigms, though they continue to have the support of organization-wide expectations.

Experience outside organizations is also potentially desirable. Individuals whose roles require spanning organizational boundaries to deal with external agencies must learn to operate effectively in multiple worlds (Strauss, 1962). Executives whose outside activities bring them in cooperative contact with diverse groups can also learn to use extraparadigm influence. More than a hundred United States cities now have programs that bring leaders from different sectors together to examine community problems and to build leadership networks (see Brown, Benroth, and Gaertner, 1983). Many corporations explicitly recognize the value of executive effectiveness outside corporate walls. Research suggests that an "inner circle" of externally linked corporate executives wields great influence in the United States and the United Kingdom (Useem, 1984). External experience is not enough, since work with other executives who largely share one's initial assumptions may not provide opportunities to deal with real diversity. Learning to negotiate credibility, formulate common visions, organize decisions, and empower others who have different values, interests, and ideologies is critical (and more difficult than dealing with others who are similar). The learning potential of executive work with a multicultural neighborhood organization or a joint union-government-management committee, from this perspective, is higher than that of work with a trade association or a business roundtable.

The development of extraparadigm influence mechanisms and skills in community partnerships has important implications for large-scale social problem solving. Both the invisible hand of the free market and the omnipotent controllers of centralized planning have serious drawbacks as problem-solving mechanisms for modern societies. Trist (1983) has argued that self-regulating institutions at the interorganizational level, intermediate between competing firms and regulating governments, offer a viable alternative to the exploitation of unregulated free markets or bureaucratic ossification of overcentralized planning. Interorganizational networks and community partnerships are social forms in which relatively small interventions, such as the use of third-party facilitation or the adoption of problem-solving processes, can have enormous social impacts. The National Coal Policy Project produced recommendations supported by both producers and environmentalists—an extraordinary outcome given their history of bitter conflict. Such coalitions can achieve policy breakthroughs that integrate public and private interests and mobilize multipartisan support. We need more understanding about the political, social, and economic forces that surround, shape, and facilitate interorganizational problem solving, and we need more experience with tailoring interventions that enable mutual influence outside organizational paradigms. Interventions that promote effective operation of such partnerships can yield large social gains at very small costs.

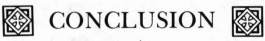

❖ CONCLUSION ❖

Functions
of Executive Power:
Exploring New Approaches

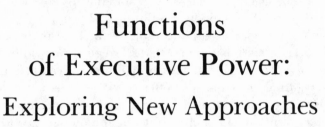

Suresh Srivastva, Frank J. Barrett

> It struck me what quality went to form a man of achievement, especially in literature, and which Shakespeare possessed so enormously—I mean *negative capability*, that is, when a man is capable of being in uncertainties, mysteries, doubts, without any irritable reaching after fact and reason.
>
> ——*John Keats*

> The test of a first-rate intelligence is the ability to hold two opposed ideas in mind at the same time and still retain ability to function.   ——*F. Scott Fitzgerald*

In looking back over these statements, we are struck by the fascination with the topic of "power" and the energy with which attendants at the symposium, authors and students alike, attempted to grasp its significance. Against this background we propose a normative theory of executive power as a summary of this book. We propose that, to view the process of power in its fullness and to be a "powerful executive," one needs to have a kind of double vision. When Keats spoke of "negative capability," he was referring to Shakespeare's ability to understand experience from a number of different human perspectives and present each character's passions, believing equally in all at once. Fitzgerald, an avid reader of Keats, was trying to capture the same phenomenon when he praised the ability to believe in apparently contradictory viewpoints, all aesthetically valid, and not be crippled by the awareness, but to "retain ability to function," to continue to dream, to see possibility and beauty. It is this talent for multiple envisioning, combined with the ability to move forward, that makes executives powerful. And yet "executive power" is more than this. And herein lies the challenge for understanding it. The observer of "executive power" needs to see and understand the multiple perspectives of various actors in interaction and yet to see the process of interaction itself, the "spaces in between" actors. We propose, then, to view executive power from an ecological stance, as an evolving system of interacting subunits.

A traditional view has power distributed vertically, in greater increments as one moves up the hierarchy, with executives who "know" issuing directives, more or less unilaterally, to less knowledgeable subordinates. This view seems to us too constricted and exclusive; power is here regarded essentially as political maneuvering among more or less "powerful" stakeholders. This kind of power in organizations weakens the executive power of the system. A dominating boss, wielding authority and enjoying control over submissive subordinates, is like a knight wielding a sharp, double-edged sword. But, instead of a hilt, this sword has a sharp blade on the other end. Thus, as the "knight" proudly expands his authority and grips the sword more tightly, he cuts into his own flesh and draws his own blood. Let us therefore abandon a vertical view of systems glorified in organizational charts and propose the image of a circle. Power cannot be found at any one point in the circle. Rather, power is relational, moving in pulsating rhythms. Power moves outward—a centrifugal, expansive force, spreading throughout the organization as it seeks consensus and inclusive agreement. It then draws inward, a centripetal force, pulling members together in a cooperative mode, with the alluring force of a common vision within which they can appreciate their own significance.

Executive power is not something that can be measured in outputs or outcomes. It cannot be seen by observing who makes what decisions. Executive power is a movement, a process of strengthening and nurturing members in an inclusive system, increasing the vitality and power of interconnected participants. It is in the process of implementing ideas and nurturing members' potential for creating ideas that power exists. The process of empowerment is the product of power in the making.

As we said earlier, perhaps the key to executive power is in the way that executives choose *to see*. The powerful executive is a seer of possibilities, of the potential for human growth and development. It is this ability to see human potential that is the soul of an empowered system, the electrical current that charges it with vitality—for merely seeing possibility in others nurtures the very potential envisioned. In seeing this potential, powerful executives do not focus on the present absence of abilities that may exist at a later date; rather, they see the intrinsic, awakening wisdom in members. The empowered system, then, is a system full of hope. It is not filled with hope based on unfounded expectations, nor is it a hope that focuses only on achieving something better than the present. It is a hope that values the richness of possibility inherent in the present, grounded in and informed by an awareness of what the system is capable of now. The powerful executive has trust in the capacity of the human spirit to create and re-create itself. This kind of hope rallies energy and activates more power in the system.

Executive power, then, operates with a commitment to human development and encourages the unleashing of members' passions and excitements. By investing in members' creative energy and supporting the development of core ideas, executive power has an infinite capacity to increase throughout the system. Executive power exists in a system to the extent that executives seek consensus, command cooperation, and create culture.

Dialogue and Consensus Seeking

Dialogue is the only way, not only in the vital questions of political order, but in all expressions of our being. Only by virtue of faith, however, does dialogue have power and meaning: by faith in man and his possibilities, by the faith that I can only

become truly myself when other men also become
themselves [Karl Jaspers].

The most essential manifestations of executive power are
embodied in the system's processes of building and maintaining
consensus. An organization that fosters social arrangements to
facilitate the seeking of consensus is valuing the system's most
essential resource—participants' ideas. The powerful executive
recognizes that the idea is the basic unit of value. Consensus is the
manifestation of power because, when members *truly* consent, the
driving mechanism that produces action is internalized. Consensus
is the *source* of power because real authority to act is created when
members collectively entrust the executive, who only then can make
plans and commit resources with the confidence that members will
execute action. Barnard (1938), in his book *The Functions of the
Executive*, recognized that real authority resides in the organizational membership: "The decision as to whether an order has
authority or not lies with the persons to whom it is addressed and
does not reside in 'persons of authority' or those who issue these
orders" (p. 163). Hence, the source of organizational authority is
members' consent. The powerful executive actively seeks consensus,
not only because of the directive power of agreement and shared
understanding of reality among members but also because the
authority by which the executive acts is the very consent of the
governed.

To understand an organization's activities and purposes, one
must understand the process by which consent is created. The
executive seeks *genuine* consensus by listening closely. In fact, the
more members are able to articulate ideas and share different
perspectives through creative, experimental social arrangements,
the more executive power the system possesses. By *genuine*
consensus we mean that the system does not attempt to force
agreement by adopting procedures that "flatten" or simplify
perspectives. We do not suggest, for example, that collective voting
by itself constitutes consensus. Voting, by presenting two mutually
competing choices so that one side "wins," can be an inadequate
means of building a common view because it polarizes members. It
is a short-cut method of decision making and does not facilitate

arrangements whereby members can achieve a shared understanding, a realization of commonality and mutuality with which many can identify. Voting creates a segmented organization. Nor should the executives, in the hope of avoiding conflict, try to eliminate a multiplicity of shared ideas. A collection of opposing viewpoints is preferable to automatic agreement, which deprives an organization of creative vitality. An organization has executive power to the extent that it nurtures ideas from various perspectives and values the creative potential in bringing together the diverse.

An empowered system supports the articulation and transmission of ideas among members by devoting time to meetings and forums where reciprocal exchanges can occur. Such arrangements enhance a free flow of information and open accessibility of members. The organization supports consensus seeking when members are free to interact, unencumbered by the disempowering baggage of titles, status, functions, and divisions. Genuine consensus seeking is the entitlement of the traditionally disenfranchised.

If consensus seeking is reaching outward and listening, the centrifugal widening movement of executive power, then the articulation of a shared understanding is the centripetal, inclusive, drawing together of diverse members. The powerful executive is both an *attentive listener,* seeking to hear commonalities that underlie diversity, and a *clear articulator* of shared agreement. His ability to envision helps to shape agreement and mutual understanding, so that diverse members can identify their part in the vision. His ability to articulate is based on his ability to see relationships and connections among diverse ideas, to see wholes even when ideas are presented to him in parts.

Powerful executives are at once buoys and anchors. They have the gift of buoyancy, floating and rising with the emergence of members' ideas, borne and sustained by consensus; and they are anchors, the shapers, the foundations that provide stability in stormy, unstable environments by holding firmly onto a common vision, giving members a fixed purpose around which to safely direct energy.

Recent theorists have brought attention to the primacy of meaning making in organizations. Given unstable and changing environments as well as complex and various technologies, some of the important defining characteristics of an organization are the consensually shared perceptions and definitions of the world, the shared paradigm. Pfeffer (1981a, p. 13) discusses the importance of shared meaning in the organization and its role in membership commitment: "One of the results of more frequent communication intensity is likely to be the development through informational social influence of a more common set of understandings about the organization and its environment. These understandings, these shared meanings, provide organizational participants with a sense of belonging and identity as well as demarcating the organization from its environment and assisting in the control and commitment of those within the organization." Through the construction of shared understandings, often formulated after action has been taken (Weick, 1969), participants' behavior becomes sensible and meaningful to themselves. Without processes of meaning creation, patterns of behavior are likely to become unstable, unfocused, and seemingly purposeless. Organizational structures and coalitions begin to fall apart unless consensus and shared beliefs are actively renewed and reformed. Executive power, then, is functioning when members are creating a shared understanding by seeking consensus. When meaning is being created by members, power is expanding throughout the organization because a "group will," built through the passionate involvement of members, is the force that moves the system, and with richer understanding members are capable of deeper involvement and personal commitment.

Simply engaging in organizational activities does not mean that we know what we are about or where we are headed. Hence, we *discover* what we are doing and should be doing through consensus processes. While the traditional bureaucratic modes of organizing are based on the view that order is imposed, we believe that executive power is functioning when order is discovered and created through seeking consensus, by building dialogue: "The basic sense-making device used within the organization is assumed to be talking to discover thinking. How can I know what I think until I see what I say? The action of talking is the occasion for defining the articulating cognitions" (Weick, 1969, p. 165). Executive power is functioning when members are talking, sharing ideas and feelings, influencing and being influenced, seeking consensus together with an overarching ideology that only through the voluntary contributions of its members can this organization develop. In this sense, all members are thought of as "executives" because—through their efforts, their ability to develop, and their commitment to learning—they help the organization realize its potential.

With this in mind, we would like to put forth a few propositions that highlight the functioning of executive power.

Proposition 1: Executive power is embodied in the process of seeking consensus. The outcome of seeking consensus is members' growth, increasing ability to work together, and emergent consent. We use the term "seeking" consensus rather than "achieving" consensus deliberately, because consensus is not so much achieved as it is discovered. A consensus decision does not occur in a moment that can be witnessed. In fact, it is difficult to determine *when* consensus occurs, because members' perceptions and understandings are forming in the process of restless, continuous dialogue. Engaging in dialogue is itself *transformative*. Ideas are delicate, fragile creatures and rarely appear neatly packaged and integrated. Yet many initially outrageous and impossible notions become realities, for ideas are social creations, rarely the product of a lone genius. Others' contributions uncover unimagined possibilities and implications, which enrich and enliven an idea. Further, the process of articulating perceptions contributes to their formation: one often discovers one's perceptions while in the act of expression, empowered by others' listening. Therefore, seeking genuine consensus does not involve seeking views that exist a priori; rather, the process is primary.

Members themselves develop and learn in the process of seeking consensus, as their awareness is heightened and their thinking sharpened. Just as a writer develops in the process of writing and not after the book is finished, so, too, members grow and learn in the process of sharing ideas and not after the ideas are implemented. Similarly, members grow as a social unit and improve their participation skills. They experience increasing self-direction, satisfaction in working together, improved ability to cope with frustration and ambiguity, and an increasing ability to articulate ideas.

Proposition 2: An organization legitimizes consensus seeking when members have a sense that the organization is an open-ended, evolving system. When all parties are able to express ideas freely and to engage in open dialogue in an effort to move the organization ahead, executive power is in action. When an organization is imbued with executive power, all members have the right to participate actively in the initiation, maintenance, and transformation of organizational activities; and participants are united in the belief that they share in the creation of organizational reality, that their voluntary contributions are essential in the determination of organization activities. The fundamental ideology at the root of this principle is a belief in the open, evolutionary process of organizing, a sense that the organization is not a closed, determined structure but is in a perpetual state of becoming. This underlying assumption that the organization is permeable, transformable, and responsive to human effort heightens the urgency in seeking consensus, because members come to believe that the system cannot achieve its potential without their contributions. An empowered system is full of reminders that members are potent contributors to the movement of the organization.

Guiding values and ideas emerge through the creative interplay of individuals and groups when members are free to engage in open dialogue, without arbitrary barriers to interaction. An egalitarian spirit permeates the consensus-seeking process because *all* members become active inquirers into potentialities. Hence, executive power functions at its best when all parties are actively seeking consensus and providing resources for others to continue the search by helping each other create meaning and build shared agreement. Executive power is maintained through the management of agreement among diverse yet interdependent stakeholders; in this sense, the substance of executive power is found in political processes of coalition formation, when ideas are negotiated, and forums wherein participation and decision making are encouraged.

When executive power is functioning, participants do not dispassionately carry out prescribed roles. Committed to the ideal that an organization's continued excellence depends on the voluntary contributions of members, they feel free to oppose as well as propose ideas and to interact and exchange ideas in a variety of situations and settings. They do not relate to each other merely as role functionaries but are able to appreciate each other's complexity; they are serious together and laugh together, they play and work together. It is a melding of the person and the role that encourages this enactment. When members can relate to each other holistically, able to appreciate each other's priorities and to understand resistances in areas of disagreement, a climate is created wherein members are able to separate disagreement about ideas from the overall relationship. They can disagree and refrain from judging. They tolerate each other's different styles because they *live with* each other. Because they respect each other's competence and relate to each other holistically, they can engage in a free exchange of ideas; but the glue that holds their relationships together is an overriding desire to build a common vision. The consensus process, then, is like a marriage: members are free to disagree but are united by respect for the whole.

Proposition 3: Executive power is extended throughout a system through processes of affirmation. Affirmation is an invitation for members to share ideas and participate in seeking consensus. Current literature emphasizes that, when a participant has an innovative idea, he or she needs to stay aggressively committed to it, to be an "ideal champion" (Peters and Waterman, 1982), to be clear and persistent in overcoming inevitable obstacles (Kanter, 1983). We would like to speak to the other side of this process. Innovations emerge when members genuinely *seek* consensus—that is, when members are attentive to each other's ideas and affirm voluntary contributions. By providing consensual validation for each other's experiences, members feel affirmed and entrusted to continue risking opinions and feelings. When everyone is forwarding opinions and expressing feelings, no room is being made for shared understandings; multiple isolation perpetuates. Such a climate fosters collective agreement by acquiescence. Consensus can begin only when someone is listening. To be heard is to be empowered. Executive power begins to take action when members validate each other's experience in a spirit of mutual reciprocity. A spirit of affirmation is the contagion that furthers dialogue exchanges and the building of shared agreement, for the more one values the contributions of others, the greater affirmation one is able to receive for one's own contributions. The more one makes room to be influenced by others, the more opportunity others are able to offer for the articulation of one's ideas.

Feelings of impotence and inefficacy sabotage consensus seeking. The system's capacity for executive power increases, however, when members experience their own potency in contributing to the direction of the organization. As members sense the emergent quality of consensus and the permeable, responsive nature of each other's understanding, they respect the consensus process and are able to invest the best in themselves, aware that they can bring out the best in each other.

Enhancement of Cooperation

Innovations and ideas that fail are often the result of failed cooperation. The functioning of executive power in a given situation commands cooperation. One must recognize the conditions that challenge the implementation of ideas: people in different departments, with different interests, experience different environments and use different technologies. The powerful executive is aware of different stakeholders in the system and the validity of their perspectives. The more that organization members can appreciate the *validity of others' experiences* and perceptions, the greater the capacity for cooperative action in the system and the greater the system's capacity for executive power.

Because powerful executives are aware of others' worlds of experience, they devote time to anticipating the possible effects, the intended and unintended consequences, that will occur when an interdependent system takes action. They devote time to considering whose support is necessary in order to implement an innovative idea and whose skills are needed to fulfill a plan of action. They know who can be relied on for support and where they might meet resistance. The powerful executive is respectful of members' resistance. He does not avoid conflicts but listens to those who predict consequences that he might not have anticipated. Executive power is in action when various stakeholders take the time to consider each other's needs, discuss alternative means toward attaining goals, and achieve inclusive solutions that serve the interests of many.

In an empowered system, members share and listen; the powerful executive creates an informative and well-informed network. He commands cooperation by negotiating, by educating, by listening to others' needs. Knowing that he can no longer rely on the chain of command and other bureaucratic tools to see that ideas are implemented, he must enlist the support of peers, subordinates, and superordinates alike. In negotiating projects, the powerful executive does not compromise by settling on the least common denominator among diverse interests. Rather, he remains persistent and clear in his vision as he strives to maintain excitement and a spirit of discovery while creating conditions for feasibility.

The irony is that the powerful executive commands cooperation by asking for help. Having said that, we must qualify: It is not a request that belies or creates one-way dependency. Dependency weakens executive power. In order to "command" cooperation, there needs to be a foundation of trust, of mutual respect for one another's competence, that is not found in dependency relationships. By appreciating the full worth in the other's experience, regardless of status or title, powerful executives promote and support the other's *autonomy*. The more that members support each other's autonomous integrity and see each other as separate centers of experience, the greater the capacity for cooperative action and executive power in the system. This egalitarian spirit is what makes the process more than a purely political game in which members acquire and use leverage to persuade others to cooperate.

A system characterized by executive power supports cooperative action among members by creating social structures that are not limited to convenient categories of level, division, function, or department. Rather, cooperation must occur in social arrangements that cross all boundaries, through temporary networking structures: task forces, committees, ad hoc teams, coalitions. An organization fosters a cooperative mode when it allows and encourages the committing of resources, time, energy, and personnel to various parts of the system.

Proposition 4: The more the diverse members experience themselves as contributors to a collective agreement, the greater their willingness to cooperate. The greater the diversity of ideas shared in a system, the better the quality of meaning and purposefulness attached to the vision. A variety of perspectives enhances not only the quality and precision of the idea but the *depth* as well, because the impetus for executive power is members' identification with the organization's actions. When members can identify their part in the creation of organizational priorities, they feel committed to action, to fulfill the blueprint that they helped design. In a system of shared governance, it is this quality to command cooperation that makes the organization *more efficient* than a bureaucratic mode of governance.

Control and ownership are not passed down from above but are internalized and drive members to do what is necessary to further collective interest. Driven by an understanding of what is necessary and the will to act as they see fit (and not as others demand), members become responsible to themselves. Under Weber's typology the worker's need for stability and certainty is met when he or she takes on a prescribed role and receives focused direction from above. We propose that when executive power is functioning, members create their own security and stability. Having contributed and having witnessed others contribute to shared understanding, members know how an agreement is reached. Within this framework for understanding diverse actions, members are free to perceive a world worthy of their investment.

In the functioning of executive power, the voice of authority is the voice not of coercion but of clarification; members' understanding is the guide to action. They act as one would follow a recipe when cooking: once committed to the production, one does what is necessary to complete the task. There is no violation to personal integrity in completing a task.

When executive power is functioning, the overriding drive of a shared agreement for direction and the spirit of furthering excellence offset feelings of turfism and competition that can occur in segmented organizations. Members are more able to cross lines of authority, divisions, and functions to assist each other, because they do not see these lines as boundaries. Feelings of joint authorship and commitment to a vision of excellence unite diverse stakeholders when executive power is functioning.

The spirit of cooperation creates more opportunities for cooperation. Under conditions of complexity, members build a system of increasingly intensive task-based interdependency. As members build inclusive task designs in which they sense their creative energies invested in their work, conditions for cooperative action are enhanced and the system's executive power increases.

Proposition 5: Cooperation is enhanced when members feel that they are preserving the unity and integrity of the group or organization. Under the shadow of a perceived threat, such as "Either we increase production or we go down the drain," resistance to cooperation is quickly forgotten as members unite around the most basic of social goals: self-preservation of the group. The same spirit can be engendered in more positive ways, in response to an opportunity or a challenge. When members feel that they are renewing the life of the group or enhancing its integrity, cooperation is heightened.

Proposition 6: The more members actively cooperate in fulfilling organizational goals, the more they develop feelings of trust and openness, and the more they promote one another's integrity and autonomy.

Recent participation literature notes the need for a spirit of trust in an organization to enhance cooperation among members. The fact is that action *precedes* awareness; experience gives rise to sentiment. The more members cooperate with each other toward the accomplishment of an agreed-upon goal, the more opportunities they have for developing trust and openness. Therefore, it is the creation of tasks that require interdependent cooperation that facilitates trust, and not vice versa.

Under bureaucratic norms of instrumental rationality, personal autonomy is feared because it can lead to chaos and normlessness: permission to act is granted or not granted, as leaders see fit. Under norms of executive power, permission is not a favor for some to grant to others. As members experience the impact of their contributions, they give permission to themselves to think, act, and feel. By developing respect for their own competence and ideas, they are free to respect the ideas of others. When members are free to contribute, a deep-seated respect for individual worth emerges, and members develop an awareness of and tolerance for the unique tempo of each individual. People are valued not only for their achievements but for what they are and what they become.

Transmission of Organizational Culture

Culture transmits the values that are held in esteem by the organization. Executive power functions when executives create a meaningful culture of hope and possibility. Such a culture—a shared system of language, symbols, myths, and rituals—fosters in members a sense of their significance by reminding them of their common vision and the cooperative actions that resulted in proud achievement. Powerful executives communicate through symbols their high investment in members' potential. By committing resources to an idea in its early stages, executives symbolize their faith in members' capabilities. Physical settings marked by openness and accessibility help to create a sense of interconnectedness among diverse members. One of the most significant indicators of the values of a social system is the way that members use time. Spending extended time periods in dialogue exchanges and consensus building sends a message to newcomers and current members that their perspectives and preferences are impotant resources. Powerful executives, by means of the culture that they help to create, convey to the organization's members that these executives approach new ideas and possibilities with curiosity, not with suspicion. They reinforce norms at all levels of the system by their supportive behavior, acting as midwives, assisting in the difficult birthing process of ideas. Stories and myths about past successes build a shared history with which members are proud to identify and also engender a sense that they, too, can be makers of history.

It is culture that makes a group of individuals an interconnected system and more than a temporary collection of individuals. Culture perpetuates the system by providing a stable core of meaning that seems timeless, allowing members to channel their energies and enjoy a sense of higher purposefulness and belonging. Culture is the genetic blueprint for intergenerational continuity, the collective creed that inspires passionate involvement and creative contributions, as members cooperate without sacrificing autonomy.

Executive power is embodied in the *management of organizational spirit and meaning.* Through the management of belief systems, values, ideals, and ideologies, executives are powerful to the extent that they can help form an organizational culture where people feel there is something serious, meaningful, and significant about their existence as organizational participants.

Proposition 7: The greater the extent to which executives create a culture in which members feel they are making significant contributions to an organization devoted to excellence, the greater the system's capacity for executive power. In organizations where executive power is nourishing the culture, members feel that they are contributing to the excellence of an evolving system, moving toward the "cutting edge" of new discoveries and important contributions to society. Such norms of spiritual significance are reinforced by myths, symbols, and rituals that communicate the sense that this system has achieved success as a result of the contributions of its membership and that its future legacy is in the hands of present members. It is this spirit of excellence, a commitment to a superordinate ideal, that sustains the seeking of consensus and commands cooperation. An empowering culture creates a spirit of inclusion, a sense of partnership and interdependence. An egalitarian spirit enhances the commitment to consensus processes and furthers reciprocal interactions free of arbitrary barriers that inhibit participation. In such an environment, members are able to strive for consensus, to stay invested in negotiation processes, to participate in open-ended forums without rushing to premature resolution, because of their commitment to this ideal. In a sense, the creation of a culture of norms and beliefs is the most powerful mechanism executives have.

Proposition 8: The greater the extent to which the organization values its history so that members feel empowered in the present, the greater the executive power in the system. The socialization process communicates to members that they belong to an organization with a proud history. This history, communicated by symbols and stories of past accomplishments, satisfies members' need to be related to a larger purpose outside oneself. Executive power is enhanced when history is conveyed in such a way that members do not accept the givenness of present structures. Rather, they are encouraged to inquire into history, so that they understand how the organization evolved and begin to realize that apparently permanent and immutable social arrangements are actually the result of human consent. Generally, organizations foster a human cosmogony (Srivastva and Barrett, 1985), a story of how and why social structures were created by man and emerged as manifestations of human intentionality, so that present members feel empowered to become creators and so that, through seeking consensus, they can shape organizational activities that enhance the system. Personal empowerment is strengthened by this realization: Not only has history made man, man has made history.

Proposition 9: Executive power is enhanced when members adopt cultural norms that promote a generative language that, in turn, fosters reciprocity. Language reveals our relational stance to one another. One of the hazards of modern bureaucratic rationality is that many have adopted a language of possession (Illich, 1973), a language that in the bureaucratic arena actively subordinates others: "Have him report to my office," "One of my assistants will get back to you." Such language is binary; it closes off possibility and ends dialogue.

Under norms of executive power, we imagine a system of interrelationships marked by mutual reciprocity and openness to learning, reflected in a generative language that at once communicates information and support for the other. Bureaucratic rationality promotes a language in which those on top are responsible for unilaterally communicating information to subordinates: "You got that?" or "Is that clear?" We imagine a collaborative language in which both parties take responsibility for understanding; knowledge is not passed from a wise superior to a receptacle-subordinate. We imagine a language that supports caring and sharing; members meet in the "center" to create meaning: "I wonder what you think about this." In an empowered system, generative language allows members to challenge one another in an egalitarian spirit, one that confirms Paulo Freire's image of the student-teacher relationship: "Through dialogue, the teacher of the students and students of the teacher cease to exist and a new term emerges: teacher-student with student-teachers. The teacher is no longer the one who teaches, but one who is himself taught in dialogue with the students, who, in turn, while being taught, also teach" (Freire, 1974, p. 67).

Conclusion

The picture of executive power we have painted is an image of what an organization can evolve to. We know that such an image is not easily realized, but, in fact, every system must have some of these qualities in order to survive. Even as we recognize the capacity of humans to destroy each other, we must not forget man's most remarkable gifts: man is the only organism capable of consciously directing his own evolution. While other creatures must change their frameworks to adapt to the environment, man can change the environment to suit himself. We are capable of creating richer social arrangements for ourselves. The rational-bureaucratic mode of organizing prides itself on patterns of predictability and calculability of results. Yet such a system actually eliminates our uniquely human capacity for spontaneity and creativity. "The fact that man is capable of action means that the unexpected can be expected from him, that he is able to perform that which is infinitely improbable" (Arendt, 1969, p. 178).

We are not speaking here of some potentials that lie within each of us, waiting to be realized. They are not *in* us. Such a shrunken, modern psychological view of man fails to realize that achieving potentiality is a social phenomenon. Wisdom happens in interaction; it emerges in the space between actors. Once we make efforts to refrain from usual assumptions, to look at each other not in terms of what we do but what we are capable of, we create conditions to further the emergence of wisdom among us.

The hope lies in the way we creatively manage ourselves in interaction, the way we choose to organize. Executive power can function to initiate, maintain, and transform relationships in such a way that refreshing potentialities emerge in the spaces between us. We can manage our workplace so as to encourage and support the seeking of shared agreement, to enhance cooperation, and to create cultures in which we experience our own potency.

References

Ackoff, R. L. *Redesigning the Future.* New York: Wiley, 1974.

Allison, G. T. *Essence of Decision: Explaining the Cuban Missile Crisis.* Boston: Little, Brown, 1971.

Andrews, K. *The Concept of Corporate Strategy.* Homewood, Ill.: Irwin, 1971.

Ansbacher, H., and Ansbacher, R. *The Individual Psychology of Alfred Adler.* New York: Basic Books, 1956.

Ansoff, M. I. *Corporate Strategy.* New York: McGraw-Hill, 1965.

Arendt, H. *The Human Condition.* New York: Doubleday, 1969.

Argyris, C. *Intervention Theory and Method: A Behavioral Science View.* Reading, Mass.: Addison-Wesley, 1970.

Arnold, D. "A Process Model of Subcultures." In D. O. Arnold (ed.), *The Sociology of Subcultures.* Berkeley, Calif.: Glendessary Press, 1970.

Astley, W. G., and Rosen, M. "Organizations: A Politico-Symbolic Dialectic." Unpublished paper, Wharton School, University of Pennsylvania, 1983.

Astley, W. G., and Sachdeva, P. S. "Structural Sources of Intraorganizational Power: A Theoretical Synthesis." *Academy of Management Review,* 1984, *9* (1), 104–113.

Bachrach, P., and Baratz, M. S. "Two Faces of Power." *American Political Science Review,* 1962, *56,* 947–952.

Bales, R. F. "Adaptive and Integrative Changes as Sources of Strain in Social Systems." In A. P. Hare and others (eds.), *Small Groups.* New York: Knopf, 1955.

331

Barnard, C. *The Functions of the Executive.* Cambridge, Mass.: Harvard University Press, 1938.

Bass, B. M. *Leadership and Performance Beyond Expectations.* New York: Free Press, 1985.

Becker, H. S. "Culture: A Sociological View." *Yale Review,* 1982, *71,* 513-527.

Becker, H. S., Greer, B., Hughes, E. C., and Strauss, A. *Boys in White: Student Culture in Medical School.* Chicago: University of Chicago Press, 1961.

Beckhard, R., and Harris, R. *Organizational Transitions: Managing Complex Change.* Reading, Mass.: Addison-Wesley, 1977.

Beer, M. *Organization Change and Development: A Systems View.* Santa Monica, Calif.: Goodyear, 1980.

Bell, D. *The Coming of Post-Industrial Society.* New York: Basic Books, 1973.

Bell, M. J. *The World from Brown's Lounge.* Urbana: University of Illinois Press, 1983.

Bennis, W. "A Funny Thing Happened on the Way to the Future." *American Psychologist,* 1970, *25* (7), 595-608.

Bennis, W. "The Artform of Leadership." In S. Srivastva (ed.), *The Executive Mind: New Insights on Managerial Thought and Action.* San Francisco: Jossey-Bass, 1983.

Berger, P. L. (ed.). *The Human Shape of Work.* Chicago: Contemporary Books, 1964.

Berger, P. L., and Luckman, T. *The Social Construction of Reality.* New York: Doubleday, 1967.

Bergmann, A. "Industrial Democracy in Germany: The Battle for Power." *Journal of General Management,* Summer 1975, pp. 20-29.

Berlew, D. E. "Leadership and Organizational Excitement." *California Management Review,* 1974, *17* (2), 21-30.

Berlew, D. E., and LeClere, W. "Social Intervention in Curaçao: A Case Study." *Journal of Applied Behavioral Science,* 1974, *10* (1), 29-52.

Beveridge, W. *Social Insurance and the Allied Services.* London: His Majesty's Stationery Office, 1942.

Beyer, J. "Ideologies, Values and Decision-Making in Organizations." In P. Nystrom and W. H. Starbuck (eds.), *Handbook of Organizational Design.* Vol. 2. New York: Oxford University Press, 1981.

Bion, W. *Experiences in Groups, and Other Papers.* London: Tavistock Publications, 1961.

Blake, R., and Mouton, J. S. *The Managerial Grid.* Houston: Gulf Publishing, 1964.

Blake, R., and Mouton, J. S. *Consultation.* Reading, Mass.: Addison-Wesley, 1976.

Blanchard, K., and Johnson, S. *The One Minute Manager.* New York: Morrow, 1982.

Boswell, J. S. *Business Policies in the Making.* London: Allen & Unwin, 1983.

Bott, E. *Family and Social Network.* London: Tavistock Publications, 1957.

Bourgeois, L. J., and Brodwin, D. R. "Strategic Implementation: Five Approaches to an Elusive Phenomenon." *Strategic Management Journal,* 1984, *5,* 241-264.

Bower, J. L. *Managing the Resource Allocation Process.* Cambridge, Mass.: Harvard University Press, 1970.

Bridger, H. "Northfield Revisited." In M. Pines (ed.), *Bion and Group Psychotherapy.* London: Routledge & Kegan Paul, 1985.

Brown, L. D. "Can Haves and Have-Nots Cooperate? Two Efforts to Bridge a Social Gap." *Journal of Applied Behavioral Science,* 1977, *13,* 211-224.

Brown, L. D. "Planned Change in Underorganized Systems." In T. G. Cummings (ed.), *Systems Theory for Organization Development.* New York: Wiley, 1980.

Brown, L. D., Benroth, L., and Gaertner, G. "Expanding Metropolitan Leadership Networks: An Urban Quasi-Experiment." Paper presented at meeting of the Academy of Management, Dallas, Aug. 1983.

Brown, L. D., and Brown, J. C. "Organizational Microcosms and Ideological Negotiation." In M. B. Bazerman and R. E. Lewicki (eds.), *Negotiating in Organizations.* Beverly Hills, Calif.: Sage, 1983.

Brown, L. D., and Tandon, R. "Ideology and Political Economy in Inquiry: Action Research and Participatory Research." *Journal of Applied Behavioral Science*, 1983, *19*, 277–294.

Brunsson, N. "The Irrationality of Action and Action Rationality: Decisions, Ideologies and Organizational Action." *Journal of Management Studies*, 1982, *19* (1), 29–44.

Burke, W. W. *Organization Development: Principles and Practice*. Boston: Little, Brown, 1982.

Burke, W. W. "Conversations with Harold K. Sperlich." *Organizational Dynamics*, 1984, *12* (4), 23–36.

Burke, W. W., and Myers, R. A. *Assessment of Executive Competence*. Washington, D.C.: National Aeronautics and Space Administration, 1982.

Burns, J. M. *Leadership*. New York: Harper & Row, 1978.

Cavan, S. *Liquor License*. Hawthorne, N.Y.: Aldine, 1966.

Chandler, A. D. *Strategy and Structure: Chapters in the History of the American Industrial Enterprise*. Cambridge, Mass.: MIT Press, 1962.

Chandler, A. D. "Rise and Evolution of Big Business." In G. Porter (ed.), *Encyclopedia of American Economic History*. New York: Scribner's, 1980.

Child, J. "Organizational Structure, Environment and Performance: The Role of Strategic Choice." *Sociology*, 1972, *6* (1), 1–22.

Cohen, A. *Two-Dimensional Man*. Berkeley: University of California Press, 1974.

Cohen, A. *The Management of Myths*. Manchester, England: Manchester University Press, 1975.

Committee for Economic Development. *Public-Private Partnership: An Opportunity for Urban Communities*. New York: Committee for Economic Development, 1982.

Corti, E. C. *The Rise of the House of Rothschild*. London: Gollancz, 1928.

Cowles, V. *The Rothschilds: A Family of Fortune*. London: Weidenfeld & Nicolson, 1973.

Crenson, M. A. *The Un-Politics of Air Pollution: A Study of Non-Decision-Making in the Cities*. Baltimore: Johns Hopkins University Press, 1971.

Crozier, M. *The Bureaucratic Phenomenon.* Chicago: University of Chicago Press, 1964.

Csikszentmihalyi, M., and Graef, R. "Feeling Free." *Psychology Today,* Dec. 1979, pp. 84–99.

Curtis, M. *The Great Political Theories.* New York: Avon Books, 1961.

Dalton, G., Barnes, L. B., and Zaleznik, A. *The Distribution of Authority in Formal Organizations.* Cambridge, Mass.: MIT Press, 1968.

Dalton, M. *Men Who Manage.* New York: Wiley, 1959.

Deal, T., and Kennedy, A. A. *Corporate Cultures.* Reading, Mass.: Addison-Wesley, 1982.

Dickson, J. W. "Beliefs About Work and Rationales for Participations." *Human Relations,* 1983, *36,* 911–931.

Doi, T. *The Anatomy of Dependence.* Tokyo: Kodansha, 1973.

Edelman, M. *The Symbolic Uses of Politics.* Urbana: University of Illinois Press, 1964.

Eiseman, J. W. "Reconciling Incompatible Positions." *Journal of Applied Behavioral Science,* 1978, 14, 133–150.

Elden, M. "Democratizing Organizations: A Challenge to Organization Development." In R. Tannenbaum, F. Massarik, and N. Margulies (ed.), *Leadership and Organization.* San Francisco: Jossey-Bass, 1985.

Emery, F. E. "Sociotechnical Foundations for a New Social Order?" *Human Relations,* 1982, *35,* 1095–1122.

Emery, F. E., and Thorsrud, E. *Form and Content in Industrial Democracy.* London: Tavistock Publications, 1969.

Emery, F. E., and Trist, E. L. "The Causal Texture of Organizational Environments." *Human Relations,* 1965, *18,* 21–32.

Erez, M., Earley, P. C., and Hulin, C. L. "The Impact of Participation on Goal Acceptance and Performance: A Two-Step Model." *Academy of Management Journal,* 1985, *28* (1), 50–66.

Erikson, E. H. *Childhood and Society.* (2nd ed.) New York: Norton, 1963.

Etzioni, A. *Comparative Analysis of Complex Organizations.* (Rev. ed.) New York: Free Press, 1975. (Originally published 1961.)

Fisher, R., and Ury, W. *Getting to Yes: Negotiating Agreement Without Giving In.* Boston: Houghton Mifflin, 1981.

Freire, P. *Pedagogy of the Oppressed.* New York: Seabury Press, 1974.

French, J.R.P., and Raven, B. "The Bases of Social Power." In D. Cartwright (ed.), *Studies in Social Power.* Ann Arbor: Institute for Social Research, University of Michigan, 1959.

French, W., Bell, C., and Zawacki, R. *Organization Development: Theory, Practice, and Research.* Plano, Tex.: Business Publications, 1978.

Friedlander, F., and Pickle, H. "Components of Effectiveness in Small Organizations." *Administrative Science Quarterly,* 1968, *13,* 289-304.

Fromm, E. *The Fear of Freedom.* London: Routledge & Kegan Paul, 1960. (Published in the United States as *Escape from Freedom.* Originally published 1941.)

Gabarro, J. J., and Kotter, J. P. "Managing Your Boss." *Harvard Business Review,* 1980, *58* (1), 92-100.

Galbraith, J. *Designing Complex Organizations.* Reading, Mass.: Addison-Wesley, 1973.

Galbraith, J. *Organization Design.* Reading, Mass.: Addison-Wesley, 1977.

Garson, G. "The Codetermination Model of Workers' Participation: Where Is It Leading?" *Sloan Management Review,* 1977, *18,* 63-78.

Gaventa, J. *Power and Powerlessness: Quiescence and Rebellion in an Appalachian Valley.* Urbana: University of Illinois Press, 1980.

Goffman, E. *The Presentation of Self in Everyday Life.* New York: Doubleday, 1959.

Goffman, E. *Interaction Ritual.* Hawthorne, N.Y.: Aldine, 1967.

Goldthorpe, J. H., and others. "The Affluent Worker and the Thesis of Embourgeoisement: Some Preliminary Research Findings." *Sociology,* 1967, *1* (1), 11-31.

Golembiewski, R. T. *Approaches to Planned Change.* (2 vols.) New York: Dekker, 1979a.

Golembiewski, R. T. *You Seem to Have Given Up on Us. . . , You Don't Seem to Care About the Authority.* Boston: Intercollegiate Case Clearing House, 1979b.

Golembiewski, R. T. *Mass Transit Management: Case Studies of the Metropolitan Atlanta Rapid Transit Authority.* Washington, D.C.: University Research and Training Program, Urban Mass Transportation Administration, U.S. Department of Transportation, 1981.

Golembiewski, R. T., and Kiepper, A. "MARTA: Toward an Effective, Open Giant." *Public Administration Review,* 1976, *36* (1), 46-60.

Golembiewski, R. T., and Kiepper, A. "Lessons from a Fast-Paced Public Project: Perspectives on Doing Better the Next Time Around." *Public Administration Review,* 1983a, *43* (6), 547-556.

Golembiewski, R. T., and Kiepper, A. "Organizational Transition in a Fast-Paced Public Project: Personal Perspectives of MARTA Executives." *Public Administration Review,* 1983b, *43* (3), 246-254.

Gordon, A. W. "Organizational Development and Individual Rights." *Journal of Applied Behavioral Science,* 1984, *20* (4), 423-440.

Gottshalk, L. A., and Davidson, R. S. "Sensitivity Groups, Encounter Groups, Training Groups, Marathon Groups, and the Laboratory Movement." In H. Kaplan and B. Sadock (eds.), *Sensitivity Through Encounter and Marathon.* New York: Dutton, 1972.

Gouldner, A. *The Coming Crisis of Western Sociology.* New York: Basic Books, 1970.

Governor's Task Force on Private Initiatives. *Report.* Boston: Office of the Governor, 1982.

Greiner, L. E. "Evolution and Revolution as Organizations Grow." *Harvard Business Review,* 1974, *50* (4), 37-46.

Gricar, B. G., and Brown, L. D. "Conflict, Power and Organization in a Changing Community." *Human Relations,* 1981, *34,* 877-893.

Gricar, G. B., and Hay, T. M. "Political Limits to a National Consensus on Coal Policy." Unpublished paper, Pennsylvania State University, 1984.

Grinyer, P. H., and Spender, J. C. "Recipes, Crises and Adaptations in Mature Businesses." *International Studies of Management and Organization,* 1979, *9* (3), 113-133.

Hackman, J. R. "The Design of Work in the 1980s." *Organizational Dynamics*, 1978, *7*, 3–17.

Hackman, J. R., and Oldham, G. "Development of the Job Diagnostic Survey." *Journal of Applied Psychology*, 1975, *60*, 159–170.

Hackman, J. R., and Oldham, G. *Work Redesign*. Reading, Mass.: Addison-Wesley, 1980.

Hall, J. "To Achieve or Not: The Manager's Choice." *California Management Review*, 1976, *18* (4), 5–18.

Hardy, C. "*Organisational Closures: A Political Perspective.*" Unpublished doctoral dissertation, Warwick University, 1982.

Hardy, C. *Managing Organisational Closure*. Epping, Essex, England: Gower Press, 1985.

Hardy, C., and Pettigrew, A. M. "The Use of Power in Managerial Strategies for Change." In R. S. Rosenbloom (ed.), *Research on Technological Innovation, Management and Policy*. Vol. 2, Greenwich, Conn.: JAI Press, 1985.

Harrison, R. "Understanding Your Organization's Character." *Harvard Business Review*, 1972, *50* (3), 119–128.

Harrison, R. "Strategies for a New Age." *Human Resource Management*, 1983, *22* (3), 209–235.

Hart, D. K., and Scott, W. G. "The Organizational Imperative." *Administration and Society*, 1975, *7* (3), 259–285.

Hetzler, S. A. "Variations in Role-Playing Patterns Among Different Echelons of Bureaucratic Leaders." *American Sociological Review*, 1955, *20*, 700–706.

Hickson, D. J., and others. "A Strategic Contingencies Theory of Intra-Organizational Power." *Administrative Science Quarterly*, 1971, *16*, 216–229.

Hill, P. *Towards a New Philosophy of Management*. Epping, Essex, England: Gower Press, 1971.

Hofstede, G. "Alienation at the Top." *Organizational Dynamics*, 1976, *4* (3).

Hofstede, G. *Culture's Consequences: International Differences in Work-Related Values*. Beverly Hills, Calif.: Sage, 1980.

Holdaway, S. *Inside the British Police*. Oxford, England: Blackwell, 1983.

House, J. S. *Work Stress and Social Support.* Reading, Mass.: Addison-Wesley, 1981.

Huff, A. S. "Industry Influences on Strategy Reformulation." *Strategic Management Journal,* 1982, *3,* 119–131.

Illich, I. *Tools for Conviviality.* New York: Harper & Row, 1973.

Irwin, J. *Scenes.* Beverly Hills, Calif.: Sage, 1977.

Janis, I. L. *Victims of Groupthink.* Boston: Houghton Mifflin, 1972.

Jaques, E. "Social Systems as a Defence Against Persecutory and Depressive Anxiety." In M. Klein and others (eds.), *New Directions in Psycho-Analysis.* London: Tavistock Publications, 1955.

Johnston, A. V. "Revolution by Involvement." *Accountancy Age,* 1975, *7,* p. 11.

Jonsson, S. A., and Lundin, R. A. "Myths and Wishful Thinking as Management Tools." In P. C. Nystrom and W. H. Starbuck (eds.), *Prescriptive Models of Organizations.* Amsterdam: North-Holland, 1977.

Kanter, R. M. *Men and Women of the Corporation.* New York: Basic Books, 1977.

Kanter, R. M. "Power Failure in Management Circuits." *Harvard Business Review,* 1979, *57* (4), 65–75.

Kanter, R. M. *The Change Masters: Innovation for Productivity in the American Corporation.* New York: Simon & Schuster, 1983.

Kaplan, A. *The Conduct of Inquiry.* San Francisco: Chandler, 1964.

Katz, R. "Time and Work: Toward an Integrative Perspective." In L. L. Cummings and B. M. Staw (eds.), *Research in Organizational Behavior.* Vol. 2. Greenwich, Conn.: JAI Press, 1980.

Kerr, S., and Jermier, J. M. "Substitutes for Leadership: Their Meaning and Measurement." *Organizational Behavior and Human Performance,* 1978, *22,* 375–403.

Keynes, J. M. "Economic Possibilities for Our Grandchildren." In E. S. Phelps (ed.), *The Goal of Economic Growth.* New York: Norton, 1969. (Originally published 1930.)

Khaleelee, O., and Miller, E. J. "Making the Post-Dependent Society." Unpublished paper, 1983.

Khaleelee, O., and Miller, E. J. *The Future of Work: A Report of the West Yorkshire Talkabout, July–November 1983.* London: Work & Society, 1984.

Khaleelee, O., and Miller, E. J. "Beyond the Small Group: Society as an Intelligible Field of Study." In M. Pines (ed.), *Bion and Group Psychotherapy*. London: Routledge & Kegan Paul, 1985.

King, W. R., and Cleland, D. T. *Strategic Planning and Policy*. New York: D. Van Nostrand, 1978.

Kipnis, D. *The Powerholders*. Chicago: University of Chicago Press, 1976.

Kipnis, D., Schmidt, S., and Wilkinson, I. "Interorganizational Influence Tactics: Explorations in Getting One's Way." *Journal of Applied Psychology*, 1980, *65*, 440-452.

Klein, M. "Some Theoretical Conclusions Regarding the Emotional Life of the Infant." In M. Klein and others (eds.), *Developments in Psychoanalysis*. London: Hogarth Press, 1952.

Klein, M. "Our Adult World and Its Roots in Infancy." *Human Relations*, 1959, *12*, 291-303.

Kotter, J. P. "Power, Success and Organizational Effectiveness." *Organizational Dynamics*, 1978, *6* (3), 27-40.

Kotter, J. P. *Power in Management*. Saranac Lake, N.Y.: American Management Associations, 1979.

Kotter, J. P. *The General Managers*. New York: Free Press, 1982.

Kotter, J. P. *Power and Influence*. New York: Free Press, 1985.

Kotter, J. P., and Schlesinger, L. "Choosing Strategies for Change." *Harvard Business Review*, 1979, *57* (2), 106-114.

Kralj, J. "Is There a Role for Managers?" *Journal of General Management*, Winter 1976, pp. 7-16.

Langer, E., Blank, A., and Chanowitz, B. "The Mindlessness of Ostensibly Thoughtful Action: The Role of Placebic Information in Interpersonal Interaction." *Journal of Personality and Social Psychology*, 1978, *36*, 635-642.

Laumann, E. P., Galaskiewicz, J., and Marsden, P. V. "Community Structures as Interorganizational Linkages." *Annual Review of Sociology*, 1978, *4*, 455-484.

Lawrence, P. R., and Lorsch, J. W. *Organization and Environment*. Boston: Division of Research, Graduate School of Business Administration, Harvard University, 1967.

Lawrence, W. G. "A Concept for Today: Management of Oneself in Role." In W. G. Lawrence (ed.), *Exploring Individual and Organizational Boundaries*. London: Wiley, 1979.

Lawrence, W. G. *Some Psychic and Political Dimensions of Work Experiences.* Occasional Paper. London: Tavistock Institute of Human Relations, 1982.

Lawrence, W. G., and Miller, E. J. "Epilogue." In E. J. Miller (ed.), *Task and Organization.* London: Wiley, 1976.

Lawrence, W. G., and Miller, E. J. "Psychic and Political Constraints on the Growth of Industrial Democracies." In M. Pines and L. Rafaelsen (eds.), *The Individual and the Group.* Vol. 1: *Theory.* New York: Plenum, 1982.

Leach, E. "Ritual." In D. L. Sills (ed.), *International Encyclopedia of Social Sciences.* Vol. 13. New York: Free Press, 1968.

LeMasters, E. E. *Blue Collar Aristocrats.* Madison: University of Wisconsin Press, 1975.

Likert, R. *New Patterns of Management.* New York: McGraw-Hill, 1961.

Lithman, Y. G. "Feeling Good and Getting Smashed: On the Symbols of Alcohol and Drunkenness Among Canadian Indians." *Ethnos,* 1979, *44,* 119-133.

Lodge, G. C. *The New American Ideology.* New York: Knopf, 1975.

Lorsch, J. W., and Allen, S. A. *Managing Diversity and Interdependence.* Boston: Harvard Business School, 1973.

Lorsch, J. W., and Barnes, L. B. *Managers and Their Careers.* Homewood, Ill.: Irwin, 1972.

Lorsch, J. W., and Morse, J. *Organizations and Their Members.* New York: Harper & Row, 1974.

Louis, M. R. "Uncovering the Fundamentals of Organizational Behavior." *Organizational Behavior Teaching Review,* 1984, *9,* 4-7.

Louis, M. R. "An Investigator's Guide to Workplace Culture: Assumptions, Choice Points, and Alternatives." In P. Frost and others (eds.), *Organizational Culture: The Meaning of Life in the Workplace.* Beverly Hills, Calif.: Sage, 1985.

Lukes, S. *Power: A Radical View.* London: Macmillan, 1974.

Lukes, S. "Political Ritual and Social Integration." *Sociology,* 1975, *9,* 289-308.

MacAndrew, C. R., and Edgerton, G. *Drunken Comportment.* Hawthorne, N.Y.: Aldine, 1969.

McCall, M. *Power, Influence and Authority: The Hazards of Carrying a Sword.* Technical Report no. 10. Greensboro, N.C.: Center for Creative Leadership, 1978.

McClelland, D. C. "The Two Faces of Power." In D. Kolb and others (eds.), *Organizational Psychology, A Book of Readings.* Englewood Cliffs, N.J.: Prentice-Hall, 1979.

McClelland, D. C. *Power: The Inner Experience.* New York: Irvington, 1975.

McClelland, D. C., and Burnham, D. H. "Power Is the Great Motivator." *Harvard Business Review,* 1976, *54* (2), 100-110.

McClelland, D. C., Davis, W. N., Kalin, R., and Wanner, E. *The Drinking Man.* New York: Free Press, 1972.

McClelland, D. C., Rhinesmith, S., and Kristensen, R. "The Effects of Power Training for Staffs of Community Action Agencies." *Journal of Applied Behavioral Science,* 1975, *11,* 92-115.

McDonald, A. "Conflict at the Summit: A Deadly Game." *Harvard Business Review,* 1972, *50* (2), 60.

McMurray, R. N. "Power and the Ambitious Executive." *Harvard Business Review,* 1973, *51* (6), 140-145.

Manning, P. K. *Police Work.* Cambridge, Mass.: MIT Press, 1977.

Manning, P. K. *The Narc's Game.* Cambridge, Mass.: MIT Press, 1980.

March, J. "The Power of Power." In D. Easton (ed.), *Varieties of Political Theory.* Englewood Cliffs, N.J.: Prentice-Hall, 1966.

March, J. G., and Olsen, J. P. "Organizing Political Life: What Administrative Reorganization Tells Us About Governing." *American Political Science Review,* 1983, *77* (2), 281-296.

Markley, O. W., and Harman, W. W. (eds.). *Changing Images of Man.* Oxford, England: Pergamon Press, 1982.

Martin, J. "Stories and Scripts in Organizational Settings." In A. H. Hastorf and A. M. Isen (eds.), *Cognitive Social Psychology.* New York: Elsevier Science, 1982.

Maslow, A. H. *Motivation and Personality.* (2nd ed.) New York: Harper & Row, 1970.

Mason, R. *Participatory and Workplace Democracy.* Carbondale: Southern Illinois University Press, 1982.

May, R. *Power and Innocence.* New York: Norton, 1972.

Mechanic, D. "Sources of Power of Lower Participants in Complex Organizations." *Administrative Science Quarterly,* 1962, *7,* 349-364.

Menzies, I.E.P.M. "A Case-Study in the Functioning of Social Systems as a Defence Against Anxiety." *Human Relations,* 1960, *13,* 95-121.

Milgram, S. *Obedience to Authority.* New York: Harper & Row, 1974.

Miller, D. "Evolution and Revolution: A Quantum View of Structural Change in Organizations." *Journal of Management Studies,* 1982, *19* (2), 131-151.

Miller, D., and Friesen, P. "Momentum and Revolution in Organizational Adaptation." *Academy of Management Journal,* 1980, *23,* 591-614.

Miller, D., and Friesen, P. "Structural Change and Performance: Quantum vs. Piecemeal-Incremental Approaches." *Academy of Management Journal,* 1982, *25* (4), 867-892.

Miller, E. J. "Socio-Technical Systems in Weaving, 1953-1970: A Follow-Up Study." *Human Relations,* 1975, *28,* 348-386.

Miller, E. J. "Organisational Development and Industrial Democracy: A Current Case Study." In C. L. Cooper (ed.), *Organisational Development in the U.K. and U.S.A.* London: Macmillan, 1977.

Miller, E. J. "Autonomy, Dependency and Organisational Change." In D. Towell and C. Harries (eds.), *Innovation in Patient Care.* London: Croom Helm, 1979a.

Miller, E. J. "Open Systems Revisited: A Proposition About Development and Change." In W. G. Lawrence (ed.), *Exploring Individual and Organisational Boundaries.* London: Wiley, 1979b.

Miller, E. J. *Work and Creativity.* Occasional Paper. London: Tavistock Institute of Human Relations, 1983.

Miller, E. J., and Rice, A. K. *Systems of Organisation: Task and Sentient Systems and Their Boundary Control.* London: Tavistock Publications, 1967.

Miller, G. *Living Systems.* New York: McGraw-Hill, 1978.

Mintzberg, H. "Patterns in Strategy Formation." *Management Science,* 1978, *24,* 934-948.

Mintzberg, H. *The Structuring of Organizations*. Englewood Cliffs, N.J.: Prentice-Hall, 1979.

Mintzberg, H. *The Nature of Managerial Work*. Englewood Cliffs, N.J.: Prentice-Hall, 1980.

Mintzberg, H. *Power in and Around Organizations*. Englewood Cliffs, N.J.: Prentice-Hall, 1983.

Mirvis, P. H. "The Art of Assessing the Quality of Life at Work." In E. Lawler, D. Nadler, and C. Cammandt (eds.), *Organizational Assessment*. New York: Wiley-Interscience, 1980.

Mirvis, P. H., and Berg, D. N. (eds.). *Failures in Organization Development and Change: Cases and Essays for Learning*. New York: Wiley, 1977.

Neilsen, E. H. "The Human Side of Growth." *Organizational Dynamics*, 1978, pp. 61–80.

Neilsen, E. H. "Applying a Group Development Model to Managing a Class." *Exchange: The Organizational Behavior Teaching Journal*, 1979, *2* (4), 9–16.

Neumann, J. "Future Directions in Workplace Democracy." Candidacy paper, Department of Organizational Behavior, Case Western Reserve University, 1983.

Nord, W. "A Marxist Critique of Humanistic Psychology." *Journal of Humanistic Psychology*, 1977, *17* (1), 75–83.

Normann, R. *Management for Growth*. London: Wiley, 1977.

Ouchi, W. G. *Theory Z*. Reading, Mass.: Addison-Wesley, 1981.

Pascale, R., and Athos, A. *The Art of Japanese Management*. New York: Simon & Schuster, 1981.

Pasmore, W., Haldeman, J., Francis, C., and Shani, A. "Sociotechnical Systems: A North American Reflection on Empirical Studies of the Seventies." *Human Relations*, 1982, *35*, 1179–1204.

Peele, S. "The Cultural Context of Psychological Approaches to Alcoholism." *American Psychologist*, 1984, *39*, 1337–1351.

Perrow, C. *Complex Organizations: A Critical Essay*. Glenview, Ill.: Scott, Foresman, 1972.

Perrucci, R., and Pilisuk, M. "Leaders and Ruling Elites." *American Sociological Review*, 1970, *35*, 1040–1075.

Peters, T. "Symbols, Patterns, and Settings." *Organizational Dynamics*, Autumn 1978, pp. 3–23.

Peters, T. J., and Waterman, R. H., Jr. *In Search of Excellence: Lessons from America's Best-Run Corporations.* New York: Harper & Row, 1982.

Pettigrew, A. M. "Information Control as a Power Resource." *Sociology,* 1972, *6,* 187–204.

Pettigrew, A. M. *The Politics of Organizational Decision Making.* London: Tavistock, 1973.

Pettigrew, A. M. "Towards a Political Theory of Organizational Intervention." *Human Relations,* 1975, *28* (3), 191–208.

Pettigrew, A. M. "Strategy Formulation as a Political Process." *International Studies of Management and Organization,* 1977, *7* (2), 78–87.

Pettigrew, A. M. "On Studying Organizational Cultures." *Administrative Science Quarterly,* 1979, *24* (4), 570–581.

Pettigrew, A. M. "Patterns of Managerial Response as Organizations Move from Rich to Poor Environments." *Educational Management Administration,* 1983, *2,* 104–114.

Pettigrew, A. M. "Contextualist Research: A Natural Way to Link Theory and Practice." Paper presented at conference on Conducting Research with Theory and Practice in Mind, University of Southern California, Los Angeles, Nov. 1984.

Pettigrew, A. M. *The Awakening Giant: Continuity and Change in Imperial Chemical Industries.* Oxford, England: Blackwell, 1985a.

Pettigrew, A. M. "Examining Change in the Long-Term Context of Culture and Politics." In J. M. Pennings and Associates, *Organizational Strategy and Change: New Views on Formulating and Implementing Strategic Decisions.* San Francisco: Jossey-Bass, 1985b.

Pfeffer, J. "Management as Symbolic Action." In L. L. Cummings and B. M. Staw (eds.), *Research in Organizational Behavior.* Vol. 3. Greenwich, Conn.: JAI Press, 1981a.

Pfeffer, J. *Power in Organizations.* Marshfield, Mass.: Pitman, 1981b.

Pfeffer, J., and Salancik, G. R. *The External Control of Organizations: A Resource Dependence Perspective.* New York: Harper & Row, 1978.

Punch, M. *Policing the Inner City.* London: Macmillan, 1979.

Punch, M. (ed.). *Control in the Police Organization.* Cambridge, Mass.: MIT Press, 1983.

Punch, M. *Muddy Boots and Grubby Hands: The Politics and Ethics of Fieldwork.* Beverly Hills, Calif.: Sage, 1985.

Pym, D. "Emancipation and Organization." In N. Nicholson and T. D. Wall (eds.), *Theory and Practice of Organizational Psychology: A Collection of Original Essays.* London: Academic Press, 1982.

Quinn, J. B. *Strategies for Change: Logical Incrementation.* Homewood, Ill.: Irwin, 1980.

Quinn, J. B. "Managing Strategies Incrementally." *Omega,* 1982, *10* (6), 613–627.

Quinn, R. P., and Staines, G. L. *The Quality of Employment Survey.* Ann Arbor: Survey Research Center, University of Michigan, 1978.

Ranade, W., and Norris, P. "Democratic Consensus and the Young: A Cross National Comparison of Britain and America." *Journal of Adolescence,* 1984, *7,* 45–57.

Ranson, S., Hinings, C. R., and Greenwood, R. "The Structuring of Organizational Structures." *Administrative Science Quarterly,* 1980, *25* (1), 1–18.

Reich, R. "The Profession of Management." *New Republic,* June 27, 1981, pp. 27–32.

Report of the Committee of Inquiry on Industrial Democracy (Bullock Report). London: Her Majesty's Stationery Office, 1977.

Reuss-Ianni, E. *Two Cultures of Policing: Street Cops and Management Cops.* New Brunswick, N.J.: Transaction Books, 1983.

Rice, A. K. *Productivity and Social Organisation: The Ahmedabad Experiment.* London: Tavistock Publications, 1958.

Riemer, J. W. *Hard Hats.* Beverly Hills, Calif.: Sage, 1979.

Robertson, R. N. *History of the American Economy.* San Diego, Calif.: Harcourt Brace Jovanovich, 1955.

Roethlisberger, F., and Dickson, W. *Management and the Worker.* Cambridge, Mass.: Harvard University Press, 1939.

Rothchild-Whitt, J. "The Collectivist Organization: An Alternative to Rational-Bureaucratic Models." *American Sociological Review,* 1979, *44,* 509–527.

Roy, D. "Banana Time: Job Satisfaction and Informal Interaction." *Human Organization,* 1959-60, *18,* 158-168.

Rubinstein, J. *City Police.* New York: Farrar, Straus & Giroux, 1973.

Salancik, G., and Pfeffer, J. "Who Gets Power and How They Hold On to It." *Organizational Dynamics,* Winter 1977, pp. 2-21.

Salancik, G., and Pfeffer, J. "A Social Information Processing Approach to Job Attitudes and Task Design." *Administrative Science Quarterly,* 1978, *23* (2), 224-253.

Sarason, S. *Work, Aging and Social Change.* New York: Free Press, 1977.

Sashkin, M. *A Manager's Guide to Participative Management.* Saranac Lake, N.Y.: American Management Associations, 1982.

Sashkin, M. "Participative Management Is an Ethical Imperative." *Organizational Dynamics,* 1984, *12* (4), 4-22.

Saunders, P. *Urban Politics: A Sociological Interpretation.* Harmondsworth, Middlesex, England: Penguin, 1980.

Schein, E. H. "The Role of the Founder in the Creation of Culture." *Organizational Dynamics,* 1983.

Schein, E. H. *Organizational Culture and Leadership: A Dynamic View.* San Francisco: Jossey-Bass, 1985.

Schein, V. E. "Power and Organization Development: Little Red Riding Hood and the Big Bad Wolves." Paper presented at the Academy of Management, Kansas City, Aug. 1976.

Schutz, W. *FIRO: A Three Dimensional Theory of Interpersonal Behavior.* New York: Holt, Rinehart & Winston, 1958.

Schwartz, H. S. "Maslow and the Hierarchical Enactment of Organisational Reality." *Human Relations,* 1983, *36,* 933-956.

Selznick, P. *Leadership in Administration.* New York: Harper & Row, 1957.

Sherif, M. "Superordinate Goals in the Reduction of Intergroup Conflict." *American Journal of Sociology,* 1958, *63,* 349-358.

Smith, D. J., and Gray, J. *Police and People in London.* Vol. 4: *The Police in Action.* London: Policy Studies Institute, 1983.

Spradley, J. P. *You Owe Yourself a Drunk.* Boston: Little, Brown, 1970.

Srivastva, S., and Barrett, F. J. "A Role for Human Cosmogony in Organizations." Unpublished paper, Case Western Reserve University, Cleveland, 1985.

Srivastva, S., Obert, S. L., and Neilsen, E. H. "Organizational Analysis Through Group Processes: A Theoretical Perspective for Group Development." In C. Cooper (ed.), *Organizational Development in the U.K. and U.S.A.* London: Macmillan, 1977.

Srivastva, S., and others. *Job Satisfaction and Productivity.* Cleveland: Department of Organizational Behavior, Case Western Reserve University, 1975.

Starbuck, W. H., Greve, A., and Hedberg, B.L.T. "Responding to Crises." *Journal of Business Administration,* 1978, *9* (2), 111-137.

Stern, E. *Welfare Crisis in Britain: A Preliminary Assessment.* Occasional Paper. London: Tavistock Institute of Human Relations, 1982.

Strauss, G. "Tactics of the Lateral Relationship: The Purchasing Agent." *Administrative Science Quarterly,* 1962, *63,* 161-186.

Tannenbaum, R., and Schmidt, W. "How to Choose a Leadership Pattern." *Harvard Business Review,* 1958, *36,* 95-101.

Thomas, W. I. "The Definition of the Situation." In L. A. Coser and B. Rosenberg (eds.), *Sociological Theory.* (3rd ed.) New York: Macmillan, 1971.

Toffler, A. *The Third Wave.* New York: Morrow, 1980.

Trice, H. M. "Rites and Ceremonials in Organizational Culture." In S. B. Bacharach and S. M. Mitchell (eds.), *Perspectives on Organizational Sociology: Theory and Research.* Vol. 4. Greenwich, Conn.: JAI Press, 1984.

Trice, H. M., and Beyer, J. M. "Studying Organizational Cultures Through Rites and Ceremonies." *Academy of Management Review,* 1984, *9,* 653-669.

Trist, E. L. "Organizational Ecology." *Australian Journal of Management,* 1977, *5,* 161-173.

Trist, E. L. "New Directions of Hope." *Human Futures,* 1979, *2* (3), 176-185.

Trist, E. L. *The Evolution of Sociotechnical Systems.* Issues in the Quality of Working Life, Paper no. 2. Ontario: Quality of Working Life Centre, 1981.

Trist, E. L. "Referent Organizations and the Development of Interorganizational Domains." *Human Relations,* 1983, *36* (3), 247–268.

Trist, E. L., and Bamforth, K. "Some Social and Psychological Consequences of The Long Wall Method of Coal-Getting." *Human Relations,* 1951, *4,* 3–38.

Trist, E. L., Higgin, G., Murray, H., and Pollock, A. *Organizational Choice.* London: Tavistock Publications, 1963.

Turner V. W. *The Ritual Process.* London: Routledge & Kegan Paul, 1969.

Turner, V. W. *Dramas, Fields and Metaphors.* Ithaca, N.Y.: Cornell University Press, 1974.

Useem, M. *The Inner Circle: Large Corporations and the Rise of Business Political Activity in the U.S. and U.K.* New York: Oxford University Press, 1984.

Vaill, P. "Toward a Behavioral Description of High-Performing Systems." In M. McCall and M. Lombardo (eds.), *Leadership: Where Else Can We Go?* Durham, N.C.: Duke University Press, 1978.

Van Maanen, J. "Working the Street." In H. Jacob (ed.), *The Potential for Reform of Criminal Justice.* Beverly Hills, Calif.: Sage, 1974.

Van Maanen, J. "The Asshole." In P. K. Manning and J. Van Maanen (eds.), *Policing: A View from the Streets.* New York: Random House, 1978.

Van Maanen, J. "The Fact or Fiction of Organizational Ethnography." *Administrative Science Quarterly,* 1979, *24,* 539–550.

Van Maanen, J. "Notes on the Production of Ethnographic Data in an American Police Agency." In R. Luckman (ed.), *Law and Social Enquiry.* New York: International Center for Law in Development, 1981.

Van Maanen, J. "Fieldwork on the Beat." In J. Van Maanen, J. M. Dabbs, and R. B. Faulkner, *Varieties of Qualitative Research.* Beverly Hill, Calif.: Sage, 1982.

Van Maanen, J. "The Boss." In M. Punch (ed.), *Control in the Police Organization.* Cambridge, Mass.: MIT Press, 1983a.

Van Maanen, J. "Golden Passports: Managerial Socialization and Graduate Education." *Review of Higher Education,* Series on Organizational Studies, 1983b, *3,* 435-455.

Van Maanen, J., Miller, M. L., and Johnson, J. C. "An Occupation in Transition: Traditional and Modern Forms of Commercial Fishing." *Sociology of Work and Occupations,* 1982, *9* (2), 193-216.

Vroom, V. H., and Yetton, P. *Leadership and Decision-Making.* Pittsburgh: University of Pittsburgh Press, 1973.

Wallace, W. *The Logic of Science in Sociology.* Hawthorne, N.Y.: Aldine, 1971.

Walter, G. A. "Organizational Development and Individual Rights." *Journal of Applied Behavioral Science,* 1984, *20* (4), 423-440.

Walton, R. "How to Counter Alienation in the Plant." *Harvard Business Review,* 1972, *50,* 70-81.

Walton, R. "The Topeka Work System: Optimistic Visions, Pessimistic Hypotheses, and Reality." In R. Zager and M. Rosow (eds.), *The Innovative Organization.* Elmsford, N.Y.: Pergamon Press, 1982.

Weber, M. "The Three Types of Legitimate Rule." In A. Etzioni (ed.), *Essays on Complex Organizations.* New York: Holt, Rinehart & Winston, 1961. (Originally published 1947.)

Weick, K. *The Social Psychology of Organizing.* Reading, Mass.: Addison-Wesley, 1969.

Wessel, M. *The Rule of Reason: A New Approach to Corporate Litigation.* Reading, Mass.: Addison-Wesley, 1976.

Whitehead, A. N. *The Function of Reason.* (2nd ed.) Boston: Beacon Press, 1967. (Originally published 1933.)

Winnicott, D. W. "Ego Distortion in Terms of True and False Self." In *The Motivational Processes and the Facilitating Environment.* London: Hogarth Press, 1960.

Winnicott, D. W. *Playing and Reality.* (2nd ed.) Harmondsworth, Middlesex, England: Penguin, 1980.

Winter, D. G. *The Power Motive.* New York: Free Press, 1973.

Woodward, J. *Industrial Organisation: Theory and Practice.* London: Oxford University Press, 1965.

Wortman, M. S. "Strategic Management and Changing Leader-Follower Roles." *Journal of Applied Behavioral Science,* 1982, *18,* 371-383.

Yankelovich, D. "The New Psychological Contracts at Work." *Psychology Today,* 1978, *11* (12), 46-50.

Yankelovich, D. *New Rules.* New York: Random House, 1981.

Zaleznik, A. "Managers and Leaders: Are They Different?" *Harvard Business Review,* 1977, *55* (3), 67-78.

Zaleznik, A., and Kets de Vries, M. *Power and the Corporate Mind.* Boston: Houghton Mifflin, 1975.

Index

ALVERNO COLLEGE LIBRARY
Executive power
658.4S774

2 5050 00196556 1

169595

658.4
S774

REMOVED FROM THE
ALVERNO COLLEGE LIBRARY

Alverno College
Library Media Center
Milwaukee, Wisconsin

DEMCO